METROPOLITAN ORGANISING CAPACITY

This book is one of a series to be published by Ashgate under the auspices of EURICUR, the European Institute for Comparative Urban Research, Erasmus University Rotterdam. Titles in the series are;

Leo. H. Klaassen, Leo van den Berg and Jan van der Meer (eds.),
The City: Engine behind Economic Recovery

Leo van den Berg, H. Arjen Klink and Jan van der Meer,
Governing Metropolitan Regions

Leo van den Berg, Jan van der Borg and Jan van der Meer,
Urban Tourism

Metropolitan Organising Capacity

Experiences with Organising Major Projects in
European Cities

LEO VAN DEN BERG
ERIK BRAUN
JAN VAN DER MEER

European Institute for Comparative Urban Research
Erasmus University Rotterdam
The Netherlands

Routledge
Taylor & Francis Group

LONDON AND NEW YORK

First published 1997 by Ashgate Publishing

Reissued 2018 by Routledge
2 Park Square, Milton Park, Abingdon, Oxon, OX14 4RN
711 Third Avenue, New York, NY 10017

Routledge is an imprint of the Taylor & Francis Group, an informa business

Publisher's Note
The publisher has gone to great lengths to ensure the quality of this reprint but points out that some imperfections in the original copies may be apparent.

Disclaimer
The publisher has made every effort to trace copyright holders and welcomes correspondence from those they have been unable to contact.

A Library of Congress record exists under LC control number: 97073460

ISBN 13: 978-1-138-32123-6 (hbk)
ISBN 13: 978-0-429-45269-7 (ebk)

Contents

Preface

In 1991 the city of Eindhoven invited the European Institute for Comparative Urban Research (Euricur) to carry out an international comparative and evaluating study of experiences with management structures in eight metropolitan regions, all members of the Eurocities network. The main reason to explore these experiences was that this topic is of growing interest in many European countries. This initiative resulted among others in the volume *Governing Metropolitan Regions* by Leo van den Berg, H. Arjen van Klink and Jan van der Meer, published by Avebury, Aldershot (UK) in 1993.

Encouraged by the positive experiences with this study the city of Eindhoven launched a new proposal for a comparative study at the Annual Meeting of Eurocities in Lisbon in 1993. The aim of this new study is to get a better insight into the organising capacity of metropolitan cities. The participation of eight European cities and a grant from the European Commission made the investigation possible.

To exchange both good and bad experiences related to this subject is considered to be very useful, especially for regional and local authorities. Organising capacity has been defined here as the capacity to develop and implement strategies needed to respond to fundamental changes in society and to create conditions for a sustainable metropolitan development. Organising capacity is not restricted to the formal administrative structure; it incorporates public, private and mixed public-private networks to reach objectives that are difficult (or impossible) to obtain by public authorities alone. The investigation consists of the analysis of strategic -renewal-projects and the organising capacity incorporated in its execution. In that way fifteen projects in eight metropolitan cities in six countries have been analysed according to a theoretical framework specifically developed for this study.

The case studies have largely been accomplished by interviewing representatives of municipalities (both from core cities and from surrounding municipalities), public companies (for instance public transport companies), representatives of the private sector (Chambers of Commerce, private companies involved in the projects), project managers, etc. Without their help and information the investigation could not have been accomplished at all. We want to express our great appreciation of the welcome we received in all the participating cities and the willingness to share valuable information with us.

The research has been carried out under the supervision of a Steering Committee chaired by Drs Philip Werner (on behalf of the city of Eindhoven) and furthermore composed of - in alphabetical order - Mr Iñigo Atxutegi (on behalf of the city of Bilbao), Mr Eddy Cop (on behalf of the city of Antwerp), Mrs Ilda Curti (on behalf of the city of Turin), Mr Alberto Laplaine Guimarais (on behalf of the city of Lisbon), Mr Chris de Lange (on behalf of the city of Rotterdam), Mr Raffaelle La Monica (on behalf of the city of Bologna), Mrs Elisabeth Steinberg (on behalf of the city of Munich), Mr Sandro Testoni (on behalf of the city of Bologna), Mr Hans Verdonk (on behalf of the city of Rotterdam) and Mrs Maria Manuela Vitorio (on behalf of the city of Lisbon). Besides the representatives of the cities, Mr Harrie Jeurissen represented the Dutch Section of the Council of European Municipalities and Regions and Mr Anthony van der Ven represented the Eurocities network. The authors thank the members of the Steering Committee for their valuable remarks and pleasant cooperation.

The case studies could not have been performed, let alone completed on time, without the help of three Euricur researchers. Thanks are due to Dr H. Arjen van Klink, co-author of the case study of Turin (Chapter 9), Drs Peter M.J. Pol, co-author of the case study of Bilbao (Chapter 3), and Drs Paul Poppink, co-author of the case studies of Bologna (Chapter 4) and Rotterdam (Chapter 8) for there much-appreciated contribution to this research project. Naturally only the three authors are responsible for the contents of the full report.

Finally we like to thank Mrs Attie Elderson-De Boer for the translation of the text into English and Arianne van Bijnen, the Euricur secretary, for her indispensable help during all the phases of the investigation.

Leo van den Berg, Erik Braun and Jan van der Meer

Rotterdam, January 1997

1 Introduction, background and theoretical framework

Introduction

The position of metropolitan regions in Europe is changing drastically. Owing to fundamental developments as the globalisation of the economy, the transition to an information society, and the European integration, metropolitan competition has become a leading principle to determine the future urban system in Europe [Brunet, 1989; Parkinson et.al., 1992; Brotchie et.al., 1995; Cheshire and Gordon, 1996; and many others]. Increasingly, metropolitan regions need to organise themselves better to improve their competitive position.

Research into the functioning of administrative systems of metropolitan regions in Europe has confirmed that 'controlling capacity' on the level of the metropolitan region is indispensable [Berg, van den, Klink, van, and Meer, van der, 1993]. Indeed, the (future) prosperity of a metropolitan region depends to a high degree on its *organising capacity*. The principal aspect of that power is to be able, adequately and on the proper spatial-economic scale, to anticipate, respond to and cope with changing intra- and inter-metropolitan relations due to crucial internal and external processes of change. In that context, organising capacity can be defined as *the ability to enlist all actors involved, and with their help generate new ideas and develop and implement a policy designed to respond to fundamental developments and create conditions for sustainable development.*

1

An increasing number of academics and urban managers recognise that organising capacity is a very important element of urban management. Yet, there is still little knowledge concerning this topic. The objective of this book is to increase the insight into the practice of metropolitan organising capacity.

Background and methodology

This volume is based on the results of an international comparative investigation into the practice of organising capacity in eight European metropolitan regions. The investigation has been conducted among member cities of the *Eurocities* network. In this network of exchange, research and communication around seventy of the larger European cities (over 200,000 inhabitants) are represented. The cities of Antwerp (Belgium), Bilbao (Spain), Bologna (Italy), Eindhoven (The Netherlands), Lisbon (Portugal), Munich (Germany), Rotterdam (The Netherlands) and Turin (Italy) decided to participate, the major reason being that they were convinced of the importance of the research topic.

As table 1 indicates the group of cities offers a highly interesting mix of experiences. The population differs in number, as does the extent of and the relation to the metropolitan region, with the city of Eindhoven being the smallest (200,000 inhabitants) and the city of Munich the largest (1,300,000 inhabitants). The economic performance of the cities differs: Munich and Bologna can be counted as affluent, while Bilbao and Lisbon are trailing in development, as is confirmed by their respective 'Objective-2' and 'Objective-1' status, which entitles them to special subsidies by the European Union. The Eindhoven region too has been given the Objective-2 status (for the 1994-1996 period), owing to substantial lay-offs by the city's two leading industries. The other three cities find themselves somewhere in the middle. Most of the cities have a distinct industrial background: Bilbao (traditional large-scale basic industries such as steel industry and shipbuilding), Bologna (high representation of medium- and small-scale traditional and high-tech industry), Eindhoven (still dominated by Philips Electronics and to a lesser extent by DAF Trucks), Munich (Siemens, BMW) and Turin (FIAT). Some cities are important seaports (Rotterdam and Antwerp, and to a lesser extent Bilbao and Lisbon). Finally, the economic structure of Lisbon, the capital of Portugal is mostly service-based.

2

Table 1
Characteristics of the cities and the metropolitan areas

	Inhabitants City	Inhabitants Region	Year	Economic performance	Tertiary/ Secondary
Antwerp	466,000	1,139,000	1993	average	73/27
Bilbao	370,000	923,000	1991	poor	60/40
Bologna	400,000	900,000	1990	strong	55/36
Eindhoven	194,000	670,000	1993	average	60/33
Lisbon	664,000	2,552,000	1991	poor	81/18
Munich	1,300,000	2,400,000	1993	strong	69/25
Rotterdam	596,000	1,100,000	1993	average	71/29
Turin	956,000	1,800,000	1991	poor/average	56/44

The research has been supported by a Steering Committee composed of representatives of the participating cities, the Eurocities network and the Council of European Municipalities and Regions. Organising capacity manifests itself most in projects aimed at sustainable economic development. The eight cities have been asked to submit two projects for analysis. The projects display a variety of aspects: projects at the preparatory stage, in progress or completed, projects in the areas of economics, environment and/or transport, or projects concerned with the interface of these areas. Projects with a physical component (for instance infrastructure) or with a less tangible component (such as improvement of the economic structure or the drawing up of a strategic plan) were equally welcome. Moreover, the choice has not been limited to very successful and already completed projects but also projects that had trouble taking off, or are hampered by inertia, have been included. Seven cities have submitted two projects for the investigation. Only Lisbon has proposed one very large and comprehensive project. These fifteen projects have been analysed to assess the notion of metropolitan organising capacity.

The investigation is not so much concerned with the decision of a city or region to develop a particular project for a problem or challenge, but focuses on the process of organising and implementing these projects. The assumption is that these projects potentially contribute to a sustainable development of the metropolitan region and to the improvement of its competitive position.

To arrive at the empirical analysis, next to a study of literature, in-depth interviews were held with key persons directly or indirectly involved, like project managers, representatives of municipalities (both from core cities and surrounding municipalities), public companies (for instance public transport companies), representatives of the private sector (among others, Chambers of Commerce and private companies involved) and academics. The draft reports have been submitted to the discussion partners and to the members of the Steering Committee for verification.

The organisation of the book is as follows. In this chapter the increased need for metropolitan organising capacity is discussed and a theoretical framework is drawn up out of elements that can reveal organising capacity. These elements are: administrative structure, strategic networks, vision and strategy, leadership, political support, societal support and spatial-economic conditions. The central objective of the case studies, reported on in chapters 2 to 9, is to give substance to these elements and to explain their relationship and their role in the projects and more generally, in the metropolitan region. Each of these chapters is devoted to one participating city.

The 'city chapters' are organised as follows: first the city and its metropolitan region are briefly introduced by a socio-economic profile, including a sketch of the existing administrative structure. That introduction is followed by a description of each project, pointing out the challenge which triggered the project off, and recounting the developments until now and the expectations for the future. Then follows an analysis based on the evaluation of the elements of the theoretical framework. This analysis has to be set off against the performance of the projects investigated. Is the project successful, that is to say, does it meet the objectives?

Chances and threats: the need for organising capacity

Changes of technological, demographical, political and societal nature result in fundamental developments which spell chances for and threats to metropolitan regions. The change in competitive relations, the progressive liberalisation of world trade, and the accelerated industrialisation of countries that were predominantly agrarian shortly before, pushes larger companies to 'global sourcing' and 'global trading'. The most evident basic expression is a new international division of labour [Hall, 1995]. A growing number of eastern Asian and Latin American countries has become competitive, not only in traditional industries, but also in technically sophisticated industries, owing to a combination of modern equipment, qualified cheap labour and

4

competent management [Hall, 1995]. Globalisation is speeded up by evolving technologies of telecommunication, a distinct feature of the second fundamental development, the shift of all advanced nations from goods production and goods handling to the processing of information. This shift is perhaps as momentous as the transition from an agrarian to a manufacturing economy [Castells, 1991].

In an informational economy traditional location factors are no longer significant. The combined result of globalisation and informationalisation is that the production of services becomes increasingly detached from that of production of goods [Sassen, 1995]. The new locational logic is governed by access to information. This leads to locational disarticulation: world-wide dispersal of production and increasing concentration of (producer) services in metropolitan cities [Hall, 1995]. The clustering of services in turn, attracts other services with regard to real estate, communication, tourism, art & culture, etc. Although it might be thought that telecommunication should work opposite to concentration in major cities, centre-periphery differences seem to become even more pronounced than they used to be [Hall, 1995; Wegener, 1995; NEI/Ernst & Young, 1992]. Major metropolitan regions are the traditional points of concentration for specialised information-generating and information-exchanging activities. Increasingly, experts recognise that this concentration and interchange will remain critical to the knowledge intensive industries of the future [Stegman and Turner, 1996]. Because these cities also serve as (inter-)national transportation nodes, the process of informationalisation seems to favour these regions.

Throughout the world a fundamental shift can be observed to think about national or international economies as a system of metropolitan centered regional economies, that transcend municipal boundaries [Peirce, Johnson and Stuart Hall, 1993; Barnes and Ledebur, 1991; Ohmae, 1995; Stegman and Turner, 1996]. In Europe, national urban hierarchies have been replaced by a European system of urban regions. A major consequence is that the new dynamics of urbanisation are a function of the principle of spatial competition. Competition has become more intense and universal than ever; cities and regions vie with one another to attract new mobile investments and visitors, or to keep established economic activities. At the same time processes of policy decentralisation take place in most European countries. Furthermore, despite the fact that the European Union is not allowed to develop and implement explicit urban policies (owing to the principle of subsidiarity), the impact of European Union financing and of European Union policies in the areas of economics, social affairs, transportation and

5

environment on cities increases substantially [Berg, van den, Meer, van der and Pol, 1996].

Spatial-economic scale enlargement makes the functional metropolitan region a logical basis for present-day urban policy, intra-metropolitan competition being considered as destructive to the competitive metropolitan position in a European context. Consequently the quality of the metropolitan environment for the location of economic activities is of crucial importance. Within that environment, the emphasis is on other factors than before. In analytical terms, the environment for business location can be divided into three components: *hardware*, the concrete tangible location factors including labour, land, infrastructure and capital; *software*, the qualitative, intangible quality-of-life factors; and orgware, the handling of hardware and software [Porter, 1990]. Within this triad, a shift is taking place. 'Soft' location factors are on the wax: the quality of urban living and the residential working environment are taken into account for locational choices. Within the 'hard' location factors the accent is shifting to high-qualified labour potential, and the quality of international accessibility in terms of goods and passenger transport. Competition pushes cities to fully use their potential, that is hard- and software. Consequently orgware, the handling of hardware and software, is becoming vital in view of the growing competition among cities. A major problem concerning organising capacity is the absence in most European metropolitan regions of a management at the proper functional level [Berg, van den, Klink, van and Meer, van der, 1993]. Needless to say that this is counter productive for the areas involved. In view of the extending spatial-economic scale and the lack of adequate government at that same scale, *orgware* or a well developed organising capacity might become an extremely important metropolitan locational advantage.

The spatial scale is widening not only in economic terms but also with respect to environmental and transport questions. Environmental pollution does not stop at municipal borders. The regulation of the emission of harmful substances, the processing of waste and the conservation or creation of green areas for instance, all demand to be taken up on at least the functional metropolitan level. Of course, some environmental questions (greenhouse effect) are best approached on the world-wide, European or sometimes national scale. However, on the metropolitan level too, the coordination of environmental questions appears necessary. One condition for metropolitan environmental quality is that neighbouring municipalities come to an agreement about the type of business activity to be attracted.

Transport problems have exceeded local boundaries much longer. Here, too, coordination on the metropolitan, regional, national or European level is imperative. To direct complex transport flows between city and ring, from and to the metropolitan region, calls by definition for adjustment on the metropolitan level. Rotterdam's mainport function, for instance, has implications for the entire functional (transport) region with respect to the hinterland connections (opening up by road, rail connections, etc.).

Joint metropolitan approach to economic, environmental and transport problems is not only required by the fundamental developments sketched above, but also prevents intra-metropolitan inconsistency and inefficiency. Indeed, a metropolitan approach permits (economic) scale advantages for the design, coordination and implementation of policy.

In that context, *orgware*, or organising capacity -the ability to develop and implement an integral strategy- becomes a dominant factor towards a sustainable ecological and socio-economic development. To the analogy of Nijkamp & Vleugel's pentagon model (1993)[1], the number of determinants of metropolitan development can be extended to five. To *hardware* (infrastructure, labour and capital), *software* (qualitative factors) and *orgware* (the way to handle the remaining factors), can be added *finware* (financial arrangements and financing) and *ecoware* (environmental aspects). Jointly, these five components determine for the most part a sustainable metropolitan development, with orgware representing the handling and exploitation of potentials with respect to the other components.

The components are 'pieces of the same puzzle'. To recognise the impact of the separate elements and their relation is vital. Only such knowledge makes integrated response to changing locational criteria possible. The same holds true on the sectorial level: to try for sustainable economic development calls for an insight into the relations between environment, transport and economy (see figure 1). In that view, metropolitan sustainable development need not lead to a rigid trade-off between environmental quality and metropolitan economic growth. The quality of the living environment is a location factor of growing importance and attracts additional economic activity; it is thus a determinant of economic growth. On the other hand, economic growth can generate financial resources that can be used for the benefit of the environment. The relation between the economy and the environment is a matter of selectiveness (for instance with respect to business acquisition or expansion), negative environmental effects being limited and environmental-protective activities encouraged.

7

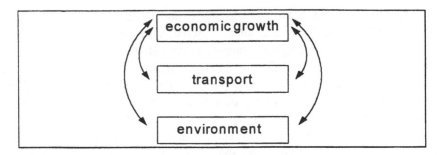

Figure 1   'Pieces of the same puzzle'

Accessibility (both physical and communicative) is a necessary condition for metropolitan economic development. The efficient direction of transport flows is therefore a crucial supporting function, as are adequate infrastructural provisions. Economic growth generates transport flows and transport facilitates further economic growth. On the other hand, transport flows have inherent negative effects on the environment (air pollution, noise, sacrifice of greenery in favour of the road network). To strike the right balance is more and more vital in that context. Once more adjustment (for instance among different modalities) and selectiveness (for instance with respect to the direction of transport flows in the metropolitan region) are key notions.

The factor that binds all the above mentioned policy aspects together is a vision of metropolitan development, producing strategies and concrete objectives. Organising capacity in the metropolitan region is necessary but not sufficient: a vision translated into a strategy for the future metropolitan development integrates different aspects and prevents inconsistencies. The overall metropolitan development vision is translated into related, consistent strategies for separate aspects. No need to argue that a vision upon the integral metropolitan development is an absolute condition for sustainable economic development. Moreover the vision *directs* the organising capacity. Without vision, efficient and effective organising capacity is a utopia, an 'unguided missile'. We will take that matter up next.

Towards a theoretical framework for organising capacity

This chapter defines organising capacity as the ability to enlist all actors involved, and with their help generate new ideas and develop and implement a policy designed to respond to fundamental developments and create conditions for sustainable development. The first pillar of organising capacity is the formal institutional framework (*the administrative organisation*) and the role of the various public actors within this framework. However, organising capacity is not just a matter of (local) government and traditional planning procedures, other public and private actors are involved as well. *Strategic networks* -among public actors, between public and private actors, or among private actors- as a means to cope with the dynamics of today's urban society, have become equally important. At the same time, networks call for more co-ordination. *Leadership* of key persons or organisations is necessary to utilise the potential of new and existing networks and to direct the efforts of the parties involved. Networks lack a formal (legal) hierarchical structure. Therefore incentives to induce co-operation are crucial. Chances and threats to the metropolitan economy (*spatial-economic conditions*) could provide a joint rationale for collaboration. The shift in 'hard' and 'soft' location factors results in increased interdependency between social, economic, environmental, transportation aspects. Consequently revitalisation strategies should promote integrality. An integral *vision* of metropolitan development, translated into *strategies* and concrete objectives safeguards integrality and prevents inconsistencies in planning. Moreover, in a competitive environment networking among public and private actors is not sufficient. It is extremely important to organise support among the 'interest groups' and 'target groups' involved. They have to be made aware of the necessity and attractivity of policy proposals or projects. Nowadays *political support* as well as *societal support* can be decisive for projects to succeed.

Administrative organisation

For the role of the public administration the publication 'Governing Metropolitan Regions' [Berg, van den, Klink van, and Meer, van der, 1993] offers a lead. This study analysed administrative structures in eight European metropolitan regions[2] and compared the practical solutions adopted by these metropolitan regions to match their administrative structure to the enlarged spatial-economic scale. The analysis was mainly based on the evaluation of five criteria: adequacy of the spatial scale, competence, integrality, democratic content, and efficiency/effectiveness. One major conclusion from this investigation is that *co-operativeness* of the municipalities involved is a necessary condition for the performance of any metropolitan administrative model. That means that not only *formal competence* is decisive, but that a co-operative environment, providing a breeding ground for *material competence*, can lend substance to the decisiveness of the metropolitan administrative structure. However, organising capacity concerns more than the adequate functioning of public administration. To implement a suitable administrative structure, in which local and metropolitan authorities operate in harmony, is an important first step but there are more steps to make.

In the investigation the administrative structure is taken into consideration. How is the administration in the metropolitan region structured? In theory, two extremes and a number of intermediary gradations can be imagined: at one end a strong hierarchical structure with much power concentrated in a metropolitan government, with hardly any autonomy on the local level; on the other, a horizontal structure without any metropolitan controlling capacity, local authorities sailing their own course without giving much thought to metropolitan wide problems. In practice, the horizontal structure will b e the rule rather than the exception. In none of the eight cities an authority on the level of the metropolitan region does exist. In four metropolitan regions (Bologna, Eindhoven and Rotterdam) preliminaries are in progress or the law provides for it (Lisbon).

Strategic networks

Because of the complexity, dynamics and diversity of present society, government on the basis of one-way traffic between public and private actors is no longer satisfactory. In other words: urban management is not just a matter of the formal public administration. Activities related to 'governing efforts' are by definition interaction processes between public actors and public or private target groups or individuals involved. Governing is mainly a process of steering, influencing and balancing these activities (Kooiman, 1993). Kooiman (1993) defines the patterns developing from the governing activities of social, political and administrative actors as *governance*. Governance covers both the day-to-day effect of governing and the structure within which governing proceeds.

Interactive governance implies that the staging of partnerships with other than local and metropolitan authorities becomes increasingly important. Metropolitan and local authorities must actively enlist representatives from the (other) public or semi-public sectors as well as representatives from the private sector that influence metropolitan development directly or indirectly. With respect to organising capacity this must be extended to a *partnership culture*, in which mutual co-operativeness between the involved public and private actors can flourish. In this way organising capacity is closely related to steering in what we will indicate here as *strategic networks*. Strategic networks can be conceived of as patterns of interaction between mutually dependent actors that evolve around policy problems or projects. That strategy springs from networks of public, semi-public and private actors, with their own interests, objectives and perceptions, who for the realisation of their objectives depend on others, is by no means a new notion. Less common is, however, the exploitation of strategic networks. On the other hand, public-private partnerships are a frequently chosen option for metropolitan revitalisation and other projects. Public-private partnership is in fact nothing else but joint government by public-private networks (Kouwenhoven, 1991).

Why are strategic networks gaining importance? The governance structure has to stimulate network building around strategic themes to do justice to the specific nature and spatial scale of each theme. Strategic networks thus become important *complements* to the formal administrative structure. Besides, strategic networks can create broad support for setting and accomplishing policy objectives (metropolitan competitive position, quality of life, etc.), thus enhancing metropolitan decision power.

When is governance through strategic networks a likely option? Networks vary widely in nature and contents. Moreover, the concept of a network is variously interpreted. Jarillo (1993) relates the notion of network particularly to businesses, to indicate an arrangement of relations among companies (along with market relations, vertical integration and bureaucracy). The interpretation of network need not be so narrow, however. A network consists of the total of relations among (public and private) organisations, institutions and persons, the relations being marked by a degree of two-way dynamics. Mutual relations among participants, or interdependency among (activities of) actors, form the backbone of the network. The mutual dependency need not necessarily be symmetrical. The fact that authorities can wield more power than the other partners need not be an obstacle: interdependency does not imply balance of power.

Various factors determine the performance of such networks: target convergence, willingness to co-operate, basis of confidence and flexibility. Although all these aspects are important characteristics of strategic networks the investigation concentrates on the creation and the composition of these networks and whether the network contributed to the progress of the project.

That qualification has been split into two elements:

11

- the actual willingness to co-operate within existing administrative structures ('public networks'), such as the willingness of various departments within a public institution or various municipalities within a metropolitan region to work together, and the co-operation between various administrative tiers to develop and implement a specific project;
- the remaining public-private as well as private networks. Have the right actors been enlisted in the project, 'birds of different feathers' and from different sectors, if necessary?

Leadership

The investigation into the functioning of metropolitan administration (Berg, van den, Klink, van, Meer, van der, 1993) has revealed that apart from the five criteria[3], leadership of key persons within the administrative organisation is equally important. With regard to strategic networks leadership is even more important. In the investigation the assumption is that the leadership and the entrepreneurial spirit of key figures or key institutions contribute substantially to the successful designing, development and implementation of projects. There must be leadership, whether relying on specific competencies (the position in the administrative hierarchy, financial capabilities, specific know how or other powers) or on the charisma of public or private individuals who fulfil the function of 'project-puller' successfully. The existence of clear leadership performed by an institution, a company or a specific person does promote the starting-up and the execution of a project in the direction desired.

Spatial-economic conditions

Yet another conclusion from Van den Berg, Van Klink and Van der Meer (1993) is that spatial-economic conditions -opportunities and threats for the metropolitan economy- can be considered important for the success of a metropolitan government. One can expect that the same applies to the formation and co-operativeness within strategic networks. In the investigation the hypothesis is that spatial-economic problems and obstacles can induce parties in the region to collaborate. These problems may 'bind' actors together and thus be an important incentive to collaborate. The hypothesis is that without (the recognition of) significant problems in a city or region, the creation of organising capacity is more troublesome.

12

Vision and strategy

As said earlier integrality becomes increasingly important. The factor that binds all policy aspects together is a vision of metropolitan development, producing strategies and concrete objectives. A vision is a prerequisite to integrate different aspects and to prevent inconsistencies. An overall metropolitan vision must be translated into related, consistent strategies for separate aspects. No need to argue that a vision upon the integral metropolitan development is an absolute condition for sustainable development. Without vision, efficient and effective organising capacity is a utopia, an 'unguided missile'. An important aspect in the investigation is therefore whether the project fits into a broadly supported comprehensive vision and strategy, and, with respect to the project itself, have concrete goals been formulated and is there a clear strategy of implementation? If a distinct vision and a well elaborated strategy are lacking on the metropolitan as well as on the project level this has to be considered as a negative condition for creating organising capacity.

Political support

The elbowroom of public and private actors in urban development is determined in the local political circles and sometimes on a national or even supra-national level. The research covers support, either from 'higher' government levels (supra-national, national or regional authorities) or from local politicians within the local or regional council(s). This support helps to bring about positive collaboration on the local level. Proper presentation and communication of the policy problem and the solution envisaged is of paramount importance. The financial support and scope granted by the 'higher' administrative levels to the local governors is an additional condition for creating organising capacity.

Societal support

No matter how valuable a project might be for sustainable metropolitan development, lack of support of those directly involved or interested, notably the population or specific market parties (for instance private investors) can limit the chances of successful implementation. If a sound communication strategy has been properly implemented from the start of the project, in accordance with the scope and impact of the project, and leading to broad support, then this element contributes to the organising capacity.

Figure 2 recapitulates the elements that contribute to organising capacity. The hypothesis is that the performance is the result of the interaction of all elements in the scheme. Together they make up a *dynamic system*. As a consequence, the coherence among them is especially important. For lack of cohesion, the performance of a project can be disappointing, despite a positive evaluation of most of the separate elements.

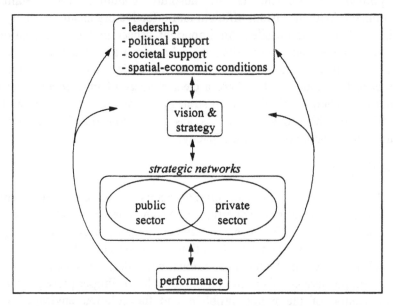

Figure 2   Theoretical framework of organising capacity

Performance implies an assessment. All projects have been developed to face a challenge with implications for both the city and the metropolitan region. The projects are instruments to make the most of opportunities or to turn against clear threats. The actors involved have had certain expectations concerning the performance of the projects: the projects need to attain objectives to contribute to a balanced and sustainable metropolitan development. In sum, the performance of a project deals with the question: is the metropolitan region capable of organising the project in accordance with the objectives that have been set beforehand and what is the contribution of the elements of organising capacity to the progress of the project? Notably, most of the projects are still in progress. In that case, the study has addressed the question whether the project is 'on track' to attain its objectives.

Notes

---

[1] Nijkamp & Vleugel (1993) introduced a pentagon model with respect to 'missing links and networks' related to (international) transport and communication networks, which distinguishes hard, soft, org, fin, and eco ware. We believe that this 'pentagon prism of concerns' can also be used in a wider context.

[2] Antwerp, Birmingham, Frankfurt, Lille, Lisbon, Rotterdam, Strasbourg and Valencia.

[3] Scale adequacy, competence, integrality, democracy and efficiency/effectiveness.

2 Antwerp

Introduction

The city of Antwerp is the main economic centre and the largest city of the Region of Flanders. Antwerp owes its international character to a rich cultural-historical past and its favourable situation in north-western Europe, which has also enabled the port to develop into one of the greatest of the world. Moreover, Antwerp accommodates the second most important chemical complex in the world (after Houston), and is the world's principal diamond centre. With nearly half a million inhabitants, the city qualifies itself as 'a metropolis of human dimensions'. The functional urban region of Antwerp counts some 1.1 million residents.

Next the chapter sketches a profile of Antwerp and explain the administrative structure, to provide a spatial and socio-economic background for the two projects that have been selected for analysis. After that general introduction, the two projects will be dealt with separately. One is the *Strategic Plan for the Region of Antwerp*, the other an information-technology project entitled *Antwerp, an Intelligent City*. Both projects will be briefly described and then analysed according to the theoretical framework presented in chapter one.

Profile

Population

In 1993, Antwerp had about 462,000 inhabitants. In 1983, seven suburbs had been merged with the city of Antwerp'. Just before that merger the population was 187,000. In 1970, 550,000 people lived in that same area. So, between 1970 and 1993, the agglomeration lost 88,000 inhabitants. The conclusion is warranted that in the period since 1970, Antwerp, like most other major cities in north-west Europe, has suffered from suburbanisation: an exodus of people from the city to the surrounding ring and more remote places. Commuter relations are one cause of a strong socio-economic interplay within the functional urban region of Antwerp, consisting of 39 municipalities and accommodating 1,139,000 residents (1993). This functional urban region, based on socio-economic orientation (commuter relations) has no formal status, and is slightly larger than the Antwerp Metropolitan District (30 municipalities and 934,000 inhabitants in 1993).

Reurbanisation, or new growth in the central city after years of population losses, a trend that has been manifest in various cities in north-west Europe since the mid-1980s, is not perceptible in Antwerp, for during the past decade the population of Antwerp has slightly dropped each year by some 2,500 persons).

The city of Antwerp has a relatively aged population: almost 19 per cent are over 65, and only 16 per cent are under 15. The number of persons drawing state benefits increases fast. The number of foreigners is also on the wax and amounted to 13 per cent in 1993. In the pre-1983 part of Antwerp and the district Borgerhout the percentages are considerably higher (up to 20).

Economic structure and development

Economically, the Antwerp region is the pivot of Flanders. Some indicators presented in table 1 give an impression of the relative position of the Antwerp region within Flanders.

Especially since 1981, the shares of some economic indicators have declined. Thus, in economic development, the Antwerp region has slightly trailed behind Flanders and Belgium as a whole.

18

Table 1

Shares of Antwerp region within Flanders region with respect to some indicators

Indicator	Antwerp's share within Flanders region
Population	20%
Employment	25%
Unemployment	20%
Gross product	22%
Value added of business companies	31%
Investments	26%
Exports	40%

Especially since 1981, the shares of some economic indicators have declined. Thus, in economic development, the Antwerp region has slightly trailed behind Flanders and Belgium as a whole.

Strong points of the region are its favourable geographic location within the Paris-London-Randstad-Ruhr Area quadrangle (50 km from Brussels), the good multi-modal accessibility, the presence of a world port, a sound industrial base and a varied service sector, a high-grade, productive and flexible labour force and an attractive quality of life in terms of culture and residential distinction. As weak points must be counted the dependency of local and regional companies on foreign decision centres, the relatively feeble technology base, the lack of consistency in government policy in the past, and the poorly defined Antwerp image [MVPA, 1992]. To that must be added the fact that the importance of the favourable physical situation has waned with the arrival of new communication techniques, the increasing congestion, and the lack of financial resources to carry out the policy measures considered necessary.

The production structure is dominated by the port and a range of port-related industries and transport services. The port is the second-largest of Europe in terms of transhipment (almost 110 million tons a year), and growing fast (by 14 million tons in five years). It defines itself more and more as a general-cargo port. Especially the container sector is growing fast. Among the port-related industries, notably the chemical industry, the oil refineries and car assembly are of importance.

Antwerp is a major international diamond centre. The diamond trade accounts for half of the world's total and seven per cent of total Belgian exports. Besides, the tourist sector received a strong impulse in 1993, when Antwerp was the cultural capital of Europe. Table 2 gives an insight into the employment structure of the city in 1982 and 1992. The well-known pattern of a manufacturing sector declining in terms of employment, and a growing service sector (except for transport) is confirmed in Antwerp.

The development of employment has varied with the international business cycle. The number of jobs declined by 15,000 (more than five per cent) between 1980 and 1984. A period of partial recovery (by 9,000 jobs) followed, which lasted until 1990. Since then, the number of jobs has once more declined by 4,000 to the 1992 level.

From the point of view of the Antwerp Metropolitan District the situation appears to be less alarming. Since the early 1980s, the decline of jobs in the city has been more than compensated by the net growth of 23,000 jobs in the 38 towns of the Antwerp Metropolitan District. There has been a shift of jobs from the central city to the ring towns due to the lack of space in the central city, urban policy measures and the process of suburbanisation [Vranken en Abdeljelil, 1995].

Unemployment in Antwerp shows considerable fluctuation. The number of unemployed drawing full benefits amounted to 25,000 by the end of 1993, that is 11 per cent of those insured against unemployment (source: VDAB). Unemployment among young people is 15 per cent. After 1986 (the earliest comparison opportunity by the current definition) unemployment dropped fast from 19,300 (1986) to 14,500 in the economic peak year 1989. Afterwards, there was a rapid decline in employment, especially in 1992 (by 4,200) and in 1993 (by 3,200).

Urban problems and policies

Like many other major European cities, Antwerp suffers the repercussions of its economic success. While the Antwerp region as a whole can be qualified as prosperous, there is an increasingly serious social discrepancy. Between the tourist-oriented historic inner city and the office-oriented parts of the city on the one hand and the suburban residential cores mostly accommodating the well-to-do, areas have developed where poverty reigns. Although the various policy levels are well aware of the onerous social developments, the necessary about-turn has so far failed to set in for lack of means and coordinated efforts.

Table 2
Employment structure of the city of Antwerp
(jobs x 1,000, 1982 and 1992)

	1982		1992		1982-1992
	Jobs	%	Jobs	%	Jobs
Agriculture, hunting, fishery	0.1	0.0	0.2	0.1	+0.1
Energy, water	6.1	2.5	4.7	1.9	-1.4
Non-energy minerals	3.7	1.5	2.8	1.2	-0.9
Chemical industry	8.9	3.7	10.6	4.4	+1.7
Metal and optical industry	33.5	13.8	25.8	10.6	-7.7
Other industries	16.3	6.7	12.5	5.1	-3.8
Construction	10.4	4.3	9.6	3.9	-0.8
Total agriculture and industry	79.1	32.6	66.2	27.2	-12.9
Trade, hotels & catering, repair	34.1	14.1	35.8	14.7	+1.7
Transport, communication	39.1	16.1	35.1	14.4	-4.0
Banking, insurance	23.7	9.8	35.8	14.7	+12.0
Other services	66.8	27.5	70.3	28.9	+3.5
Total trade and services	163.6	67.4	176.9	72.8	+13.3
Total	242.7	100	243.1	100	+0.3

Source: Statistisch Jaarboek 1993, Stad Antwerpen

The city of Antwerp is in dire financial straits. The merger of 1983 has not brought Antwerp the expected financial advantages. Currently, the city of Antwerp can afford only about one third of the total investments the separate municipalities could make before the merger. Antwerp found out that there was no hope of financial support from the State, and had to seek its own way out of its predicament. A drastic reorganisation took care of a substantial portion of the debt load, but what with the structural budget cut and the increasing number of underprivileged who appealed to municipal social security in the 1980s, the financial picture had little chance of picking up.

For the coalition of parties now constituting the local government, to close the gap between citizens and politics is the first priority. That gap is seen partly as the consequence of the municipal merger in 1983, when the disappearance of seven town councils greatly diminished direct communication between citizens and government. That was not conducive to the citizens' trust in the government. Work is now in progress to give the district councils their own responsibilities and budgets.

The municipal government which took office in 1995 has set the following policy priorities [Stad Antwerpen, not dated c]:

1. to decentralise policy and politics, thus closing the gap between government and citizen;
2. to get to grips with the feelings of insecurity and the social problems;
3. to restore the environmental balance;
4. to improve democracy: the citizen as partner of the government;
5. to reduce deprivation by fighting poverty and improving housing in the underprivileged neighbourhoods;
6. to make Antwerp more than ever a metropolis, a centre of international fame, and place it more than ever in the maritime, economic and cultural vanguard.
7. From the above listing, internal affairs (political and administrative decentralisation, more participation of citizens in policy) and the progressive social problems are put before the stimulation of economic competitive power. As in other major cities, in Antwerp the fear prevails that the progressive concentration of social problems in the central city, in addition to the scant financial opportunities to fight it adequately, will in time have adverse consequences for economic development.

Administrative structure

Since the early 1970s, Belgium has been involved in a process of federalisation. The Constitution of 1993 marks the beginning of Belgium as a federal state. The preliminaries of federalisation were completed on May 21, 1995, when the first direct elections for the two federal Chambers, the three regional parliaments (for the Regions of Flanders and Wallonia and the

Brussels Capital Region) and three Community parliaments (one for each of the three official languages Dutch, French and German) were held.

The Communities are responsible for person-linked matters such as culture, social and medical welfare, social aid and support payments, and education. The Regions are charged with spatial, land-linked matters such as regional and economic development, national housing, traffic and transport, energy and environment. Like the Regions, the Communities are public bodies with independent legislative and executive powers and their own services.

The Flemish Region and Community decided to merge into one Flemish Council. The competencies of the Flemish Council comprise: economics (with the exception of monetary and fiscal policy), public works and infra-structure (with the exception of railways and international aviation), education and training, spatial planning and agriculture, culture, scientific policy, social policy (but social security is a federal matter), housing policy, local administration, and foreign policy as far as the council's own authority is concerned.

The nine Belgian Provinces (the level between the municipalities and the Regions and Communities) have only limited tasks. Their budgets are for instance considerably smaller than those of the larger cities, such as Antwerp. Traditionally the national government has had a great deal of influence on the local level. Since the federalisation most tasks and responsibilities have passed to the Regions.

Although the merger with seven suburban municipalities (in 1983) widened the scope for local administration, it appears to have been insufficient for an effective and efficient development of the entire urban region [Berg, van den, Klink, van, Meer, van der, 1993]. Even more than before the merger, the suburbs that 'managed' to keep out of it are loath to cooperate with Antwerp. The current competitive relations between Antwerp and its suburbs make the symbiosis of core and ring all but impossible. Especially the city of Antwerp suffers from that situation: lack of space for industrial expansion, a lopsided division of costs (to the disadvantage of Antwerp) and benefits (for the surrounding municipalities), etc..

Since the early 1990s, important changes have taken place in the Antwerp administration. External pressures and internal forces induced two newly appointed top officials (the chief executive and his deputy) to initiate a campaign (labelled 'City on the Move') for what is called 'a customer-friendly public enterprise par excellence', aiming at optimum use of human resources and a holistic view of urban management [Vandekerckhove, 1995].

The initiators opted for a 'learning organisation' that flexibly adjusts to changes and allows for self-correction in the course of the transformation process. Meanwhile important steps have been taken to reform the administration. The next objective is to consolidate what has been achieved until now, and to fix the 'City on the Move'-ideas in the minds of all staff members.

Strategic plan for the region of Antwerp

The challenge

Such well-known phenomena as the internationalisation of the private sector, the fast-changing international communication possibilities, and the disappearance of the European inner frontiers have increased competition among urban regions in Europe. Traditionally strong economic positions are increasingly under pressure. That pressure is not determined exclusively by external forces. Internal factors as well, notably the concentration of deprived groups, threaten before long to put the positions of central cities as locomotives of the regional economy in jeopardy. At first, the effects of that process are felt mainly in the central cities themselves, but in the end the entire functional region will find its economic development gradually trailing.

Alarmed by the lagging economic performance as compared with that of Flanders as a whole, representatives of the Antwerp business community, united in the Chamber of Commerce, felt the need for initiatives to stem that tendency. At the same time, political circumstances (the rise of an extreme right-wing group) as well as other considerations woke the municipal authorities to the absolute necessity of an energetic and effective social-economic revitalisation of the city.

Those considerations in particular led in 1990 to a collective initiative of the president of the Chamber of Commerce and the Mayor of Antwerp to design a broadly supported strategy of long-term promotion of the Antwerp economy. To realise that joint initiative, the two initiators (namely, the Chamber of Commerce and the city of Antwerp) created the 'Maatschappij voor de Vernieuwing en Promotie van Antwerpen' (MVPA, Society for the Renovation and Promotion of Antwerp).

The Main Branch Antwerp of Belgium's National Bank was invited to take part in this initiative and to supervise the first important challenge: drawing up a strategy for the Antwerp region.

At the end of 1992 the 'Strategic Plan for the Region of Antwerp' was presented to and formally accepted by the Antwerp municipal council. The objective of the SPRA was defined as 'to develop clear strategic objectives for the region'. The plan is an inventory of strong and weak elements in the economic structure and the regional living and location environment, and a review of actions considered necessary, stipulating the actors most qualified for their execution.

So far, the inventory of activities has not yet been followed up by an explicit strategy in the shape of priorities set, a time schedule, a financing plan, or something of the kind.

An important effect is, however, that the SPRA has created conditions to meet the need for a 'general consensus' in the Antwerp region between private and public parties on the strategic options to be pursued. The MVPA functions as a consultative platform on which the various private and public partners meet regularly, not only on the top level, but also in workgroups occupied with the elaboration of specific elements of the plan. Especially the shaping of that consultative body has been a strong point of the plan.

In April 1995, a survey of actions realised and in progress was published. In some sectors appealing results had been attained, but in others next to nothing had been achieved (MVPA, 1995).

That the suburban municipalities of the Antwerp Metropolitan District are not taking part in the MVPA is a serious obstacle to an effective and efficient implementation of some parts of the plan.

Meanwhile, the two initiators of the SPRA have been replaced by their successors. The 'locomotive function' lies primarily with the Chamber of Commerce. The municipal government's contribution is mostly a beneficent attitude towards the initiative. Although the coalition agreement of the entirely new political coalition (that came into office in the beginning of 1995) contains -as is natural- many elements also treated in the SPRA, the latter does not seem to be formally or informally integrated in the municipal policy.

In what follows, we will successively discuss the making of the plan, the structure and method of the MVPA, the contents of the plan, present situation and expected development; next, the organising capacity with respect to the SPRA will be analysed by the criteria mentioned in chapter 1.

The making of the plan

The stagnating Antwerp economy and the worldwide tendencies that put urban positions in jeopardy, by the end of the 1980s gave rise, in Antwerp as in other cities, to increasing demands for a long-term vision. Meanwhile, much energy had already been invested in studies to that effect. While many of these were valuable, they lacked coherence. Changes were urged in many reports, but rarely carried through. The need developed to put the findings of the many studies together and on that basis draw up a clear review of strong and weak points and of actions considered necessary.

Political motives were involved as well. Antwerp was confronted with a fast rise of an extreme right-wing party. To stop that tendency, an energetic social-economic policy, widely supported by private enterprise in Antwerp and by social organisations, seemed the right method.

An interesting role is played by the National Bank of Belgium. The Bank does not seem directly concerned with the Antwerp ups and downs, but precisely its independent and objective position coupled with its good reputation and the availability of extensive -economic- databanks have been the reason to invite its Antwerp Branch to organise the drawing-up of the plan. Its very lack of political or commercial interests made it possible to circumvent any sore feelings among the different Antwerp partners. The Bank organised meetings to discuss the various partial themes and, together with research fellows from the University of Antwerp, drew up the SPRA. By its active efforts, the Bank became a motive force of the pullers of the plan.

Although the three formal leaders of the operation (the president of the Chamber of Commerce, the Mayor and a director of the Bank) met regularly, the preparations as far as the content was concerned were consciously kept out of the political circuit, for fear of early leaks to the press, with possible negative effects. The implication was that the Chamber of Commerce and the National Bank were the leaders as far as the contents of the plan was concerned. Only very shortly before the official presentation was the plan submitted to the municipal government. In an 'academic session' (solemn gathering), the final plan was formally presented (by the two initiators) to the top people of the Antwerp community. The plan was for the most part received positively in the press. The board and council of the municipality intrinsically backed the plan, although the political reception could not be called particularly enthusiastic.

A serious handicap, inherent to the administrative structure described above and to the ensuing lack of cooperativeness among the local authorities in the Antwerp region, is the aloofness of the suburban municipalities. All burgomasters had been invited and indeed got themselves informally represented in the workgroups, but in practice the suburbs have detached themselves from the plan, so that the title Strategic Plan for the Region of Antwerp is not quite justified.

Structure and method

To carry out the activities effectively in a formal framework, the MVPA was founded in the summer of 1990. The MVPA is a non-profit foundation, erected to organise the prepare the plan and afterwards promote and guide its execution. The MVPA has an Executive Board (15 members), chaired by the president of the Chamber of Commerce. The municipality appoints the deputy chairman. The current deputy chairman is the alderman for financial affairs (1996). The Board meets about ten times a year. At the moment, three (out of ten) aldermen have seats on the Board. Besides, there is the General Assembly (some 50 persons from all sectors of society), which meets once or twice a year.

The daily management and the support of the implementation are in the hands of the Strategic Cell, Finally some working groups support the progress of the sectorial programmes of the SPRA. There are now working groups active in the fields of telematics & informatics, mobility & transport, tourism, small and medium-size companies (the PLATO-project), labourmarket, education and environment.

The Strategic Cell has at present a coordinator (appointed by the president of the MVPA and paid by the MVPA, thanks to a subsidy by the Province of Antwerp, and very recently by the Flanders Region) receives secretarial and informative support from the city of Antwerp. The (commercial) General Bank provides office room. In addition, five persons are coordinating or managing the implementation of specific parts the SPRA. They are financed by the Chamber, the City and by public and private companies involved. The resources of the implementing organisations must be qualified as 'very modest'.

Besides stimulating the activities, the MVPA functions mainly as a forum for the discussion of matters put forward by the principal decision makers. Previously, they often did not know one another's attitudes and plans, so that

Antwerp addressed the outside world in (too) many voices. Especially the forum function is a successful product of the activities in the SPRA-setting.

Contents of the plan

The first move was to define the functional urban region of Antwerp by a social-economic criterion (commuter relations). In that way a Metropolitan Region of 39 municipalities was identified, which admittedly does not coincide with any existing statistic or administrative division.

On the basis of Michal Porter's theory of competition, the principal seven economic sectors and seven types of location condition ('umbrella determinants') within the regional economy were identified. As key economic sectors emerged: harbour, manufacturing industry, diamond, tourism, telematics, small and medium-size companies, and ecology. The critical location factors selected were: residential climate, education, labour market, spatial planning, infrastructure, research & development, and promotion.

Next, SWOT[1]-analyses were performed on the fourteen selected domains with the help of existing and new research results, a comparison of strategic plans for cities and regions in Belgium and abroad, extensive surveys, and the results of discussion meetings and interviews. Moreover, for all these domains long-term objectives were formulated and action points (several hundred) defined under stipulation of the actors responsible for implementation, and wherever possible the estimated cost.

Efforts have been made to get the greatest possible input from the parties and citizens involved. Among other things, a survey was held among 471 business companies and institutions (including the 39 burgomasters of the region) and among 1250 citizens of the region. There was a 25-percent response, which was considered a success.

The plan is first and foremost an extensive inventory, on the basis of which proposals for necessary actions have been formulated. What the present plan lacks is the second step, namely, particulars of the implementation envisaged (priority setting, time schedule, cost budgets, etc.). One reason could be that obviously many actions, especially those concerning accessibility, fall outside the competency of Antwerp or the Antwerp private sector. However, even for the 'indigenous' activities there is no formal execution scheme.

All political parties, including the present coalition partners, expressed themselves in favour of the plan at the time of the elections (end of 1994). However, so far the municipal government has not reacted to (repeated) requests for explicit priorities. The new president of the Chamber of Commerce (in office since 1994) will have to pull the plan and from a recent newspaper interview [Gazet van Antwerpen, edition of 29 September, 1995] actually plans to do so. Without the input of the Chamber, the SPRA would be in jeopardy.

In the interview, the new president formulated the priorities of the Chamber of Commerce. First of all, some bottlenecks in road, train and water connections around Antwerp have to be removed, and Antwerp Airport (an awkward political question) be granted a chance of development. Furthermore the president believes that the various interest groups in and outside Antwerp have not yet fully understood the necessity of a strategic approach.

While the main lines of the plan are still hanging somewhat in the air, in some segments good results have been achieved. Sometimes the successes are due to efforts in the framework of the SPRA, but not all the realisations are direct effects of the SPRA (for instance the Water Agreements between the Netherlands and Flanders, which happen to fall outside the competency of Antwerp), or are continuations of activities taken in hand earlier (such as the project entitled 'Antwerp; An Intelligent City', which will be elaborately discussed later on).

The projects realised are listed in a recent review (MVPA, 1995). Notably in the sector Telematics & Informatics encouraging results have been registered, as will be explained in the discussion of the second project. In the sector of small-scale enterprise some projects are also proceeding satisfactorily, such as the PLATO-project, initiated by the Chamber of Commerce. PLATO is a guidance programme for small and medium-size companies with growth potential. It had already proved a good formula outside the Antwerp region. By now 120 selected companies have been under guidance and a second round has begun.

The future of the SPRA seems to depend on answers to the following questions:
1. Does the municipal government intend to do more than look on beneficently, and to set clear policy priorities within the SPRA?
2. Are the suburban municipalities willing to collaborate with Antwerp?

3. Will the present leaders go on making active efforts to implement the plan?

A great obstacle to the implementation is the lack of resources and competencies for the essential parts of the plan. There are no funds to set a good team to work on the active promotion of the implementation. The present input is considered to be on too small a scale for that purpose.

The municipal government so far has not squarely backed the plan nor defended it towards other levels of government. Unless its attitude is changed shortly, the plan does not seem to be long-lived. That has in fact been confirmed by the present chairman of the MVPA (and president of the Chamber of Commerce) when he stated that "a concrete stand is expected today" [Gazet van Antwerpen, 29 September, 1995]. In his eyes, the new local government should be given a fair chance, but will shortly have to show the political courage to make choices.

Nor does the necessary condition of participation by the region seem near fulfilment. The impression prevails that the authorities of the suburbs do understand the need for cooperation, but lack the courage or the will to put it before their political rank and file. A positive development is that the Flemish government, wishing to stimulate the drawing-up of strategic regional plans, has initiated the founding of regional platforms for municipalities (participation on a voluntarily basis) to reach a common regional vision. The MVPA was recognised in May 1995 as the proper organ for the region of Antwerp to elaborate the initiative. In fact, that proposal was launched very recently, so that any endeavour to estimate its chance of success would be premature.

Analysis of the organising capacity

Now we will analyse the Strategic Plan for the Region of Antwerp by the elements of organising capacity defined earlier (in chapter 1).

Vision and strategy

The SPRA has sprung from the widely accepted and long-confirmed vision that Antwerp has to develop into the European transport and distribution centre of North-West Europe. To make good that ambitious objective, a strategic approach was held indispensable. The MVPA was founded as an instrument of effective implementation. The MVPA (a public-private initiative) has taken in hand the organisation of drawing up the SPRA. Long-term sectorial objectives and a long list of action points have admittedly been defined. However it has so far failed to produce a well-formulated strategy. What remains lacking is a clear stand with respect to the priorities, and a time chart and financial analysis.

The Chamber of Commerce as well as other agencies (like the public/private tandem MVPA/SPRA) have to leave the making of choices to the municipal government. The previous council, which retired from office at the end of 1994, failed to make them, nor has the present local government so far proceeded to do so, despite repeated urging by the other partner, the Chamber of Commerce as representative of private enterprise.

Perhaps the political priorities do not quite coincide with those held by the private sector. The 1995-2000 Coalition agreement [City of Antwerp, not dated c] stresses the social aspects, among them the harmonious society, the social equilibrium, employment, safety, and democracy. Private enterprise focuses on improving the production environment, more in particular the accessibility of Antwerp, which is vital for a centre of transport, distribution and trade.

Administrative structure

The necessary condition of cooperativeness on the level of the functional region is not met in the region of Antwerp, at any rate as far as administrative collaboration is concerned. It has been said that the relation between Antwerp and the suburbs has not been satisfactory since the merger of 1983. It does not seem likely that that situation will soon change in favour of collaboration, although "the city will do everything to open the political debate around the theme of 'region building' [City of Antwerp, not dated c]. The MVPA has meanwhile started, in an informal manner, to establish relations and create a base of confidence. Perhaps the new initiative of the Flemish government to create regional platforms for the formulation of strategic regional plans has a chance of success. Given the voluntary character of the participation and the present awkward relationship, strategic cooperativeness on the level of the urban region still seems a long way off.

Besides the lack of public-public partnership, the lack of financial scope for an effective new policy or for financial support to such initiatives as the SPRA, is an obstacle to the Antwerp government. The situation is inherent to the method of municipal financing.

Strategic networks

In Antwerp the Chamber of Commerce can be regarded as a strategic network, because, contrary to the situation in some other countries (among which Germany, France, the Netherlands), the Belgian Chambers of Commerce (like those in the United Kingdom, for instance) have no public functions, but act mostly as protectors of the interests of private enterprise, on which they are largely dependent for their revenues. The joint creation of the MVPA is a good step towards a new strategic network. As a consultative platform, where the top people from political circles, the private sector, the academe, the social organisations, employers' and employees' associations can meet and discuss the future of Antwerp, the MVPA may be very useful. Such an institutional consultation structure may serve to create synergetic effects on the one hand and avoid counterproductive actions on the other. Politically, a growing understanding of each other's motives may help to reach clear choices regarding the future position of Antwerp.

Within Antwerp, public and private parties were more and more experiencing the lack of insight into each other's views of urban development as a serious deficiency. The interaction between public and private networks was obviously limited. In the city whose citizens and agencies until a short time ago had little interest for one another's interests, economic and political factors have brought about the conviction that in the event collaboration is for everybody's good.

The SPRA is in the main a matter of interaction between the municipal government and the Chamber of Commerce. Indeed, one reason to create the MVPA was the wish to institutionalise that interaction. That does not concern the interaction between private and public sectors, nor for that among parts within those sectors. For those purposes annual Industrial Top-Level Talks are staged and a permanent consultancy structure for telecommunication and informatics has been arranged. Besides, the consultative communication with various Flemish ministries (among others, the ministries of Employment and Spatial Planning, Traffic and Transport) has been intensified.

Leadership

Although the (past) mayor and the (past) president of the Chamber of Commerce are explicitly mentioned as initiators, the impression prevails that it is in particular the president of the Chamber of Commerce who, jointly with the representative of the Bank of Belgium, has put the SPRA on the rails. At the moment the plan is mostly kept in motion by the Chamber. The municipal government is admittedly pleased with the initiative and backs its contents, but has not made the plan its own. The municipal coalition agreement for 1995-2000 does not even once refer to the SPRA. The MVPA is mentioned only as the place where the consultation between the private and public sectors will be activated.

Now that both initiators have retired from office, the best opportunity to keep the plan on the move seems to have been missed. Both new leaders first have to get acquainted with the matter and then show themselves willing to function as the new locomotives. The new president of the Chamber seems to be willing to play the part. Whether the new mayor is as willing, is uncertain. The consequence will be an even stronger shift of leadership to the Chamber.

Another problem is the (quantitatively) small staff of the MVPA's executive body. Too small for important progress to be expected within short.

Spatial economic conditions

Although the region of Antwerp has an 'impressive economic potential' [MVPA, 1992], the SPRA owes its existence to an economic growth that lags behind that of the whole of Flanders. The wish to conserve and possibly reinforce competitive power and employment was among the reasons to draw up the plan. The threats to the economy come notably from the worsening congestion and the lack of public resources to maintain and extend the infrastructure, and from the absence of an optimum regional policy.

Political support

The 1994 elections brought to an end a long period (70 years) of socialist leadership. The success of an extreme right-wing party has been interpreted predominantly as an expression of dissatisfaction and doubt and thus as a warning signal to the politicians that fundamental changes were in order. The new coalition, consisting of four parties (without the extreme right-wing party, the second-largest by the 1994 election results), has put the recovery of the citizen's confidence in the governors' policy in the forefront of its plans. The greatest priority is given to involving the citizen more than before in decision making, investing in environmental measures, social concern, and the problems of safety and society.

The new administration faces the difficult task of pursuing, with limited resources, a new policy that is acceptable to all four participating parties. The situation will not give rise to instant drastic intervention. Only after a period of exploration can a distinct stand be expected.

Meanwhile, the options of the new government seem to flank the SPRA, no integration of the two being in sight for the time being. The important question is what attitude the new mayor is going to take. The coming months seem decisive for the SPRA.

On the supra-regional level, the federalisation process has to be taken into account. The recently installed Flemish government still has to prove itself, and is not likely to put a matter as touchy as region-building instantly on the agenda. Besides, a metropolitan region of Antwerp is looked upon as a huge power factor within the Flemish Region, and finally the general opinion is that the Flemish members of parliament are not really familiar with metropolitan problems.

Performance

The strength of the plan lies in the blend of opinions and the functioning as a forum for decision makers from the public and private sectors to meet and consult with one another. That function is considered of great value by the parties involved. Before 1992, such a platform was lacking.

The Chamber of Commerce, as representative of private enterprise, is the engine behind the plan, which by now has stimulated a few sectors (telecommunication, among others), but so far has had little influence.

The municipal government has its own options, which in many respects run parallel to those of the SPRA. Until today, it has taken a beneficent view of the SPRA without making the plan its own. The platform function is highly appreciated. For the moment the authorities' political priorities seem to differ from those of the Chamber of Commerce (that is, the private sector in Antwerp). Moreover, the government has too little elbow room to be really innovating, and quite a few necessary actions are outside the competency of Antwerp or the Antwerp region, especially with regard to infrastructural improvement.

Actually, the name Strategic Plan for the Region of Antwerp lacks validity in two respects. First, the plan is primarily a strategic *vision*, which needs further elaboration before it can be called a strategy. Second, the region is not involved, so that it is primarily a plan of the city of Antwerp.

The coming six months seem decisive for the future of the SPRA. Much depends on the attitude of the Antwerp council with respect to the elaboration.

'Antwerp, an intelligent city'

The challenge

'Information technology, burotics, telecommunication, telematics are the basis of the rapid evolution to an information society. They are part and parcel of our society. They contribute to the unstoppable development of a digitalized multimedia society' [ICA, not dated]. To give substance to that challenge is the essence of the project 'Antwerp, an Intelligent City' (henceforth to be called AIC-project). The AIC-project is meant to create a technological framework for the city to develop 'intelligently' in the years to come.

The driving force behind the AIC-project is the Antwerp Information Technology Centre (ICA). Without the ICA, which a few years ago was given the chance of shaping total information supply within public Antwerp, the AIC-project (or a comparable project) probably would not have been launched as fast, and Antwerp would not have taken the lead in applied telematics and informatics which it now has, both nationally and internationally. The ICA and the AIC-project are inseparable. Because without ICA there would have been no AIC, the former will now be discussed in some detail.

One of the first ideas maturing within the ICA was the construction of a glass-fibre network to link all the participating public services and companies. That would not only greatly raise the quality and speed of communication, but also open the possibility of saving on the cost of data transmission among the many buildings scattered across Antwerp in which public services are housed. In the 'old' situation, the transmission was accomplished from modem to modem through telephone lines leased from Belgacom (Belgian State Telephone Company) for which the usual tariff was charged. The ICA estimated that the construction costs of the glass-fibre network could be retrieved in 20 years. However, the 'shareholders' were not instantly convinced of the ultimate usefulness of such a network.

The momentum for the definite breakthrough of the ICA came in 1992, when the Antwerp city council approved the proposal to construct a glass-fibre network (MANAP, Metropolitan Area Network Antwerp). The decisive arguments in favour of construction were the investment in the future (in the form of many and manifold multimedia applications) and the possibility of a drastic cut on (internal) telephone expenses, which would considerably reduce the retrieval time of investment in the MANAP, and lead to great savings afterwards. The financial argument derived from the permission to make use of a 'private' network for internal telephone traffic, even between different locations. Up till then that had been a privilege of Belgacom.

Especially the added value to be gained from future uses was an additional argument to combine the public initiatives for further development and application of telematics & informatics in the project 'Antwerp Intelligent City'.

How the ICA came about

In 1985 the decision was taken, on the basis of the findings of an external consultancy bureau, to merge the informatics services of the two principal public organisations within Antwerp, those of the municipality and the OCMW (social welfare centre). The fact was recognised that the two services, unable to respond in good time to changes in the information supply, were functioning inefficiently. The informatics lag, added to the need to reduce the municipal budget, led to the political decision to carry through a drastic reform. From the merger of the two services developed the ICA, which in a short time evolved to an advanced information service.

The ICA found accommodation with the intercommunity body CIPAL (Information Technology Centre for the Antwerp and Limburg Provinces). In 1988 the ICA was granted independency and thus freedom of action. In the legal sense, the 'CIPAL-ICA' (ICA for short) is an intercommunity body, a non-profit organisation supplying services to members.

After a reorganisation, work was begun with a staff of 20 persons, to which in one year's time were added a hundred others, with adequate knowledge of and experience in informatics. That helped the renovation process enormously. In a relatively short time the lag could be turned into a leading place before many another public agency, thanks to the fast creation of an extremely advanced informatics service. At present the ICA employs a staff of over 150.

The ICA Board of Governors counts twelve members, four members of the municipality, four from the OCMW management and four from the intercommunity body CIPAL, which emphasises that the ICA is primarily a public agency. Nevertheless, its action freedom is great. The fact that everybody, political or non-political, is in favour of the project, makes matters easier.

When in 1992 the possibility was opened to organise one's own telephone communication, the investment in the construction of the MANAP came to be considered acceptable from a political point of view as well. For instance, the municipality rents telephone lines for the control of traffic lights. These telephone lines are in use around the clock. Therefore, very much can be saved by leading internal telephone communication (about three fifths of total telephone traffic among the over 400(!) public offices) through a self-controlled glass-fibre network.

In 1998, when the liberalisation of telephone traffic within the EU will be complete, use of the 'private' network between the municipality, OCMW and Port Authority (that recently joined the project, thus becoming the third public partner) will also be permitted, as will be connections with the 'outside world', outside the public agencies. At the moment, that kind of telephone communication is still in the hands of Belgacom.

With a view to Antwerp applications, the ICA has launched a joint venture with the following partners:

- Alcatel Bell (private company, supplies the switchboard);
- Integan (intercommunity body for cable television, lays the cable);
- Telindus (private company, delivers peripheral equipment).

Much to the advantage of the project appeared to be the participation of the Antwerp-located company Alcatel Bell, a private company (originally Belgian, now French), specialised in informatics and telematics applications. This company recognised the usefulness of experimenting with the kind of application ICA had in mind. Alcatel Bell developed the equipment. For Alcatel Bell, this practical experiment helped towards the development of market-oriented and practice-tested products. The advantage for Antwerp in that situation was that the Alcatel Bell technicians were standing by around the clock to identify any teething troubles -not at all unusual in experiments-, put them right, and go on to improve the system. The close collaboration with that company has therefore contributed much to the success.

Another windfall was Antwerp's designation as Cultural Capital of Europe during the year 1993. That designation inspired drastic changes in the traffic infrastructure. By good coordination with the public-works department, wherever a street was broken up, a piece of glass-fibre cable was put in, thus saving much digging. A glass-fibre network to a length of over 40 km was laid in record time. The ultimate length now foreseen is 55 km (under the surface of the city of Antwerp).

Telematics and informatics are looked upon as one of the seven 'flagships' of the SPRA (see the project first dealt with above) primary reasons being the presence of international prominent telematics companies in the region, among which a few high-tech ones, the availability of specialised university education, and the progressive telematics policy pursued by the local authorities, including the OCMW and the Port Authority.

From the SWOT-analysis of the position of the Antwerp telematics & Informatics sector, the following long-term objectives were derived in the SPRA [IMVPA, 1992]:

1. to promote collaboration between the public, academic and private partners involved   towards a common vision;
2. to develop Antwerp to the most advanced region in the area of telematics;
3. to build and extend a high-grade telecommunication network that can be connected to local, regional, national and international networks;
4. to elaborate the concept of 'Intelligent City' as an attraction factor for existing and new-to-attract companies.

To attain these objectives, the following 'strategic action points' were considered necessary by the composers of the SPRA:

1. creation of a permanent consultative platform for telematics & informatics;
2. creation of a tele-communication centre;
3. construction of a Metropolitan Area Network (expansion of the existing system for high-speed transfer of all types of text, sound, image, etc.);
4. consolidation of the specialised education supply;
5. region promotion: 'Antwerp Informatics City'.

The AIC-project can be regarded as a contribution from the public sector to the SPRA. Meanwhile, through the ICA and the AIC-project several of the planned activities in the area of telematics and informatics have been realised. The ideas of the ICA and the ideas formulated in the SPRA run parallel. The AIC-project makes as such an important contribution to this element of the SPRA. Moreover, as a result of the collaboration with the ICA, the Alcatel Bell company delegated a staff member to stimulate the execution of the telematics and informatics programme as formulated in the SPRA.

The ICA is moreover a significant instrument for the participation of Antwerp in international networks (such as Telecities, City-YRN, Magica, and others), and the acquisition of subsidies from the European technological funds.

The role of the ICA with respect to private enterprise is still limited, although successes have meanwhile been recorded with the EDIGO-project (application of electronic data interchange with small- and medium sized companies). Four out of the five principal Antwerp suppliers of equipment/software take part in this project.

Finally, the Antwerp experiences draw many visitors, on whom some city promotion can be practised. In 1994 the ICA received 1500 interested visitors from some 30 different countries, among them EU-delegates and many suppliers of info-equipment.

Although the ICA was already functioning in the new constellation, the collaboration within the SPRA has helped towards one of the most successful developments within Antwerp.

Contents of the project 'Antwerp, Intelligent City'

The 'Antwerp-Intelligent-City' project has several dimensions. It can be viewed alternatively as [ICA, not dated]:
- a basis for Antwerp's future information systems;
- strategic tool to secure Antwerp's position as an important future economic centre;
- a framework within which parties can exchange points of view, try for cooperation, etc.;
- a laboratory for testing, shaping and adjusting novel ideas and new technologies.

The leader of the AIC-project is the Antwerp aldermen for Information Technology Applications. The ICA does not receive additional financial support for the AIC-project. This project has to be fully self-supporting, and hopes to that end for European subsidies from the Technology funds.

A few concrete sub-projects, carried out under the umbrella of the AIC-project, are in the area of tele-administration, tele-education, and tele-medicine. By EU-criteria, such applications are eligible for subsidy. Other objects are video-conferencing and tele-control of the water quality in the Antwerp swimming pools.

The latest application is the supply of tele-services by the municipal departments. The installation of special booths at strategic spots in the city takes basic services closer to the citizen. That purpose counts in Antwerp as a political priority.

Not only for the municipal government but also for the OCMW, the AIC-project is extremely important. The complete OCMW-services, including eight hospitals, are joining the city departments on the MANAP. The ICA has already made considerable efforts to computerise the billing, which is a crucial part of the OCMW-operations, including the health-insurance refunds, the only income of the Belgian hospitals. Other applications are of a medical nature, for instance the electronic transfer of medical images such as X-rays. Advanced equipment for diagnosing is getting more expensive all the time and cannot be afforded by every hospital. Thanks to electronic exchange, the doctor who is treating a patient can receive the results of, say, a brain scan performed in another hospital. The long-term objective is to build up a complete electronic case history including digitalised medical images [City of Antwerp, 1994].

In recent years, other services of the OCMW have been decentralised to 30 Social Service Offices where citizens can get in touch with the OCMW, for instance for job opportunities or specific administrative forms. All applications aim at easier and more efficient information of the customer. The project receives financial support from Brussels (through the Fourth Framework Programme 1994-1998 of DG XIII).

The port has its own informatics system tailored to the transport and distribution function. The connection to the MANAP concerns notably the remaining communication.

Future

The future of the ICA opens a wealth of prospects, which is inherent to the fast evolution in the sector. Support is assured, indeed, nobody questions the value of the project. The extension possibilities are legion, not only as regards the use but also in the spatial sense.

As far as the use is concerned, negotiations are in progress to make universities, R&D-centres and comparable knowledge centres into MANAP-users. Work is also going on with interactive teletext, tourist information (EU-subsidisable), etc.

Companies can communicate through MANAP (and through Belgacom) with the authorities, but not yet among themselves. From 1998 (when telecommunication becomes fully liberalised) that will change. A high-grade telecommunication infrastructure will then be a high trump card for the Antwerp location climate.

At present, the spatial scale of ICA's operations is still limited to the city itself. The Antwerp system is unique for Belgium. The conviction is, however, that such a system is practicable only if there is adequate support, a condition which seems to be met only by the larger towns. The Flemish government takes much interest in the Antwerp experience, and contemplates a telecommunication network of its own, to compete with Belgacom. ICA has been requested to elaborate that plan.

Analysis of AIC

We shall now analyse the project 'Antwerp, an Intelligent City' with reference to the elements of organising capacity.

Vision and strategy

The AIC-project springs from the prospects of urban applications of telematics & informatics as viewed by the management of the ICA and within the SPRA. The visions the ICA and the SPRA take of the sector are perfectly compatible.

The decision rigorously to reorganise the obsolete public information service, though mostly inspired by the wish to cut expenses, can also be considered the outcome of a vision shared by the municipal and OCMW authorities. At any rate, the strategy to give the ICA as much freedom as possible has certainly stimulated the development of that informatics service. It has enabled ICA to set to work energetically, unfettered by red tape. The opportunity opened by institutional renovation, has been well used by the ICA.

ICA's strategy (to joint the company involved in looking for ever new applications, to mutual advantage) has been helped along by the liberalisation of the (internal) telephone communication and the spatial deconcentration of the government apparatus, which made considerable savings possible.

41

Administrative structure

Both the project and the implementing agency are one hundred per cent public. The specific administrative structure does not seem decisive for its success (or failure).

Strategic networks

The principal actors committed to the theme in hand are the SPRA, the Telecities Network, and the OCMW. The first two networks are informal (voluntary membership). The initiatives are private/public (SPRA) and public (Telecities). Spatially, the SPRA is limited to the city of Antwerp. Telecities is an international network of European cities. The OCMW is a formal public organisation, functioning within the city of Antwerp. As such it is not a network, but a combination of agencies occupied with social and medical services.

The implementing agency of the SPRA, the MVPA, functions primarily as a consultative platform. It has been useful in bringing together the public (ICA) and private parties within the sector telematics & informatics. As a result, the ICA is actively involved in some activities considered necessary (such as EDI-applications) in the setting of the SPRA.

Antwerp is an active member of the Telecities Network, created by Eurocities. Telecities counts some 65 members and 10 workgroups. Antwerp is represented (together with Barcelona, Bologna, The Hague, Manchester and Nice) in the supervising body, and chairs three workgroups. Telecities, subsidised by the EU, is considered a highly important initiative because it permits the formation of consortiums to apply for European subsidies, and because it offers opportunities for the exchange of knowledge. Especially the latter works highly stimulating. The cities try to top one another in activity, especially the leaders, Antwerp among them.

The OCMW, finally, is a public body, with its roots in works of charity; it coordinates agencies of social and medical service. As such it is an important 'umbrella', which for its services is profiting much from the glass-fibre cable.

The interaction between the administrative structure and the strategic networks does not seem to have been decisive for success. At the moment, the AIC-project is still exclusively a public enterprise. A few companies are directly involved, but their involvement has to do with implementation rather than strategy. The interaction with the predominantly private SPRA is excellent. There are in fact no impeding factors. All parties back the initiative.

Leadership

The initiative to launch the ICA was taken by the boards of the municipality and the OCMW. It was inspired by the malfunctioning of the informatics services and by budget cuts. As such, the public leadership does not seem decisive for the success, although the political support of the aldermen concerned has certainly make a positive impact.

The role of the ICA-management is undoubtedly important. The project has been set in motion professionally and purposefully by the ICA. By building up a qualitatively strong organisation and establish relations with significant actors (Alcatel Bell, among others), great steps forward were made possible. ICA has also ambitiously responded to the wish to define Antwerp internationally as informatics city, for instance within the Telecities network, in which Antwerp occupies a prominent place. That this also serves to promote the city, is well understood.

Spatial-economic conditions

For this project, certain spatial conditions have been significant. First, the presence in the Antwerp region of quite an important telecommunication industry. The presence of a company as Alcatel Bell proved vital to the fast development of applications through the MANAP.

Another positive factor has been the presence of the informatics department and a post-graduate telecommunications and telematics course at the University of Antwerp, through which high-educated staff become available.

Because the administrative apparatus is highly deconcentrated (a multitude of establishments scattered across Antwerp), the glass-fibre network has saved a lot on communication expenses. The savings would have been far less under more spatial concentration.

The impression is that the informatics services of the port on the one hand and those of the city and the OCMW on the other have neither influenced nor reinforced each other. The reason probably is that the two organisations have divergent needs. Notably in the field of transport and distribution, the logistic services have been greatly improved by the introduction of telematics and informatics. A harbour town like Antwerpen can be expected to take the lead in that respect. Rightly, therefore, the SPRA mentions the 'electronic monitoring of shipping and treatment of data flows' as a strong point under the heading 'port' [MVPA, 1992]. Still, the ICA has been developed separately from the port, and the port services waited until two years ago to join the glass-fibre network.

Political support

The attitude of politicians was without exception positive, irrespective of political colour. All parties recognised that a positive urban development requires an up-to-date communication technology. The AIC-project accordingly seems to be above discussion. That is unquestionably due, among other things, to the adequate approach of the ICA.

The improved communication possibilities between citizen and authorities that are now being prepared, are a policy priority for the present city administration. The priority points 'improvement of the environment' and 'reinforcement of the tourist sector' are also furthered by the applications offered by the MANAP (such as quality control of the water in swimming pools , and interactive tourist-information pillars).

Finally, the city of Antwerp desires a wider international qualification than that of a harbour city. Eurocities/Telecities offers opportunities to that effect, and a successful appeal has also been made to the European technology funds.

Performance

From the above, the performance of the ICA and the AIC-project appears to be highly positive. The most important results can be described as follows;
- the lag in informatics of the public agencies (municipality and OCMW) could be turned into a leading position in the area of telematics and informatics applications;
- much money can be saved on public communication expenses;
- the MANAP offers many future applications, the more so after the liberalisation of telephone services in 1998, also for private uses.
- the AIC-project is helpful in realising the priority policy aim to bring 'government closer to the citizen';
- within the sector Telematics & Informatics of the SPRA much progress has been made. thanks in particular to the AIC-project;
- internationally (for instance in the context of Telecities) Antwerp can indeed rightfully define itself as an 'intelligent city'.

Conclusions

For several years, the economic development of the city of Antwerp has lagged behind that of Flanders as a whole. Since Antwerp is the unquestioned economic gravity centre of Flanders, that lag, which moreover threatened to become structural, has incited the Antwerp private sector and the local government to work more intimately together. The impression is that formerly the collaboration was not optimum and that the tendency to put individual interests first was characteristic of the Antwerp situation. That was confirmed in a recent interview with the current president of the Antwerp Chamber of Commerce [Gazet van Antwerpen, 29 September, 1995). The involvement of various parties with the Antwerp ups and downs was allegedly underdeveloped for that very reason. That in the end this would be to the detriment of the general interest seems finally to have penetrated to the major parties within Antwerp, among them the municipal government, other important public bodies such as the Port Authority, and the Antwerp private sector represented in the Chamber of Commerce.

The insight that separate functioning can be counterproductive and therefore should be prevented, found expression, among other things, in the joint founding of the Maatschappij voor de Vernieuwing en Promotie van Antwerpen (MVPA: Society for the renovation and promotion of Antwerp), a non-profit public-private organisation, for the purpose of drawing up the Strategic Plan for the Region of Antwerp (SPRA) and promoting its execution. This plan was to result in a widely supported future vision, to be made concrete in a number of (main) objectives and necessary actions.

The exercise of drawing up the plan can be qualified as successful. Under the leadership of the strictly neutral National Bank of Belgium, many parties have given evidence of their involvement by taking part in some way in the realisation of the plan. The MVPA appears to function well as a platform for consultation between the public and private executives within Antwerp, and the many intentions laid down in the SPRA are an inspiration. Meanwhile, appealing successes have been achieved in several sectors, successes which without the new approach of consultation might have been reached less smoothly or not at all.

So far the result is positive. However, there are many matters that have not yet been taken in hand to the satisfaction of the parties involved. One such matter is the lack of cooperativeness among the governments of suburban municipalities, which are not really on speaking terms with the government of the central city. The consequence is that the SPRA is primarily an

45

Antwerp plan rather than a plan for the region. Particularly in the Antwerp situation, better adjustment and collaboration between the (impoverished) central town, which has to solve most of the regional problems, and the (mostly affluent) suburbs, is urgently needed. The suburban municipalities have so far tended to put their own interest first. That attitude, mostly induced by short-term political motives, has to be characterised as shortsighted.

A second handicap of the strategic plan is that it got stuck in the inventory of a multitude of actions considered necessary. What lacks is the strategy itself, set forth in priorities set, actions scheduled in time, financial consequences, etc. The Chamber of Commerce has stated that to specify these matters is primarily a task of the municipal government. So far, the latter has not taken that task in hand. Intrinsically, the municipality backs the contents of the SPRA and praises the collaboration achieved, but has formulated its policy priorities in isolation from the SPRA. The plan is not even mentioned in the policy intentions.

A third handicap is that many of the actions deemed necessary (especially the infrastructural improvements wanted by the private sector) lie for the greater part outside the direct competency of the city of Antwerp. Relevant decisions have to be taken on the national or Flemish Regional level.

Three years have passed since the SPRA was presented. For the private parties represented by the Chamber of Commerce, it is now time to get down to business lest the plan fails. If the plan as such remains 'floating in the air', the cautiously built-up organising capacity between public and private parties may be put in jeopardy. .

Some elements of the plan have indeed been taken up successfully. One is the project 'Antwerp, an Intelligent City', the second of the projects treated here. This information-technology project is the positive result of the strategic reorientation of two public automation services. Thanks to their merger into one new, advanced informatics service, which was given great freedom of action, and a decisive and energetic approach, the arrears which Antwerp had incurred in that field were turned into a lead. By now, Antwerp counts as leader in the area of telematics & Informatics applications among the European cities.

The most important results so far are the construction of an urban glass-fibre network with unique possibilities, expected to produce in time a considerable reduction of communication costs for the public bodies connected, and an enormous improvement of data transmission especially in the medical sphere. Even more challenging are the future uses, among which

46

the possibility to bring municipal basic services close to the citizens (through special booths), further automation of medical data, tourist information, environmental monitoring, etc.

Notably from 1998 onwards, when free telecommunication within the EU becomes a fact, the glass-fibre network will be able to prove its full worth. For the moment the project is a public matter, but from 1998 it will be free to give access to the private sector as well.

The successes are due to the fact that the project is politically insensitive: everybody understands that in the area of communication, where a wealth of new applications can be expected, the least one can do is to keep abreast. That the investment in the network can be recovered from the revenues is another important factor. That the municipal council approved the construction as early as 1992 is a credit to the persuasive power of the initiators.

Favourable secondary factors were the manifestation 'Antwerp, Cultural Capital of Europe 1993 (which facilitated the laying of the cable), spatial deconcentration of government services (permitted a great cut in telephone expenses), and the presence in Antwerp of some market leaders in the telematics & informatics industry (favourable to the joint developing/testing of user options).

To conclude, from the Antwerp administrative situation and from the projects investigated, the regional organising capacity in the wide sense, as far as interaction and 'intra-action' between public and private parties are concerned, is at a stage of development. The foundations have been laid, but the building is not yet complete, although here and there elements have come into their own. The parties concerned will have to exert themselves not to be left with a half-finished building. Mark that external parties (notably the Flemish government) have their own responsibility with respect to the Antwerp developments.

For the time being there seems little chance of the unfortunate administrative relations within the region taking a turn for the better. That makes it all the more necessary to reinforce the strategic networks. Possibly, by the indirect road, namely through the strategic networks, the attitude of the authorities within the Antwerp region can be influenced in such a way that the organising capacity of the Antwerp region is strengthened.

Abbreviations used

AIC	Antwerp an Intelligent City
ICA	Information Technology Centre Antwerp
MANAP	Metropolitan Area Network Antwerp
MVPA	Maatschappij voor de Vernieuwing en Promotie van Antwerpen
SPRA	Strategisch Plan Regio Antwerpen
SWOT	Strengths, Weaknesses, Opportuniti
OCMW	Openbaar Centrum van Maatschappelijk Werk
CIPAL	Centrum voor Informatica van de Provincies Antwerpen en Limburg

Note

---

[1] Overview of Strengths, Weaknesses, Opportunities and Threats.

3 Bilbao[1]

Introduction

In the last century and until the 1980s of the present century, the metropolitan region of Bilbao was highly prosperous, thanks to its traditional industries such as shipbuilding, coal mining and steel factories. When those industries fell into a rapid decline, however, the region landed into serious socio-economic problems, and perforce had to set its sights on new economic activities. Since the second half of the 1980s a revitalisation programme has been actively pursued. To facilitate the transition process of the region, two specific organisations were created that are central to this chapter: Bilbao Metropoli-30 and Bilbao Ría-2000. Next, the chapter will sketch the socio-economic developments in the region, followed by a discussion of its specific administrative structure. After that, the chapter describes the organisation Bilbao Metropoli-30 and the strategic plan designed for the region, followed by an analysis of Bilbao Metropoli-30. The chapter continues with a description and an analysis of the activities of Bilbao Ría-2000. Finally, we draws some conclusions from the chapter.

Profile

The metropolitan area of Bilbao is the urban agglomeration located in the Bajo Nervión in the Basque country and formed by 30 municipalities with a total area of 498 square kilometres and almost one million people. Bilbao is the capital of the Bizkaia province and accommodates four fifths of its total population, and 44.4 per cent of the Basque Country's inhabitants. Six of the

49

thirty municipalities exceed 50,000 inhabitants: Bilbao, Barakaldo, Getxo, Portugalete, Santurtzi and Basauri. In terms of population, Metropolitan Bilbao is the fifth most populated metropolitan area in Spain, behind Madrid, Barcelona, Valencia and Sevilla.

Two fifths of the metropolitan population are concentrated in the city of Bilbao with a density of nearly 9,000 inhabitants per square kilometre. Only a few municipalities on the left bank of the river have a higher density. Most industry of the metropolitan area is located on the left bank of the river together with most of the residential accommodations for the industrial. The principal city in this area is Barakaldo, the second city of the province of Bizkaia. Since the 1970s, the highest rate of unemployment in the region has been recorded here. Most socio-economic problems are consequently concentrated in this area. The area on the right bank of the river is the main residential area of relatively high quality outside Bilbao. Only a few industries are located here. The most important municipality in this part is Getxo; it has 85,000 inhabitants.

Between 1981 and 1991 the population in the region diminished constantly because of the drastic economic restructuring which the area underwent from the 1970s on. The Bilbao metropolis lost nearly 30,000 inhabitants between 1981 and 1991, 3.1 per cent of the total population. Some municipalities experienced even greater losses, such as Barakaldo, which in that period lost 11.4 per cent of its population (see table 1).

Table 1
Development population in the metropolitan area of Bilbao (1981-1991)

	1981	1986	1991	% (91-81)	Density
Metropolitan area	952,366	942,709	922,519	-3.1	2,240.20
Of which:					
Barakaldo	118,615	114,094	105,088	-11.4	4,153.60
Bilbao	393,759	381,506	369,839	-6.1	8,954.90
Getxo	67,793	77,856	79,954	+17.9	6,718.80
Portugalete	58,071	57,794	55,823	-3.9	17,444.60

Source: Bilbao Metropoli 30, 1994, *Informe Anual de Progreso*, Bilbao.

The demographic growth registered during the 1960s and 1970s, due to immigration and high birth rates, has been followed by the progressive ageing of the population. Births have decreased dramatically from 13,000 in 1980 to approximately 7,000 in the 1990s. But the major cause of population decline has been outmigration, even if it has lost weight from 1988 on. From those phenomena, the metropolitan area of Bilbao is expected to stabilise at around one million people.

The ageing of the population is serious. From 1981 to 1991, the share of the under 20s diminished from 34.2 to 25.5 per cent. On the opposite side, the share of the elderly (more than 65 years old) increased from 8.9 per cent in 1981 to 12.3 per cent ten years later. Still, compared to other major European cities, Bilbao is a 'youngish' urban area. The demographic dynamics has led to increases in the activity rate, with the incorporation of 165,000 new active people in one decade. The most relevant process is the change in the female activity rate which reached 27.7 per cent in 1991, eleven points above that of 1981.

The educational level of the Bilbao metropolitan population is lower than the average of Bizkaia, with a high concentration of primary studies and less-than-average proportions of secondary and university studies. Still, there was a positive evolution during the 1980s with an increase in higher-education degrees. With respect to university degrees, the market shows an excess of humanistic degrees and a certain shortage of technical and entrepreneurial students which results in a lack of adequate human resources for the market segments most related to the current processes of economic transformation.

As to the economic potential of Metropolitan Bilbao, its GDP amounts to 1,400 billion pesetas, which means half of the Basque Country's GDP. The Bilbao agglomeration is a typical example of an industrial area in decline. The crisis is mainly due to the industrial development concentrated in a few labour-intensive sectors and at a low technological level, strongly linked to the national market, besides some traditional economic links with Great Britain, Belgium and the Netherlands. Important economic activities within the metropolitan region have been shipbuilding, steel industry, hydro-electronic power companies and financial activities. The evolution of employment shows a strong decline of the industrial sector, which nevertheless still employs 31 per cent of the labour force. The decrease of industrial employment is most acute in the municipalities of Barakaldo and Sestao where the great companies in conversion, such as Altos Hornos de Vizcaya, are located. Currently the economic structure of the area shows a relative specialisation in tertiary sectors (59.5 per cent) although less than in other Spanish cities. The service activity concentrates in Bilbao city (67 per cent of the employed) and in some municipalities of the Northern area: Getxo, Sopelana, Barrika, Gorliz, Leioa and Plentzia. The construction sector currently employs 8.3 per cent of the workforce, while the primary occupation has decreased from 2.8 per cent of the population in 1981 to 0.7 per cent of the labour force of the metropolitan area.

The region's efforts to attract new foreign companies are handicapped by its rather unfortunate image due to ETA-activities. Many potential foreign investors look upon the Basque region as an instable area. That perception does no longer represent the reality. Violent attacks are virtually a thing of the past; the few attacks that are still reported, occur mostly in other parts of Spain. However, an image, once settled, takes a long time to shift. It would be a great help if some renowned foreign or international companies and/or institutions could be persuaded to settle in the region. That could work as a catalyst on the confidence of other potential investors in the region.

The metropolitan region of Bilbao has been designated as an Objective-2 region, and in that capacity is entitled to considerable financial support from the European Commission, though less than the greater part of Spain, which has been designated as an Objective-1 region. Moreover, the region has to account for more co-financing than Objective-1 regions: one half of the project costs against one quarter. Nevertheless, the European financial subsidy is important for the revitalisation of the metropolitan region of Bilbao.

Administrative structure

With regard to the Bilbao region, there are four governmental layers: the Spanish Government, the Basque Government, the County Government (diputación de Bizkaia) and the (thirty) municipalities. Following the restoration of democracy in Spain, the new constitution of 1978 firmly placed Spain on the road to decentralisation. In recognition of the regional diversity, 17 autonomous communities or regional governments were created with varying degrees of autonomy. Fifteen *Comunidades Autonomas* are located on the Spanish Mainland, among which the Basque country, the two others are the Balearic Islands and the Canary Islands. The Communities have their own parliaments and legislative responsibilities. The parliaments are elected directly by the population once every four years. The Basque region has a relatively high degree of autonomy. The Basque government itself virtually governs in sectors like education, health, culture and housing, on which it spends more than three fifths of its annual budget. With respect to such policy areas as research, industrial policy and transport and communications, economic agreements (*Concierto Económico*) are concluded every five years with the Spanish central government, stating allocations and responsibilities.

The Spanish Ministry of Public Works, Transportation and Environment (MOPTA) of the central government has progressively assumed the role of major public actor in large urban areas. In the early 1990s a special department of Urban Planning and Territorial Coordination was created to integrate sectorial plans and coordinate them with the plans of cities. In the Basque country the County Governments are responsible for tax legislation and the collection of taxes. Afterwards, part of the collected money is given to the Basque Government and the Spanish Government. Because the tax collector resides relatively near to the citizen, the degree of tax evasion is rather low. Though the tax rates in the Basque country are in general lower than in other Spanish regions, in total the taxes received by inhabitant are higher, because of the efficiency of the system. The County Governments are the supervisors of the municipalities in their jurisdiction as well as autonomous administrative bodies with a task load of their own. They are responsible, among other things, for secondary roads, agriculture, forestry, and culture.

In the 1960s, the State created administrative bodies on the level of the metropolitan area in the urban regions of Madrid, Barcelona, Valencia and Bilbao (*the Greater Bilbao Public Cooperation*). These bodies occupied themselves with a limited number of matters concerning the entire urban area. The agglomeration governments came directly under the State government. Especially in regions enjoying relative autonomy, such as Catalonia and the Basque country, there was great resistance to these bodies on account of their centralist nature en the lack of democratic legitimacy. After the Franco-period, these public bodies were dismantled.

The powers and autonomy of municipal government have also widened and strengthened since 1979. The Local Finance Bill (1988) envisaged the creation of a self-sufficient system of local finance, but this has not come off owing to the strength of the communities which play an important role in cities. The municipalities draw income from their own taxes (corporate tax and property tax) and from transfers of the County Council. Local government has become more complex as a result of the division of functions between different tiers of government. This has led to difficulties at places where local and regional tiers are controlled by different political parties.

Bilbao Metropoli-30

Bilbao Metropoli-30 was set up in 1991 as a public-private partnership to accompany the revitalisation process of Metropolitan Bilbao. There was general concern that without an independent organisation to accompany it, the strategic plan for the revitalisation of the region would be abandoned. The tasks of Bilbao Metropoli-30 are to carry out studies, research and training plans on elements of the revitalisation plan, to commercialise and to market activities outside the radius of the metropolitan area, to create awareness of the strategies of the redevelopment plan, to finance and sponsor several activities, to coordinate projects and to lobby towards the Spanish and the European Government. Furthermore, the organisation fosters the cooperation between the public sector and the private sector to reach joint solutions about problems of mutual interest that affect the metropolitan area of Bilbao.

Bilbao Metropoli-30 was founded by 19 institutions, among which the Basque government, the County Council, the Bilbao City Council and the Association of Basque Municipalities, the two universities of the Bilbao region, the Chamber of Commerce of Bilbao, the Port of Bilbao and some private companies. The participation is informal and voluntary. Bilbao Metropoli-30 is a relatively small organisation; there are only eight people on the payroll. Although the organisation has limited resources (it is funded by contributions of the members) and limited powers, it has great influence on the revitalisation of the urban region. The association currently counts more than eighty partners. These are, among others, Basque institutions, public, semi-public and private companies from both the industrial and the service sector, associations, technology centres, universities and media firms.

Bilbao Metropoli-30 seems to have contributed substantially to the revitalisation process of the region as main developer of the regional strategic plan. One of its main achievements has been to create awareness in- and outside the region of the urgent need of the transition process and of the economic potential of the region. It has helped to attract new economic activities, such as the European Software Institute. Moreover, Bilbao Metropoli-30 plays a role in raising additional national and European funds for the revitalisation process. The organisation has also helped to generate a kind of metropolitan sense, a feeling of solidarity among the population of the metropolitan region. This metropolitan sense is important for the societal support needed for the activities to be carried out in the framework of the revitalisation plan.

Strategic plan for the revitalisation of the metropolitan area of Bilbao

The strategic plan for the revitalisation of the metropolitan area of Bilbao was initiated by the Ministry of Economic Affairs of the Basque Country and the County Council of Bizkaia. The revitalisation plan for the region started to be drawn up in 1989 and was completed in 1992. The plan consists of four stages: exploration and identification of critical subjects, internal and external analysis, determination of targets, aims and strategies, and, finally, preparation and implementation of the plans to be effected. The first stages of the plan were carried out by Andersen Consulting.

Eight critical elements for the strategic plan have been distinguished. For each of them a special (public-private) task force was appointed to set priorities. Furthermore, 88 indicators have been defined by which to judge these elements and compare the results with developments in other cities and other old industrial areas involved in a process of economic transition. Every year a statistical yearbook is composed stating the scores by these indicators. The eight critical elements are (1) training of human resources, (2) transformation into an advanced service metropolis, (3) mobility and accessibility, (4) environmental regeneration, (5) urban regeneration, (6) culture, (7) cooperation between the public and private sectors, (8) social actions. They will be briefly discussed below.

1.   Training human resources
The training and retraining of human resources on behalf of new promising economic sectors is considered the most important element of the revitalisation plan. Attention will be given notably to the relation between training courses and openings on the labour market. The gap between the two is regarded as one cause of the high unemployment rate in the region. A training policy aimed at qualifying human resources for the new sectors and for the needs of a neo-industrial society has been developed.

2.   Transformation into an advanced service metropolis
Until the 1980s, the regional economy of the metropolitan area of Bilbao had been based first and foremost on labour-intensive basic industries. Because many of these activities have fallen into decline or been lost, attempts are made to find new activities with growth potentials for the region. Although much has been done in the last few years towards full technological renovation and adjustment of the productive capacity, there are still many problems pending, such as:

- insufficient investment in R and D;
- insufficient industrial diversification;
- insufficient presence in external markets;
- insufficient incorporation of productive services (such as technology, design, distribution, marketing) in the industrial process;
- insufficient development of business services;
- lack of adequate locations for business services.

Efforts are made to attract new service activities, among which high-tech ones, which are on the one hand grafted onto the industrial tradition of the region and on the other may enhance the competitiveness of the industries still in existence. Besides, Bilbao tries to attract companies dealing with aeronautics, computer software, environmental techniques, and other service activities.

3. Mobility and accessibility

To create an appealing location climate for new economic activity, the internal and external accessibility of the metropolitan area has to be improved. The metropolitan area of Bilbao faces some problems with respect to its accessibility. Because the road networks of the different subareas are not properly coordinated, the Bilbao municipality has become excessively centralised, with negative impacts on accessibility and internal traffic. Furthermore, public transport is inadequate and the lack of coordination between the different modes does not encourage people to leave private transportation for bus or tram. Table 2 reproduces the investment plans for new infrastructure. In November 1995 the first line of the new underground railway on the right bank of the river was opened. The expectation is for the underground to cut individual car traffic in the city by 15 per cent. The next step towards improved internal accessibility will be the construction of a metropolitan railway line on the left bank. However, for that line there are no funds available just now. Financial support has been requested from the Spanish central government. To complete the new system of metropolitan railways, a new intermodal terminal will be built in the centre of Bilbao.

One tool to improve external access to other European metropolises is the link with the European high-speed railway network. The European Union has put the High-Speed Railway-line from Bilbao through Vitoria to the French border on its list of priority TransEuropean Networks. Negotiations with Madrid about the financing of that project are underway.

Table 2
Infrastructure investment plans (in million pesetas)

Projects	Cost	Status
Metropolitan rail	93,00	partly realised/ partly planned
Intermodal station	40,00	plan
Enlargement of the external port	100,00	under construction
Access to the metropolitan area	35,00	plan
Railway	333,00	plan
Abandoibarra south variant (railways)	30,00	plan
Airport of Sondika	10,00	plan

Source: Bilbao Metropoli-30, 1994

Since 1991, work to build a new port has been in progress. In the event, there will be one large new harbour zone. At the moment, the harbour of Bilbao is still spread among nine different areas, of which two in the city of Bilbao. The total costs of the project amount to 100,000 million pesetas. It is financed in part from European resources. In 1997, the first part of the project will be realised, and in 2002 the entire project has to be finished. The new port area will have an extra kilometre of docks and will provide 1.5 million square metres of new space for the location of new (logistic) firms.

According to the plans, the airport of Sondika will be extended. The present airport accommodates 1.4 million passengers a year. However, the expectation is that in ten years' time the number of passengers will grow to two million. Investments in the airport are made by the Spanish central government.

4. *Environmental regeneration*
In the 1970s, Bilbao was declared one of the worst polluted areas of Spain. Since then, the quality of the air has improved because many industries have been closed down. Especially the amount of SO^2 has greatly decreased. The new economic activities generate relatively few emissions. Since 1993, gasification works have been carried out, promoted by Bilbogas. The substitution of natural gas for gas-oil will help to reduce air pollution. Currently, traffic is the main generator of emissions.

The 'iron river', the backbone of the city, is heavily polluted. In the 1980s a cleansing plan was drawn up. The total costs of the project, which consists of several plans, are estimated at 94.9 MECU. The plan will be carried out with the help of ERDF-funds (33.1 MECU). The project is funded by a consortium of municipalities along the river. The river is a potential leisure resort for the city. There is a project for a pleasure port for city residents near the sea.

Efforts are made to reduce and recycle the volume of waste that is generated in the metropolitan area. In Bilbao new recycling techniques are being developed. From the Cohesion Fund, more money can be spent on environmental measures.

5. Urban regeneration

For the first time in its history, a detailed spatial plan has been drawn up for the city[2]. Some important elements of the plan are proposals to convert old industrial zones in the centre into appealing multi-functional locations with cultural activities, parks, houses and modern economic activities. In particular the re-development of locations along the river banks, where no new industries are permitted, is hoped to have a beneficial effect on the residential and location climate of Bilbao.

6. Culture

The point of reference for the city. Moreover, the attraction of this institute can have a positive influence on the image of the region. Besides, in the Abandoibarra area a conference cultural function of the city will be notably strengthened by the erection of the Guggenheim Museum, which also has establishments in New York and Venice. The striking design of the new museum will become a significant and concert hall will be established. In the near future, this area will become the cultural centre of the region. Ten years ago there were hardly any theatres in the region. Currently, the metropolitan area boasts seven public theatres, with an average capacity of one thousand people.

7. Cooperation between the public and private sectors

Closer cooperation between the public and the private sectors is an essential element of the revitalisation plan. Inspired in particular by American experiences (Pittsburgh), Bilbao tries to improve the achievements of the management of the public sector by private techniques. The relatively young workforce of the Bilbao public management is receptive to these new techniques. The aim is to improve the competitiveness of the city. For indeed, the achievements of the private sector are related to the attitude of the public sector.

8. Social actions

In 1993, the revitalisation plan was revised to include social actions. There was a general consciousness that this was essential to make the plan a success. The aim of the social actions is to involve everyone in the economic revitalisation. One instrument to that effect is to publish a statistical yearbook as an important means of communication with the citizens. Other social actions are improvement of housing and training of human resources.

Example of a newly attracted economic activity: ESI

One achievement of Bilbao Metropoli-30 is its help in attracting the European Software Insititute (ESI). This institute is important for the strategy of economic diversification and for the image building of the region. ESI functions also as a catalyst for related activities. It has already stimulated the location of several high-technology companies in its direct vicinity. More than forty companies are at present occupied with technologically advanced activities within the Technology park, in which ESI is located.

To set up ESI was a major industrial initiative, launched by fourteen European computer software companies. In the early 1980s, Bull S.A. was the initiator of this idea. The aim is jointly to improve the competitiveness of the European software industry. To that end, an independent organisation has been founded to support the companies in this sector. The organisation intends to function as an intermediary between the suppliers and the users of the computer software. The activities of ESI are among others transfer and dissemination of information, education, training and consultancy. Some current full members of the organisation are Iberdrola, Siemens-Nixdorf, Thomson-CSF, Olivetti S.P.A. and Lloyd's Register.

The idea for the organisation was supported by the European Commission. They appreciated it and decided to promote it. A public tender was held with respect to the place of location of the organisation. 12 cities competed for this institution, among others Dublin, Glasgow, Sevilla, Paris, Pisa and Bilbao. The Basque government supported the idea and ESI was offered accommodation and land, covering almost 40 per cent of the budget of ESI. This was an important incentive to choose Bilbao as location of ESI.

Bilbao Metropoli-30: analysis

Vision and strategy

The creation and activities of Bilbao Metropoli-30 have found wide support in the region. Several public as well as private actors were involved in its founding and a wide variety of public and private actors are members. However, the public actors have taken the lead with respect to the activities of Bilbao Metropoli-30. The initiators of Bilbao Metropoli-30 were public institutions (the County Council and the Ministry of Economic Affairs of the Basque country) and the ideas with respect to the revitalisation process have mostly been developed by the public sector.

Bilbao Metropoli-30 also enjoys wide societal support. Explanations are the urgent need for strategical changes, the voluntary participation of many public and private actors and the attention Bilbao Metropoli-30 is paying to adequate communication with the local population. Good communication of the strategical aims of the organisation and its activities is considered essential for local commitment.

Bilbao Metropoli-30 seems to be the appropriate organisation to get sufficient societal support for the chosen projects. The fact is that the general public, wary of politics, tend to consider the messages of an independent, more or less neutral organisation such as Bilbao Metropoli-30 to be more reliable, more scientific, and more based on a long-term view. Therefore, Bilbao Metropoli-30 can successfully sell the message that the relatively large investments are necessary for a sound socio-economic development of the region.

The present societal support is in sharp contrast with the lack of it for the government-imposed public organisation for the entire metropolitan area, the 'Greater Bilbao Public Cooperation', during the Franco-era. That organisation lacked democratic support and met with heavy resistance in the region. By contrast, Bilbao Metropoli-30 has restored the metropolitan sense among the population of Bilbao. For some years now, people have been familiar with, and talking about a 'metropolitan area'.

An important feature of Bilbao Metropoli-30 is the drive for spatial and sectorial integrality of its activities. Great store is set by the implementation of activities in the entire functional economic region of Bilbao. The 30 municipalities involved in Bilbao Metropoli-30 constitute a highly coherent area. In principle, every municipality in the area is involved in the development of the strategic plan. The borders of the area are not fixed, however. Should the involvement of other zones in the revitalisation be desirable, then the flexible structure of the organisation makes it possible. Spatial integrality and coherence of activities essential to revitalisation is thus stimulated. The plan's comprehensive nature allows also for sectorial integrality and coherence. The strategic plan indeed provides for a wide range of activities, encompassing economic diversification, accessibility, cultural services, environmental measures, and social actions.

Administrative structure

The Spanish administrative structure is that of a strong hierarchy. Consequently, municipalities do not have much elbow room for their own strategic decisions. The possibility to influence the long-term development of the region is therefore a potent incentive to cooperate.

The three Basque government tiers involved, namely, the Basque government, the County Council, and the municipalities, all have more or less parallel objectives: the socio-economic revitalisation of the region and a more distinct profile of the region in Spain and in Europe. In other words, there is a strong feeling of solidarity, a desire to show that the region has good economic potential and knows how to capitalise it. The Basque country has a tradition of forging coalitions. An organisation such as Bilbao Metropoli-30 was therefore quite easy to set up.

The province of Bizkaia is the economic gravity centre of Basque country. The Basque government therefore puts great value on cooperation with the authorities concerned for the optimum utilisation of the economic potential. The Basque and provincial governments are the initiators of the regional partnership embodied in Bilbao Metropoli-30. Government layers are linked in solidarity vertically as well as horizontally. In general the municipalities try in their decision-making to strike a balance between their own profit and the regional interest. That is a strong point for the organising capacity of the region.

When Bilbao Metropoli-30 was first established, some members were afraid to lose competence. They were nonetheless convinced of the clear need to co-operate. They shared a clear interest in revitalising the regional economy. The strategic plan for the region outlines intended development directions for the region but does not give details for the different parts of the region. As a consequence, the municipalities involved are still competent with respect to their own economic policy. There is consensus among the municipalities about the medium-term developments, but in practice they are

61

still competing for the attraction of new companies. For instance, the cities of Bilbao and Barakaldo are both trying to draw high-technology activities to their jurisdiction. As long as it is not counterproductive, for instance because plots of land being sold at lower than "market-conforming prices", or an overcapacity in the region being invested in, some competition may turn out to be advantageous to the entire region.

Leadership

Both the revitalisation process and the Bilbao Metropoli-30 are kept going by the public sector. The public sector is at the moment the catalyst of the regional economy. The division of responsibilities between the private and public sectors has not always been like that . During the Franco-period, for instance, it was the other way round. In that period the private sector was the driving force of the regional economy. It was the private actors who determined in what direction the region was to develop; the activities of the public sector were then of secondary importance. In that period, the public infrastructure of the region was inferior, largely because the Spanish government was not inclined to invest in the Basque region. Though, the public sector has taken the lead in the revitalisation process, the private sector has been highly committed to it.

Spatial-economic conditions

The deep economic crisis of the metropolitan region of Bilbao was a great stimulus for regional collaboration. Every actor concerned understood the necessity of an intimate partnership to relieve the socio-economic misery. That was notably true of the municipalities of Bilbao and Barakaldo, which were suffering the most from the economic crisis. But also a relatively affluent municipality like Getxo unfailingly recognised the need for regional collaboration as a means to consolidate the socio-economic position of the entire region.

Political support

Municipalities have little scope to develop a strategic policy for their jurisdiction. For some of them, this was a major consideration to participate in Bilbao Metropoli-30. The municipality of Getxo, for instance, wanted to have a say in the quality of education programmes and in the long-term development of the local economy. However as an individual municipality, it is not competent in those policy areas. By joining Bilbao Metropoli-30, this and other municipalities have got hold of an important instrument for drawing up collective plans and influencing the direction of regional development.

Strategic networks

Bilbao Metropoli-30 is a public-private organisation. One of its main achievements is the regional consensus about the direction of and the choices with respect to the revitalisation process of the region. The public sector strongly encourages the revitalisation process. That the public sector initiated the revitalisation process and set up Bilbao Metropoli-30 is logical. The private sector was in a deep crisis and focused more on short-term survival. A private actor threatened with altogether stopping his activities will have trouble thinking about about long-term regional developments: 'first you have to survive, then you can philosophise'. Therefore, the most appropriate actor to initiate the revitalisation process was the public sector. However, the private sector is closely involved in the activities of Bilbao Metropoli-30.

For sound cooperation in an organisation like Bilbao Metropoli-30, municipalities need to strike a balance between the local and the regional interests. It is normal that the opinions of partners about desired development directions do not always run completely parallel. However, the necessity and the desirability of cooperation is clear to every actor involved. The fact that the Basque country can operate in relative independence from the rest of Spain is an extra stimulus, making the Basque actors more inclined to co-operate. From a feeling of solidarity and responsiveness they are anxious to improve the regional-economic situation and their national and international competitiveness.

Performance

The activities of Bilbao Metropoli-30 are focused on medium- and long-term development. The results of the envisaged economic diversification and socio-economic revitalisation of the region can only become visible in the longer run. Therefore, the results can hardly be judged after just four years of implementation. Nevertheless, in some respects changes are perceivable to which Bilbao Metropoli-30 has contributed.

One of the most important results is that all the actors concerned have committed themselves to the direction of the region's development. By reinforcing the feeling of solidarity within the urban region, Bilbao

Metropoli-30 has helped to create a climate of strong social and political support for the strategic plan. Very nearly all public and private actors as well as citizens recognise the necessity of the steps proposed.

Besides the internal promotion of activities within the urban region, Bilbao Metropoli-30 has contributed to the region's external image-building: its international marketing. Significant results are the financial subsidy for some projects from the European Commission, the attraction of the European Agency for Health and Safety at Work, the ESI, and the Guggenheim Museum.

One explanation of the success of Bilbao Metropoli-30 is its emphasis on policy (the strategic plan and the projects) rather than on the institution itself (the precise structure of the organisation). The strong regional commitment has generated a constructive climate for a collective revitalisation programme, a climate in which any matters of competency seem subordinate to the collective goal.

In the future, a more structural public organisation for the metropolitan region may be desirable. However, in the present administrative structure this will be hard to achieve. There will be tension for instance between the County (the province) and a metropolitan area. If the County loses its competency for the metropolitan area of Bilbao, its remaining jurisdiction will be small. Such a loss of competence cannot be acceptable to an organisation that is now the most powerful public actor.

Bilbao Ría-2000

The activities of Bilba Ría-2000 are aimed at developing a limited number of concrete projects envisaged in the strategic plan. It is a public-public partnership, in which public actors work together who are hierarchically dependent on one another. Since the middle of the 1980s, the various competent authorities, within their respective jurisdictions, have been working towards the transformation of Bilbao, principally in transport infrastructure, water treatment and river cleansing, and strategic economic projects. When the second phase with a greater element of urban regeneration had to be undertaken, the partners were agreed that this should be done according to a new management model, in which all the relevant authorities were to take part. The public-public organisation Bilbao Ría-2000 was founded for this purpose at the end of 1992. Bilbao Ría-2000 was set up by four government layers: the national government, the Basque government, the County Council (Diputación Foral de Bizkaia) and the City Council

(Ayuntamiento de Bilbao). Bilbao Ría-2000 works as a kind of project developer, implementing the main projects for the metropolitan region of Bilbao.

The founding of Bilbao Ría-2000 was stimulated by the Spanish government, specifically the Ministry of Public Works, Transport and Environment (MOPTA). It made Bilbao one of the priority objectives of its new City Action Policy. This policy was directed at the development of large-scale operations in town planning, transport and the environment. requiring the coordinated action of all relevant authorities. Bilbao was chosen by the MOPTA because of its problems and because much land in the centre of the city belonged to the Spanish government. The latter can be explained by the fact that several basic industrial companies, which had been closed down in the last decades, were owned by the State, along with several -now deserted- plots of land used by the national railway company and the state-owned port authority. Therefore, there was a shared interest in cooperation: the City needed the land of the State and the State needed the cooperation of the City. Another factor that contributed to the creation of Bilbao Ría-2000 was the determination of both the Basque government and the County Council to support the transformation of Bilbao, the most important metropolitan area of the Basque country, as a foundation of the Basque economy.

Bilbao Ría-2000 is a public-funded limited company. In the organisation there is a 50-50 division of interests between organisations of the central and the Basque governmental layers. The Basque interests are equally divided among the Basque government, the Bilbao City Council and the Provincial Council (see also table 3). The president of the company is the Mayor of Bilbao and its vice president is the Secretary of State for Territorial Regional Policies and Public Works. There is a Steering Board that meets every three months, consisting of 18 persons. Nine persons are representatives of state organisations and the other half are representatives of Basque public organisations (among others three ministers of the Basque government and the mayors of the main centres in the Bilbao region). The Executive Committee, which meets once a month, consists of representatives of the four public partners. Whether decisions are taken by the steering or the executive committee depends among other things on the size of the required investments, the kind of projects and the political importance. There is a relatively small executive board of 11 members. Work goes on in small project groups of two or three persons. In principle there is a separate project group for each of the four projects in which Bilbao Ría-2000 is involved. At the moment Bilbao Ría-2000 is occupied with three important projects in the city of Bilbao (Avandoibarra, Amezola and the Southern by-pass) and one project in the city of Barakaldo.

Table 3
Division of interests in Bilbao Ría-2000

Organisations of the Spanish central government	50%
Basque governmental bodies	50%
Basque government	(16.6%)
Bilbao City Council	(16.6%)
Provincial Council of Bizkaia	(16.6%)

Source: Brochure of Bilbao Ría-2000

The Abandoibarra project comprises the conversion of an old centrally located harbour area into a modern town quarter of 30 hectares. This is the most extensive and most important revitalisation project of Bilbao. Here, the new Guggenheim museum is under construction. Other objects to be realised in the area are a conference and exhibition hall, a management and business centre, a shopping mall, a hotel and several high-quality housing blocks. One third of the area has been set aside for parks.

Once the present rail-yard facilities in the Amezola-area have been moved underground, three hectares of park will be laid out on the southern edge of the city centre. The whole area covers some 10 hectares, and will be given over to quality housing in a renovated, environmentally upgraded setting. The open spaces provided for in the plan will help to relieve traffic congestion in the outlying districts of Irala and Rekalde. New road links will improve access and integrate the two areas in the city.

The third Bilbao project in which Bilbao Ría-2000 is involved is the construction of the southern by-pass. An existing railroad line skirting the town centre to the south, will be extended and upgraded (among other things with support from the European Regional Development Fund). There will be three tracks instead of two: two for passenger transport and one for freight. The southern by-pass will be used among other things to replace the present rail connection on the river bank. On the roof of the new railway linkage an avenue can be constructed: the Avenida del Ferrocarril, eliminating the barrier effect and creating an important traffic artery for the city. Two old

66

railway stations will be replaced with one new intermodal station. The rail terminal for freight transport will be moved to the new harbour area.

Bilbao Ría-2000 has recently started an urban-renewal project in Barakaldo. Half of this project is financed by the European Union, in the framework of the Community Initiative URBAN. The total investments for the project are 25 MECU. The programme combines nine different social and economic actions, among which the stimulation of small enterprise and improved access to the railway station.

Bilbao Ría-2000 is basically financed by contributions of the four public partners. In addition to the official contributions, the plan was to search for resources to supplement the budget. Therefor, it sells lucrative plots released in the town-planning actions. Furthermore, Bilbao Ría-2000 has attracted European financial support, and, with modest amounts of money, some of the members paid for projects that were carried out by Bilbao Ría-2000. At the moment, the organisation is studying new ways of participation by the private sector.

Bilbao Ría-2000: analysis

Vision and strategy

The aim of Bilbao Ría-2000 was to create a flexible organisation which could coordinate all the actions initiated by individual authorities. Its originality lies in the grouping within a single company of all public agencies, from the local to the state level, involved in the regeneration of the metropolitan area of Bilbao. The integration of all public levels in one organisation is important to create sufficient support for projects, to limit bureaucratic procedures and thus to speed up the execution of projects.

The Spanish government is one of the participating actors in Bilbao Riá 2000. To enlist the central government in the execution of projects was advisable among other reasons because the state owns plots of land that are important for the revitalisation, especially land of former state-owned industrial companies and transport companies.

From the analysis of Bilbao Metropoli-30 the fact emerged that the solidarity of the public actors in the metropolitan region of Bilbao has made the partnership easy to set up and to continue. The feeling of solidarity can be explained from the relatively independent position of the Basque country towards Spain. In such a position, the public actors involved are ready to join forces to make capital out of the regional potential and to work towards a better outward profile. The participation of the central government in an organisation such as Bilbao Ría-2000, founded explicitly to revitalise the Basque region, is remarkable in that light. The partnership proceeds well in practice; the central government understands the need for adequate collaboration with the Basque public actors and regards the partnership in Bilbao Ria-2000 as an example for other Spanish towns.

The support of the Spanish government to Bilbao Ría-2000 has been spurred on by the merger of the Ministries of Public Works and of Transport. The joining of these ministries favours a more integral approach of the State to spatial planning and transport, and in particular a broader view of the revitalisation. Matters can now be judged intersectorially. The MOPTA for instance takes a broader view of urban problems than state companies such as the national railways and the state-owned national port authority, which obviously have specific interests to defend.

Administrative structure

Bilbao Ría-2000 was founded on behalf of the execution of key projects in the metropolitan region of Bilbao. Vertical collaboration between the government levels concerned is the main characteristic of this organisation. Because of the strictly defined distribution of competencies among the four government levels, collaboration is indispensable for the decisive, fast and flexible realisation of large-scale projects. The relatively heavy hierarchical administrative structure in Spain demands such an approach.

We have pointed out the great cooperativeness of the Basque government levels. The feeling of solidarity in Basque country favours constructive work on shared objectives. Collaboration with the Spanish central government is somewhat more subtle, however. The Basques have relatively much autonomy and try to sail their own course independently from the rest of Spain. However, because the State, recognises the relevancy of a sound revitalisation of this important Spanish region and has its own direct financial interests (the plots of land it owns in Bilbao), and because the same political parties are in power in Madrid and in Basque country, the partnership between the Basque authorities and the Spanish central government has so far proceeded to full satisfaction of the actors. The mutual collaboration is strengthened by the fact that the present director of Bilbao Ría-2000 was formerly employed with the MOPTA.

Leadership

The creation of Bilbao Ría-2000 fitted into the new national urban policy, called the City Action Policy, of the MOPTA. Key elements of this policy are: to carry out large-scale projects and to involve a multiple of government layers. Bilbao being one of the larger metropolitan cities in Spain, its choice as one of the cities to implement the new national urban revitalisation programme was not illogical. The Spanish government has stimulated Bilbao Ría-2000, probably for the following reasons:
−   The Spanish government wants to have influence on and a voice in the revitalisation of the economically important Basque region;
−   The Spanish government has an interest in the optimum utilisation of plots of land it owns in the Bilbao region;
−   In comparison with the rest of the European Union, the Spanish economy is weak. Therefore, the Spanish government has every interest in supporting regions with strong economic potential, thus to stimulate the national economy.

Spatial-economic conditions

Both Bilbao Metropoli-30 and Bilbao Ria-2000 owe their existence to the dire straits in which the regional economy found itself as well as to its economic potential. Every public actor involved has an interest in using the available potentialities and setting the desired revitalisation in motion. The bad economic circumstances of the region have deepened the solidarity feelings already prevailing, thus generating a broad foundation for constructive collaboration.

Political support

That the Spanish government is involved in the activities of Bilbao Ría-2000 is a very positive development. The central government seems to have held itself somewhat aloof from the economic development of this region until the end of the 1980s. The present commitment of this important public actor is well in line, however, with developments in the European Union springing from the integration process. Because European regions increasingly compete with one another, national governments more and more try to support economically potent regions in their territories. Greater involvement on the part of Madrid in this Basque region is therefore in harmony with present trends. At the time that Bilbao Ría-2000 was set up, there was a divergence concerning governing political parties in Madrid and in the Basque country. This has supported the cooperation between the public partners involved. Both groups shared more or less the same ideas and there is a feeling of solidarity.

Strategic networks

Until now most partnerships for Bilbao Ría-2000 projects were between public actors. For the Barakaldo project, Bilbao Ría-2000 works closely together with Bilbao Metropoli-30, in an effort to involve the private sector more than in earlier projects. So far, the role of the private sector has been limited to the purchase of land. The private sector in Spain is hardly if at all participating in large-scale projects. One explanation is that pension funds and similar institutions are still in their infancy in Spain. They are reluctant to participate in large-scale development projects. Once a first step has been made by an investor, for instance a bank, more private organisations can be expected to enter the market. Another reason for the private investors' reluctance is that some of them have suffered serious losses after participating in large-scale projects. Foreign investors have so far shown little enthusiasm to invest in the region. A plausible explanation is that the region's image has been severely damaged by the activities of the ETA.

At the time Bilbao Ría-2000 was launched, the banks showed great interest in the plans. Unfortunately, the interest waned after some time and no decisions were taken actually to join the schemes. Now that some projects turn out successful, the interest of private investors is on the wax again,

Performance

The projects in which Bilbao Ría-2000 is active, are more or less on schedule. At the moment the organisation was started there were no detailed plans. But the achievements to date have been satisfactory. Moreover, there seems to be enough support for the projects in progress or planned, which is a condition for a speedy revitalisation. The success of Bilbao Ría-2000 is due to the good coordination of the governmental layers concerned. The execution of large-scale projects tends to be subject to relatively lengthy procedures, for one thing because various government levels have to be involved. By working together in one organisation, the public actors can cut the red tape. By jointly putting the objective of revitalisation first, the public actors can collaborate in a constructive way. For the MOPTA the

70

cooperation with Bilbao is the jewel in the crown of their national urban policy. It is the first urban operation in Spain that is carried out in good time.

Conclusions

The Basque country operates in relative independence from the rest of Spain. The metropolitan region of Bilbao, the economic gravity centre of Basque country, enjoys presenting itself as such. The region sets great store by international contacts, to emphasise its own special position in Spain and the strong points of the region as, among other qualifications, a business location, a congress city, and a tourist destination. In the 1970s the region fell into a deep socio-economic crisis. Traditional industry had been the motor of Basque economy since the last century. After the closure of many factories, the region counted relatively many unemployed. Besides, the region suffered from serious environmental problems, due for one thing to polluting industries. From the second half of the 1980s onwards, under the stimulation of the public sector, a revitalisation process for the region has been in progress. Important objects are the diversification of economic activities -the gravity centre has to be shifted to high-quality services-, improvement of the living environment, and enhancement of the cultural image of the urban region.

Bilbao Metropoli-30

Bilbao Metropoli-30 was set up as a public-private partnership to guide and support the revitalisation of the metropolitan region of Bilbao. The tasks of Bilbao Metropoli-30 are: to carry out studies of and research into, and develop training plans for elements of the revitalisation plan; to commercialise and market activities outside the radius of the metropolitan area; to make the public aware of the strategies of the redevelopment plan; to finance and sponsor several activities; to coordinate projects and to lobby with the Spanish and European governments. The establishment of these institutes is hoped to increase the confidence of potential foreign investors in the region. If the relatively bad image of the region (due, among other things, by ETA-activities) could be improved, more new economic activities might be drawn to the region with more ease.

There seems to be wide regional support for the activities of Bilbao Metropoli-30. The organisation has helped to generate a metropolitan awareness. In that respect the neutral character of the organisation has been important;

there are no direct political interests linked with the activities of Bilbao Metropoli-30. The participating actors are firmly committed to these activities. This can be explained in part by the solidarity felt in Basque country, among public actors -horizontally and vertically- as well as between public and private actors. Another reason for the high degree of commitment to the revitalisation plan of the region is the regional-economic situation. The deep economic crisis into which the Basque economy had fallen, was a strong incentive to collaboration.

Owing to, among other things, the feeling of solidarity and the great urgency of the revitalisation plans, the policy to be pursued is primary and the organisation secondary. In other words, problems of competency are hardly at issue; very nearly all actors are constructively occupied with drawing up schemes and carrying out the revitalisation plan.

For the municipalities concerned, another strong motive to collaborate in Bilbao Metropoli-30 was the limited scope they have for a strategic policy. The partnership enables them to exert more influence on the future socio-economic development than they might be able to individually and by the normal hierarchical avenues. Although the municipalities remain competitors, among other things for new economic activities, great store is set by inter-municipal collaboration.

The activities of Bilbao Metropoli-30 are highly integral in terms of space and sectors. The spatial integrality is attributable to the fact that the area for which the revitalisation plans are developed has not been strictly delimited. The important thing is the functional-economic cohesion in the area involved in the revitalisation. The sectorial integrality is due to the fact that the plans have essentially been designed for the socio-economic revitalisation of the entire region, and involve in principle all sectors. For that reason, the revitalisation plans have been drawn up in outlines only. They need to be elaborated in detail by the actors directly concerned. Though, the activities towards the region's revitalisation have been mainly initiated by the public sector, private actors have been highly committed to it.

Bilbao Ría-2000

The activities of Bilba Ría-2000 are aimed at developing a limited number of concrete projects envisaged in the strategic plan. It is a public-public partnership, in which public actors work together who are hierarchically dependent on one another. The actors are the municipalities where the projects are carried out (Barakaldo and Bilbao), the County Council, the

Basque Country, and the Spanish central government. The participation of the Spanish government is remarkable in the light of the relative independency of the Basques. One explanation for the participation of the Spanish central government in Bilbao Ría-2000 is that this public actor owns important stretches of land in the region. The State considers the project an interesting illustration of the new City Action Policy of the Ministry of Public Works, Transport and Environment. The partnership with the State, which so far has been fruitful, can also be explained from the circumstance that there was a divergence of ruling parties in Madrid and in the Basque country.

The partnership of Bilbao Ría-2000 is stimulated by two factors that have also been pointed out in the discussion of Bilbao Metropoli-30: the feeling of solidarity and the regional-economic conditions. The Basque solidarity reinforces the inclination jointly to take up revitalisation in a constructive spirit and the abominable regional-economic circumstances made all the public actors involved understand the need of good cooperation.

Private companies have so far hardly been involved in the project development. They are wary of participating in large-scale projects, because of some bad experiences in the past and the uncertain prospects of the region. That the implementation of projects has so far been successful could well stimulate a greater financial commitment of the private sector.

The first concrete results of the revitalisation process are gradually becoming visible through the various projects now in execution. Recently the first underground railway line was opened, which is to play a prominent part in the congestion-ridden intra-regional passenger transport. The most striking project is the new Guggenheim-museum in the Abandoibarra zone. By its breathtaking architecture, this project is to be a great stimulator for the diversification of regional activities. That and other results of the process of revitalisation now in progress look promising.

Solidarity will probably once more be the factor to stimulate permanent partnership of the actors involved. Should the regional economy be looking up, then the second motive for collaboration would lose its urgency. However, given past experience the discussion partners expect that solidarity will remain a dominant incentive for collaboration. In a recovering economy, the private actors may also come to play a part of importance.

Notes

---

[1] Co-author: drs. P.M.J. Pol

[2] Ayuntamiento de Bilbao (City Council of Bilbao), 1992, Plan General de ordenacion urbana.

4 Bologna[1]

Introduction

Bologna is the capital of the region Emilia Romagna. This region, situated in the northern part of the Italian peninsula, is in economic terms one of the most successful regions in Europe. Since the 1950s, the economy has flourished, with agriculture and industry as the most important sectors. The economic and societal development of the Bolognese area has expanded such as to cause administrative problems. To cope with these problems, a process to adapt the administrative structure to the changed circumstances has been set in motion. Concurrently, the public-transport system in the Bolognese region is being reorganised. The two developments will be discussed and analysed in this chapter.

Profile

Spatial situation

Bologna's extensive, well preserved medieval city centre, with its numerous porticoes and early predecessors of modern-day skyscrapers, lends to the city the aspect of a town that has long been an important economic, social and cultural centre. Bologna owes that position among other things to its situation near the foothills of the Apennines, on the edge of the Po-valley, one of the most important industrial and agrarian areas of Italy. The city is the capital of the Province of Bologna as well as the Region Emilia Romagna of which the province is a part. The region lies in North-Italy, and links the

75

Italian peninsula to the continent. Forty-eight per cent of the jurisdiction of the region is plain country, 26 per cent mountainous, and 26 per cent hilly.

The economic activities in the region are concentrated along the Via Emilia, an ancient Roman road stretching from Piacenza to Rimini on the Adriatic coast. That route has attracted many business entrepreneurs; the highest concentration is in the Province of Bologna. The mountainous areas have not benefited from the developments along the Via Emilia. In recent years they have been faced with depopulation, agricultural holdings being abandoned and livestock farming in a critical situation.

Population

The region as a whole, however, boasts the highest activity and employment rates in Italy. In recent years there has been in fact a shortage of labour. That generates considerable immigration from outside Italy, especially from non-EC states, with the associated problems of social integration. After the Second World War the total population displayed steady growth. This persisted until the early 1980s, after which the population stabilised at some four million inhabitants. The composition of the population is changing fast. The regional birth rate halved between 1950 and 1990, and the mortality rate dropped significantly. The result is an aging population.

Within Emilia Romagna the province of Bologna is the most densely populated, registering 246 inhabitants per square kilometre in 1990. That is well above the EC-average of 146. The population of the province grew by about one per cent a year in the 1950s and 1960s. Afterwards the growth slowed down and the population stabilised at some 900,000. The city of Bologna reached its maximum volume of about 600,000 soon after 1970, and then contracted again as the town outgrew its limits and the townspeople migrated to surrounding villages and towns. The movement was initially directed to the industrialised plain, but later shifted to the hills and mountains. At the moment Bologna counts just under 400,000 inhabitants.

Economy

The region Emilia Romagna is situated at the lower extreme of the famous 'DATAR-banana', the curved line which connects Europe's major trade and industry centres and runs from London through the Ruhr-area to Northern Italy[2]. In 1993 the region was in tenth place among the 122 Regions of the EC in terms of GDP per capita. The average GDP of the region is about 27 per cent higher than the EC-average. In Italy the region Emilia Romagna ranks second in personal income, which is about 35 per cent above the national average, as well as per capita consumption, which is about 36 per cent more than the national average.

In comparison with the European average, the economic structure of Emilia Romagna is marked by an overrepresented agricultural and industrial sectors and an underrepresented service sector. In 1990, one tenth of the employed persons worked in agriculture, 36 per cent in industry, and 55 per cent in services. The corresponding European averages at the time were 7, 33 and 60 per cent. Post-war industrialisation in the region came into swing in the 1950s, spread out along the Via Emilia. Although agriculture is still one of the most important sectors in the region, its employment rates have decreased sharply since the 1950s when the region began to industrialise. Having reached its top in the early 1970s, at about 41 per cent of the labour force, employment in the industrial sector steadily declined to the current 36 per cent. The service sector, still under-represented, has shown a significant increase in employment from the 1950s onward.

The business structure of the region is characterised by a high degree of small and medium-size companies, relatively highly specialised. Handicraft firms make up about 42 per cent of the total number. The importance of the industrial sector for the regional economy is highlighted by the share of about 90,000 industrial companies in a total number of about 320,000. The manufacturing industry is the strongest industrial sector and represents about 68,000 firms. The presence of about 8,000 cooperative companies, mainly in the agricultural sector, is another striking characteristic of the regional economy. Alongside the region's traditional products, such as food, ceramics, clothing and mechanical engineering, several new areas of production have emerged, such as robotics, biomedicine and graphic arts. The economic activities of the Region Emilia Romagna are strongly export-oriented. In 1993 the region's exports amounted to 7.4 billion lira, which is about 11 per cent of total Italian exports. With this share Emilia Romagna is the third largest exporting region in Italy, after Lombardia (32 per cent) and Veneto (12 per cent).

In several respects the Bolognese economy differs from the regional pattern. Of all provinces in Emilia Romagna, the province of Bologna has the highest concentration of firms: 22 per cent of the regional total. In comparison to the regional average, the agricultural sector is underrepresented, while the service sector is overrepresented. Six per cent of the labour force is employed in the agricultural sector, 35 per cent in industry and 58 per cent in the service sector. The unemployment rate of the province is at 5.9 per cent

(1991) somewhat lower than the regional average of 7.4 per cent (1991). The regional industry produces both investment goods and consumer goods. Among the most important investment categories are packaging machines, agriculture machines, machine tools, and buses and railway vehicles. The most important consumer goods include clothing, food, sports and luxury cars, car parts and motor cycles.

The Bolognese Trade Fair does much to facilitate international trade contacts. Presented as Italy's second most important exhibition centre after Milan, and Europe's fifth, the Bolognese Trade Fair organises annually no fewer than 26 fairs, 23 of which are international ones.

The Bolognese area boasts an extensive network of research, technology and education centres. The city is particularly proud of its university which, established in the year 1088, counts as the world's oldest. The university still attracts a great number of students: about 93,000 in the academic year 1993-1994, two fifths of whom come from other regions in Italy and from abroad. In a number of disciplines, such as medicine and biotechnology, the university is on a level with Europe's best. Some foreign universities, particularly American ones, are also represented in Bologna.

The region is a significant road and rail junction in Italy. Bologna is connected to five major railway lines and four motorways. The city also possesses an airport linking it with the principle cities in Italy and a number of large European cities. About three quarters of the goods that cross the Italian peninsula from north to south pass through the Bologna area.

Administrative structure[3]

Public administration in Italy is decentralised. Competencies are distributed among four administrative entities: State, Region, and Province and Community. The State's political and administrative activity concerns matters of national importance and relates to the four large sectors of policy: general policy, financial policy, political economy and policies inherent in such essential national services as justice, education, defence, etcetera. The State apparatus is divided into local administrative structures that usually coincide with regional or provincial boundaries. The responsibilities of the local organs of State are generally restricted to matters of minor importance.

The Regions are 20 in number; five with special autonomy for ethnic, historical and peripheral reasons and 15, among which Emilia Romagna, with ordinary autonomy. Each Region has a statute governing its organs, their relations and means of functioning within the Region itself, while the general electoral system remains under State law. The matters entrusted to the Regions are constitutionally defined. Those for the Regions with ordinary autonomy are the following: Administrative organisation, territorial planning, vocational training, public transport services, the environment and economic policy concerning small industrial companies. However, the Regions' legislative competencies are restricted by the need of the State to maintain overall unity. Legislation, control and planning are carried out by the Regional Council, which is elected by the citizens every five years. The regional administration is headed by a President.

Alongside the Regions there are other administrative entities equipped with independent political control. These are essentially the Communities and Provinces, but there may be local entities. The administrative responsibilities of the local entities may cover a wide area and there is an increasing tendency to reserve to the local level all matters concerning the citizen that are not of national importance. The Regions are contributing, through delegation, to the extension of local power. The specific attributions of the Provinces are few and of no great importance, objectively regarded. Their competencies essentially cover provincial road maintenance and construction, hunting, civil protection planning, some forms of social assistance, etcetera.

By contrast, communal powers are expanding to cover almost all matters of immediate civic importance between the citizen and the public administration. The Communities' obligatory duties concern urban planning, construction, municipal public works, preparation of industrial zones, social assistance, health and public hygiene, communal road maintenance and construction, urban transport, refuse collection, supply of water and gas, urban police, sewerage, etcetera. Obviously, then, the greater part of public functions relating to the organisation of the territory, social services and economic development are concentrated with the Communities. Italy is divided into more than 8,000 Communities varying greatly both in character and size. Obviously, therefore, the system cannot function uniformly and gives rise to some irregularities. Moves have developed, partly voluntarily and partly required by law, to form partnerships of local entities. Communities, particularly the smaller ones, often form cooperative associations, Consorzi, for the common provision of services or public works involving their respective territories. In other cases it is the law that requires association, such as for the Associazioni di Comuni for the provision of social and health services.

Città Metropolitana: a new administrative structure

Inducement

In the Bolognese area, as in other metropolitan regions in Europe, the developments increasingly pose problems to the administrative system. On the one hand the city of Bologna loses population to the suburbs and smaller communities in the first and second circle around it, while on the other hand the centre function of the city remains, or even expands with respect to employment, (public) services, cultural events, etcetera. Problems regarding traffic and public transport, the environment and public services exceed present territorial and administrative borders. The current administrative structure is considered to inhibit the planning and adjustment of policies, thus causing problems particularly in the realisation phase of policy measures.

That the current administrative structure in Italy is inadequate for the effective and efficient administration of large Metropolitan Areas is recognised by the national government. In 1990 a national law, law number 142, was issued which redefined the basis of the communal and provincial system. In this law the Regions were instructed to establish nine Metropolitan Areas. The designated areas are Bologna, Rome, Milan, Turin, Venice, Genoa, Bari, Florence and Naples. In coordination with the provinces and the municipalities the regions were to determine the boundaries of the new metropolitan areas and allocate the tasks. The law did not give explicit rules for the creation of the metropolitan areas. The Regions were to submit concrete proposals within one year after the enactment of the law. Although that period proved too short, since all of the regions failed to meet the condition, activities were at any rate started. At present the areas of Venice, Genoa and Bologna seem to have made the greatest progress.

Towards the Bologna Metropolitan Area

At the instigation of the Region Emilia Romagna, consultations were started with the Province and City of Bologna and other communities in the province to comply with law 142. The process proved difficult. Not all communities were ready and willing to yield tasks and competencies to a new administrative body. Their resistance had consequences for the delimitation of the Metropolitan Area. In the course of the consultations two alternatives emerged. The first proposed a Metropolitan Area roughly within the boundaries of the current Province of Bologna, covering 60 communities and about 900,000 inhabitants. The second suggested a Metropolitan Area comprising only the urban part of the current province, the residual part to form a new Province. In that case the Area would cover some 20 communities and about 600,000 inhabitants.

Major issues in the discussions between supporters of the two alternatives were the involvement of the city of Imola and the different natures of the agricultural hill sides and the industrialised plains. In the city of Imola, with 62,000 inhabitants the second largest city in the province, with a distinctive cultural identity linked to Romagna, strong opposition emerged against delegating powers to a metropolitan authority which was feared to be dominated by Bologna. Supporters of the larger area argued that the residual area is too little coherent to justify the formation of a separate province.

Various compromises were proposed, but a solution was not found. This was in part due to the fact that while law 142 had attributed the task to establish metropolitan authorities to the Regions, it had failed to give them adequate legal power to force a solution. In 1993 the situation changed when another national law was issued which provided for the direct election of mayors and city councils and thereby strengthened the role of these organs in regional matters. In anticipation of this law the city of Bologna had already given its mayor special competencies regarding administrative change. Once the law was passed, the Community and the Province of Bologna took over the initiative to overcome the deadlock.

The Conferenza Metropolitana

The Community and the Province began to cooperate with the mayors of the most important communities in the Province. This resulted in the proposal for the gradual establishment of a new metropolitan administrative structure. In February 1994, at the 'Conferenza Metropolitana', an agreement to that effect[4] was signed by the mayors of 50 communities and the president of the Province of Bologna, expressing their commitment actively to contribute to the establishment of a new Metropolitan Area. The other 10 communities were not yet ready at the time to join, and preferred to remain onlookers.

The signatories of the agreement recognise that a new administrative structure is required to deal adequately with such matters as territorial planning, coordination of functions and services, accessibility, public transport, environmental protection and major infrastructural projects. Besides, general principles were determined for the eventual establishment of the new metropolitan authority. The principles to which the new structure must answer are cooperation and solidarity, flexibility, progressiveness, concreteness, subsidiarity and simplification. In anticipation and preparation of the new metropolitan authority, the parties to the agreement intend to cooperate in three different fields: 1) spatial-economic matters, 2) social-cultural matters, and 3) administrative-financial matters. In these fields organisational provisions such as a decision structure, committees and offices were to be set up.

At the conference the organisational aspects were elaborated. To establish a political point of address, an assembly of all the participating parties was institutionalised. This assembly, the 'Conferenza Metropolitana', exists of the mayors of the participating communities, the presidents of both the Province and the Region, and representatives of the individual boroughs of Bologna. The Conferenza is to determine the political course, to initiate and coordinate activities and policies of the various administrative entities, and to consider all matters relevant to the Metropolitan Area, particularly the aspects of territory, environment, transport and public services. The mayor of Bologna was appointed coordinator of the entire project.

Furthermore, at the conference a common structure was created in which technicians and administrators cooperate in three committees to deal with, respectively: economic and territorial aspects; finance and administrative aspects; and social and cultural services. These committees were instructed to combine the proposals launched at the conference, develop a strategic plan, plan and initiate projects, and study the impact of the projects. The projects, which must be approved by the assembly of mayors, should be aimed at solving general problems in the metropolitan area. With regard to those problems objectives were to be set and cooperation with respect to resources was to be achieved. The committees are supported by 'workgroups' which are established for the elaboration and realisation of the individual projects. The leaders of the workgroups are appointed by the Province. The Province is also represented by several administrators. Furthermore, technicians and administrators represent the various communities. The smaller communities with small staffs are represented in the workgroups according to their interest in a particular project.

The first elections for a metropolitan council were set for the spring of 1999. The appropriate administrative structure which should be in place by that time is to be established in three phases. In the first phase, which ends in 1996, the transitory organisational structure is to be elaborated. Project teams (workgroups) are to be installed and the feasibility of harmonising the various existing administrative information systems is to be studied. Besides, operational services are to be set up regarding mobility and transport, the environment, and territorial planning. In the second phase, ending in 1998, these operational services should culminate in permanent 'Metropolitan Divisions'. In this phase experiments should be made with regard to appropriate financial structures. In the third and final phase, the organisational structure of the metropolitan authority is to be formally established.

Realisation

Since the signing of the Accord in 1994 some important developments have occurred with respect to several agreements from that Accord:

Strategic plan

The necessity of a strategic plan for integration and coordination of activities was recognised in the 1994 agreement. Activities have been started but no formal plan has yet been developed. So far, only an urban territorial plan has been drawn up, which in fact should have been a technical elaboration of the strategic plan. The urban territorial plan is actually a modified version of the zoning plan. The zoning plan is determined once every ten years. The most recent zoning plan dates from 1989, so that the next will be established in 1999; that will be the first metropolitan plan. However, in anticipation, the urban territorial plan was determined and confirmed by the Province in 1994 to facilitate the coordination and attuning of present territorial developments in the area.

The urban territorial plan thus represents the functional, infrastructural and environmental framework for development in the area of the current Province. The development of the plan is based on national law 142 issued in 1990 which transfers territorial competencies to the provinces and to metropolitan regions-to-be-formed. The Province of Bologna has appointed a committee which evaluates and integrates all the territorial plans of the individual communities. The territorial plan is the result of the work of the committee and defines in effect the new Metropolitan Area in broad, territorial, terms. It is therefore an important instrument for the establishment of the metropolitan authority.

Although the territorial plan is thus established, its guiding document, the strategic plan, is not. At present, there is agreement on the parties that should be involved, such as the business community, the university, social actors, administrators, mayors and opinion leaders, but most of these parties await action by the mayor of Bologna. This is due to the recent elections, which have brought forth a new city council and a new provincial president: a novel situation to which all parties have to readjust. This requires careful political manoeuvring and refraining from speaking one's mind too early. The outcome of that process is still uncertain, therefore.

An important aspect which parties feel ought to be addressed by the strategic plan is the stimulation of industrial networks that could enable the small industrial businesses that dominate the business structure to strengthen their international competitive position. Another aspect that should be taken up is the ongoing tertiarisation of the regional economy. Weakening of the industrial sector, which has long been a spearhead of the regional economy, ought to be prevented. A balance should be struck between the development of the industrial and service sectors.

Projects

Since the signing of the 1994 agreement the assembly of mayors has approved the start of 25 projects. Several of them were aimed at solving problems which can now be solved easier and faster. With respect to economic and territorial questions some important projects are concerned with the improvement of the road system and the development of a metropolitan railway network. The latter project will be dealt will extensively later on. In the social and cultural sector, initiatives for cultural exchanges have been launched. While formerly Bologna was the only town to take part in exchange programmes, now there are 31 communities involved. Besides, a new information system has been created for health services and a museum network established. In the administrative and financial areas institutional changes are also coming about. A new common procedure for the hiring of staff has been designed for all the communities in the metropolitan area. Finally, a new information system for public services has been installed.

The projects are carried out by the workgroups mentioned earlier. These groups meet regularly, usually once a week or every two weeks. Because communities and administrative bodies tend to be represented by technicians, the workgroups tend to focus on technical rather than political aspects. That seems conducive to fast decision making. The decisions made by the workgroups have to be confirmed by the Conferenza Metropolitana. That so far no major conflicts have arisen between technical and political aspects is in part due to the fact that practically all the administrations of the joining communities are of the same political brand. The few conflicts that do occur are usually arising and dealt with on a detailed local level. In the future the workgroups are to be transformed into regular offices, to assure continuous cooperation.

The projects are selected not according to a strategic masterplan, which is still lacking, but by their contribution to the general principles that were determined at the 1994 conference with a view to the eventual establishment of the new metropolitan authority.

Integration of services

Apart from the territorial plan and the projects that are being carried out, the framework of the Metropolitan Area is furthermore determined by the unification (merger) of large public-service companies responsible for waste disposal, energy supply and water supply. Services formerly rendered by a multiple of companies within the province, are now entrusted to one metropolitan company for each type of service. Municipal and provincial departments for internal affairs, press matters, environmental services, mobility and transport and computer services, are also being combined.

Current questions

Although the establishment of the Metropolitan Area is accepted by the majority of communities in the Province, among the inhabitants of the regional communities resistance against it is thought to be strong. For one thing, people fear that the cession of competencies from communities to the Metropolitan Area will make the distance between population and administration unduly large, especially with regard to smaller communities. For another, there are several problems which the regional communities want solved before the new metropolitan authority is installed, problems concerned with health services, the environment, and mobility.

In the last five years several of the smaller hospitals in the Province have been closed down for reasons of efficiency. As a result, sophisticated health services are now mainly concentrated in the city of Bologna. A group of smaller communities now want the remaining regional hospitals to be modernised to facilitate medical specialisation. In that way a more balanced supply of health services in the area could be achieved. The surrounding communities are also worried about the influx of people seeking medical treatment from outside the region. This strains the health system and is considered a problem. On these two arguments the public find it hard to understand why a community hospital should close down while money is directed towards hospital facilities in Bologna, where the population is declining as citizens move to the surrounding communities.

Another point of discussion is waste disposal. At present only a limited amount of the provincial waste is incinerated, while most of it is dumped at a limited number of waste-sites dispersed across the Province. The environmental problems associated with this dump are therefore attributed to only a limited number of communities. These communities want the amount of waste dumped in their surroundings diminished and plead the construction of new treatment plants and of the separated collection of waste, which allows for recycling and a reduction in the total amount of waste. Moreover, several communities which consider the quality of their own services above average, are worried that the unification of public services in the area, such as water supply, will lead to lower quality standards.

With regard to mobility, the surrounding communities consider the present railway system inadequate in two respects. With regard to the transport of goods, the connetion of the Bologna region to its main export markets, such as Germany and the Netherlands, requires improvement. This specifically concerns the accessibility of Interporto, a road-rail transhipment centre. With regard to public transport, the railway connections between the region and its centre, the city of Bologna, are considered unsatisfactory: too few stops and low frequencies resulting in too much car traffic and, consequently, poor access to health and other services.

The communities want these problems solved. They realise that to that end cooperation is required and they view a new metropolitan authority as an important means to establish and institutionalise it. The communities can now be involved in decision making through the workgroups, while in the past the city of Bologna regularly presented them with *faits accomplis*. A difficulty in that respect is that the smaller communities lack the manpower to be adequately represented in all the working groups.

While most provincial communities take a positive stand towards a new metropolitan authority, they cannot accept such an authority if Bologna remains as powerful as it is considered now. A weighty precondition for the communities to accept and hand over competencies to the new metropolitan authority is therefore the subdivision of the city of Bologna into several smaller communities. Apart from that, the enthusiasm of the communities depends on the way the above mentioned problems are solved.

Extensive communication is recognised as absolutely necessary to create societal support. Among the smaller communities the idea prevails that the

Metropolitan Area is a good long-term solution especially for such major issues as infrastructure and transport, but that for smaller, short-term matters a cooperative structure on a lower level is preferable. Discussions on that point are in progress and the outcome depends on the solutions found for the other matters pending.

Other communities

As mentioned earlier, several communities chose not to sign the 1994 agreement. The most prominent of these is Imola. The mayor of that town was in favour of joining the Metropolitan Area, but faced strong opposition in a number of policy fields. In that context the matter of the Metropolitan Area became an object of political controversy. The opposition demanded a referendum on the matter. A special committee was appointed to establish whether or not there was a legal basis for the referendum. The committee rejected the proposal. Meanwhile, elections had been held in which the mayor was re-elected and his opposition weakened. Therefore, the chances that Imola will eventually join seem to increase.

The business community

The private sector has traditionally been important in the Bologna region. That is partly due to the fact that the regional and provincial administration leave 'gaps' in the implementation of their policies. Investment in infrastructure is a case in point. For lack of funding, government investments have been decreasing for quite some time. This opened the way to joint investment by the public and private sectors, with the latter as initiator. For instance, the regional business community, represented by the organisations Assindustria Bologna and API Bologna, launched a plan to improve the road transport system in the area. The present ringroad of Bologna is very congested and there are no public funds for improvement projects. The business community took the initiative to develop a scheme for a new ringroad in cooperation with the University of Bologna, a large merchant bank and the (national) Autostrada company. That scheme is now being carried out. It will ultimately be completed within the framework of the Metropolitan Area.

Another project that is carried out on the initiative of the private sector is the intermodal transport centre Interporto, being erected on the outskirts of the city of Bologna. Interporto is a transport centre where road and rail transport can be connected. In the development of this centre the business community and the community of Bologna cooperated to get this centre developed and make the national government recognise it as part of the national main infrastructure. In that way, the project becomes attractive to investors. The development of Interporto was hampered by its projection on the territory of three communities: Bologna, Bentivoglio and San Giorgio di Piano. Since 1987 efforts had been made to establish essential infrastructural connections with the road and railway systems. The development of the Metropolitan Area has significantly improved the cooperation between the parties involved. The infrastructural connections are now being realised.

The business community also launched an initiative in the field of technical training, arguing that the education system needs improvement to be able to supply technicians with adequate technical knowledge. In cooperation with the community of Bologna a new schooling programme has been drawn up. Another point of interest of the business community is the accessibility of the airport of Bologna. The present access by road, rail and air is considered inadequate. It can be improved only if communities can be forced to cooperate. The same applies to the dispersal of trade fair and university facilities across the area.

Ample reasons, therefore, for the business community to be very much in favour of the development of a Metropolitan Area equipped with adequate legal powers. The competitiveness of the region is considered by the business community to be determined by such factors as the quality of its management, both in the public and in the private sector, simple procedures and a transparent administrative framework. In that sense the establishment of the Metropolitan Area is regarded as an important development. Already in 1991 the community organised a conference to discuss the necessity of a metropolitan administrative structure to cope with such problems as described above.

Although the business community is content with the development of the Metropolitan Area, it has misgivings as to the speed of the development and the territorial boundaries of the Metropolitan Area. The current speed of development is considered inadequate, and the problems with which the Metropolitan Area is to deal go beyond the boundaries of the Province. However, the present developments are considered a necessary first step.

Apart from initiating certain projects, the business community gives advice, consult and criticism on the development towards the Metropolitan Area. It is, however not formally involved: it has no decisive power. Because of the tendency towards further privatisation of government services such as waste disposal and the airport, the private sector will be more influential in the future.

Recognition

The 1994 agreement and the successive developments put the Region Emilia-Romagna more or less before a *fait accompli*. Therefore it legally accepted the present situation in april 1995. The territorial limits of the Metropolitan Area were determined to be those of the wide option, that is, to encompass the entire province. The Province as an administrative entity is to disappear. The Region also legally confirmed the competencies and tasks of the metropolitan authority. The most important tasks regard territorial planning, transport and accessibility matters, cultural matters, land and water control, provision of drinking water and energy, economic development and public health. The Metropolitan Area will be given the facilities, tasks and properties of the current Province and several tasks of the Region. A metropolitan mayor will be elected when the term of the present mayor of Bologna ends in 1999. By then there will no longer be a mayor of Bologna and a president of the Province of Bologna, but a metropolitan mayor and the mayors of the individual communities. The expectation is that the communities that did not sign the agreement in 1994 will eventually join the Metropolitan Area. The entire project will, however, possibly be subjected to a referendum procedure.

With regard to the use of referenda in matters of territorial change, there are developments at the national level. A new national law makes referendums permissible for certain matters, including territorial changes such as the subdivision of Bologna now foreseen. In 1997 a final decision on that score is expected. It could have consequences for the joining of Imola in the Metropolitan Area and the subdivision of Bologna. For the time being, the establishment of the Metropolitan Authority is still beset with uncertainty.

Analysis of the organising capacity

Vision and strategy

When the national government gave the Regions their new task in 1990 there was no clear vision of objectives, procedures, etcetera. To develop such a vision was left to the administrative entities involved in each particular case.

In the case of the Bolognese area these entities, namely, the Region, the Province and the various municipalities, shared the opinion that the current administrative structure was inadequate in several respects. The consensus was less perfect about the way to give shape to the new structure. The parties differed about, among other things, the tasks and competencies of the new authority, the way to take account of the different characters of cities (Imola) and country (the hills), and the present dominance of the city of Bologna. The lack of consensus had consequences for the extent of the new Metropolitan Area, for that would be determined by the municipalities willing to join in. The question was, however, whether the remaining area was large enough to justify the formation of a new province.

Clearly, the objective could not be achieved in one go. The impasse that developed was broken when in 1994 a partnership was formed of the municipalities who were in essence positively inclined towards a new authority. The partnership was intended to reach an agreement about the shaping of the new authority. In the ensuing covenant the signatories set themselves some objectives on the road to the Metropolitan Area, and laid down some general principles by which the tasks to be fulfilled in the region will be divided. Moreover the conclusion had been reached that the present municipality of Bologna would have to be split into a number of smaller ones, to reduce its present dominance over the area.

The agreements are flexible, however. The 'specifications' of the metropolitan authority are to be defined as the process advances. Given the prevailing problems of health care, waste disposal and other matters, the advance is slow and troublesome. The fact is that the process does not follow an integral strategic plan drawn up beforehand, and indicating whither the area shall develop. Admittedly an urban territorial plan has been drawn up as a framework for future spatial developments in the region, but that plan contains no integral vision of envisaged developments either.

The plans are predominantly being designed on the administrative level. There seems to be no singularly wide-spread support among the population. That does not augur well, should indeed the possibility of a referendum on the subject be opened.

Administrative structure

In the plans to form a Metropolitan Area in Bologna, the administrative structure itself is object of change. With the existing structure, it is increasingly difficult to decide on, and adjust policy measures in the region, especially in matters concerning transport, environment, spatial planning, and government services. But neither is it easy to persuade all municipalities to concede competencies to a new regional authority. Especially cities with pretence to distinction in terms of character or geographical situation, put up considerable resistance. To take the first important step towards the regional authority, the province and some municipalities concluded in 1994, on a voluntary basis, an agreement providing for collaboration in the policy areas mentioned above. That implies a choice in favour of institutional collaboration: an approach within existing structures by means of a public-public partnership.

By regional act 229 of March 1995, the Region confirmed the preceding developments. The Act determines the size of the Metropolitan Area to coincide with that of the present Province, and confers competencies on the new authority.

Although the creation of the Metropolitan Area as envisaged in the regional act of 1995 in fact implies the dissolution of the present Province of Bologna, the provincial administrative level will remains intact, but operate in an setting completely different from the present province. The tasks and competencies conferred on it are more extensive, and thus the administrative level will assume a more significant role than that of the present province. That the province has been so active towards its own abolishment, is indeed remarkable. The knowledge that its apparatus will be taken over by the new authority, may have been a motive.

Strategic networks

The new metropolitan administrative body in the Bolognese area is being prepared by a network structure in which the collaboration is institutionalised in a 'public-public partnership'. On the political level that partnership has been given shape in the assembly of mayors, a company which meets regularly and sets the political course. For the collective implementation, technical committees have been appointed for the different policy areas, in which the departments of the province and the municipalities are represented. They are responsible for the coordination and progress of the projects carried out in the setting of the agreement. The projects are actually carried out under the management of workgroups, in which the municipal and provincial departments are represented as well.

The advantage of that construction is that on the project level political factors are secondary, which makes for fast decisions. A problem is that in particular the smaller municipalities are too short of staff to be represented in all but the most relevant workgroups. By forming their own partnerships, they manage to be collectively represented in projects of less immediate relevancy.

The reform of the administrative structure in the region of Bologna is naturally a concern of administrative entities. The private sector is not involved, but does contribute in an advisory capacity, especially as far as the envisaged strategic plan is concerned. Other parties such as the university of Bologna, social actors, and opinion leaders are also involved. The municipality of Bologna dominates the interaction; indeed, in view of the political mutations, all those involved are looking to Bologna for the next action.

The regional firms are traditionally accustomed to take the initiative where they find the government failing. Remarkably, the government accepts that and supports the initiatives. That is for instance the case of the new technical training programme and the construction of a new circular road. The latter project features on the programme of preparations for the new metropolitan authority,

With the progressive privatisation in Italy, private enterprise is likely to assume a more prominent role in what have hitherto been government services. The implication is that the networks and interaction between government and private sector will become more important.

Leadership

The creation of the new metropolitan authority has been imposed by the national government, although regional administrative bodies were also aware of the desirability of a new structure. Earlier, in 1991, the private sector had urged the adjustment of the administrative structure to the increased scale of metropolitan problems. The task to initiate that adjustment was entrusted by the national government to the Emilia-Romagna Region. The Region soon discovered that it lacked the competencies to achieve the objective in one step.

In that situation, the province and the city of Bologna took over the initiative. The two parties pursued a more pragmatic course, aimed at the gradual formation of the new authority by forging a partnership of the municipalities positively inclined towards the new development. The success of that approach was such that the Region acknowledged it and on that basis decided to lay down in law the extent and tasks of the new Metropolitan authority to be created.

In partial objects of the partnership, such as the circular road and the training of technicians referred to earlier, the initiative was in fact taken by the private sector. In such cases, the collaboration has taken the form of a public-private partnership.

Spatial economic conditions

The social-geographical composition of the province of Bologna has been one reason for resistance to be put up against the formation of a new administrative authority with extensive competencies. For one thing there is a contrast between the strongly urbanised area around Bologna and the rural, more sparsely populated, hilly country to the south-west. The cities, too, are different in character. Imola feels kinship with Romagna rather than Bologna. Moreover, the relations between Bologna and the other towns in the area are often hampered by the great differences in size; Bologna is so big that the other municipalities feel dwarfed.

Spatial-economic conditions have also influenced the commitment of Rome to the formation of a new authority. Probably because of its strong economic position, the area is allowed a great deal of autonomy in the matter in hand. The chance of Rome having to give financial support is obviously considered very small.

Political support

On the national level, the political conditions evidently favoured the formation of a new administrative structure, since it was the national government that instructed the Region to undertake it. Ironically, the national government on the one hand created an impasse by withholding from the Region adequate competencies to carry it out its given task, and on the other hand made it possible to break the impasse by making mayors and municipal council directly eligible, thus giving them more influence in regional matters.

The local elections, by changing the political relations in Imola, the second city of the region, helped to bring that city around to supporting the formation of the region. The strong resistance against it at first prevailing in the Imola council, diminished when the municipal council was re-formed after the first local elections. On the other hand, shifts in several municipal councils have held up the process, especially the designing of a strategic plan for the region. People need time to reassess their positions and relations after the elections.

The circumstance that nearly all administrative bodies in the region had the same political colour has no doubt favoured the cooperativeness and been helpful towards the 1994 agreement and the ensuing developments.

However, developments on the national level still give rise to much uncertainty as to the actual region formation. There is a chance that the national government will provide for referendums about territorial changes such as the formation of the Metropolitan Area. Should a referendum actually be held, then the resistance, which is probably strong among the population of some municipalities, might well prevent the administrative changes as foreseen from being carried through.

Performance

To create a new administrative structure in the region of Bologna appears to be a long-winded and difficult process, but that is hardly surprising. After all, it is a drastic operation involving a multitude of parties: the Region, the Province, and some 60 municipalities, which all of them have to cede competencies. The top-down approach first adopted by appointing the Region as 'locomotive' proved inadequate to attain the objective at one go. Apart from the lack of competencies, the absence of a vision on the national level was to blame. In the ensuing bottom-up approach the Province and the municipality of Bologna have succeeded to generate cooperativeness by a pragmatic and gradual procedure. A fair number of problems, translated into 25 projects, could be actively taken up, on the basis of ideas expressed only in general terms about the final structure of the new administrative authority.

A disadvantage of that phased approach may be that the activities are not imbedded in a coherent, integral plan of the kind of regional development that is appropriate in view of the region's chances and threats, strengths and weaknesses. That disadvantage seems already perceptible in the obscurity surrounding some 'current issues'. The risk is that the evolution takes a course that will later be deplored. All the more reason to make haste with drawing up a directive strategic plan, which may also contribute to greater societal support for the proposed administrative changes.

The course chosen has advantages as well. Early results due to intensified cooperation may have such appeal to the general public as to pull down their opposition. As a matter of fact, the parties involved seem to recognise very well that to overcome the resistance, intimate communication with the population is indispensable.

The metropolitan railway network

The need for a more efficient public transport system

As in recent decades more and more people moved from Bologna to its suburbs and other provincial towns, with Bologna maintaining its centre function, commuter traffic in the region increased, and so did congestion and air pollution. The table below shows the number of persons daily travelling to work, by either car or public transport, in 1981 and 1991.

Between 1981 and 1991 commuter traffic from the province to Bologna increased fast, by about two fifths. Commuter traffic from Bologna to the province increased far less: by about 13 per cent. The total number of persons travelling to work within Bologna itself actually decreased by about 13 per cent. In all three categories the share of public transport fell significantly.

Most of the public transport is by bus: only one tenth of the public transport to and from Bologna is by train. This share remains the same in spite of the falling share of total public transport share.

At present the railway system in the Bolognese area consists of five regional lines from Bologna to five other cities in the Region Emilia-Romagna. Apart from these five lines, Bologna is connected to the Milan-Rome line of the national railway system. There are also two local (provincial) lines, which are not interconnected nor connected with the main railway station in Bologna. The regional and national lines are currently operated by the national railway company (SF), while the local lines are operated by the Province of Bologna. Local and provincial bus transport is operated by one, provincially owned, company (ATC).

There are no formal links between the management of these operators and, consequently, services are not attuned to one another.

The situation was considered by local authorities to be unsatisfactory in several respects. In the first place the regional rail transport is felt to be neglected by the national railway company: frequencies are too low, especially in the rush hour, and the number of stops is too small. Besides, the time tables of local railway and bus services and those of regional and inter-regional services are not in tune. Furthermore access to many stations by car and bus is considered inadequate. In view of the increase in demand for transport and the falling share of public transport the necessity for improvement of the public transport system was clear.

Table 1

From/ to	Car	1981 Public transport	Share public transport	Car	1991 Public transport	Share public transport
Province - Bologna	25,000	24,000	47%	42,000	27,000	38%
Bologna - Province	23,000	7,000	23%	28,000	6,000	17%
Within Bologna	56,000	73,000	36%	66,000	46,000	28%

Source: Workgroup SFM

The new metropolitan railway system

Initiatives for improvement were hampered by lack of financial means and lack of cooperation. Moreover, local parties traditionally held a relatively weak position vis-à-vis such strong bodies as the national railway company (SF). The announcement by the SF of plans to develop a national high-speed rail network, stretching from Milan, via Bologna, to Naples, presented an opportunity to facilitate improvements of the system. The high-speed rail project required a reorganisation of the Bologna railway junction. New, special, tracks were to be laid underground. To that end, the Bologna Central Station needed to be reconstructed. With reference to these planned adaptations, the local authorities (the Province and the Community of Bologna and the Region) asked the SF and the national minister responsible for transport to solve the local and high-speed rail problems simultaneously. They argued that high-speed rail traffic requires an efficient feeder network. Investment by the SF in an efficient local railway network would therefore be beneficial not only to the Bolognese area, but also to the high-speed rail system itself.

Despite the higher costs involved, the SF company proved receptive to the the arguments in favour of an integrated solution. In 1994 an agreement was concluded between the Province and community of Bologna, the Region Emilia-Romagna and the SF to transform the local transport system into a 'metropolitan railway system'. The agreement encompasses the construction of 13 new stations on existing lines and the modernisation of existing stations; the connection of the two local lines with Bologna central station; improved access to the stations; increased frequencies, and a connection to the fairgrounds.

In the agreement the division of costs among the parties was determined. A distinction was made between investment costs and operating costs. With regard to investment costs it was agreed upon that the SF, its daughter company for high-speed rail (TAV) and the State should finance the modernisation and construction of stations and the connection of the two lines to the central station. This requires an investment of about 150 billion lira. The local institutions finance the improvement of the access to the stations, which is estimated at 30 billion lira. The contributions of the respective parties to the operating costs have not yet been determined.

The realisation of the metropolitan railway system is projected to take five to six years, ending in 2000 - 2001. The time horizon is determined by the time needed to lay the new, underground, tracks for the high-speed train and to reconstruct Bologna Central Station. When this is completed, capacity on the existing tracks will come available for local transport. Connections of local lines with Bologna Central Station can then be established as well.

The agreement delegates the management of the project to the SF. However, the agreement takes into consideration that legal changes might lead to the formal establishment of the Metropolitan Area. As that would open prospects of local authorities to generate their own fiscal revenues, the responsibility for the project will in that case be transferred to them. Such legal change might also facilitate the establishment of a local transport authority, which would be an ideal institution to develop the metropolitan railway service. In anticipation of the Città Metropolitana, the realisation of the metropolitan railway project has been accommodated in the partnership concluded at the Conferenza Metropolitana in 1994.

Realisation

The realisation of the project requires the close cooperation of many parties. The parties involved besides the signatories of the SFM agreement, are the bus company ATC and a number of communities on whose territory adaptations to the railway system are required. For easy cooperation, the project is selected as one of the 25 projects to be realised in the framework of the Conferenza Metropolitana. The option chosen is to proceed step by step. Therefore, small-scale experiments are now carried out. On one line, from Bologna to Ferrara, frequencies will be increased, two new stations will be built and the bus system will be attuned to the rail system by an adjusted timetable and the connection of bus lines to rail line.

The project is carried out by a workgroup in which the relevant actors participate. There is regular consultation with higher administrative levels, but a transparent structure is sorely missed. Important decisions, especially concerning aspects of spatial planning, often seem difficult to make. Although the project and its outlines were approved at the Conference in 1994, political conflicts concerning minor questions are apt to arise. As the workgroup must work within current institutional structures, such problems are difficult to solve. The feeling therefore prevails that the establishment of a Metropolitan transport authority, which would encompass bus transport, would benefit the project by creating a unified structure with proper competencies and thus making for easier management and control. Although the establishment of a single transport authority is hampered for lack of funding, lack of agreement on the division of tasks and competencies, and by national government directives, the community of Bologna has taken a first step to establish a regular office for the SFM workgroup. The Community is also developing a plan for a new tram rail system within its boundaries.

Analysis of the organising capacity

Vision and strategy

The deteriorating traffic conditions notably for commuter traffic, and the simultaneous reduction of the share of public transport in it, have woken up the local authorities to the necessity of adjustment and improvement of the public-transport system. Especially in the eyes of the local government, the national railway company SF has failed to give much attention to short-distance transport. The regional railway system controlled by that company no longer meets the requirements of travellers: the frequencies are too low and there are too few stopping places. The two locally controlled lines are not connected to Bologna Central Station. Besides, the time tables of the buses and the railways are far from perfectly matched. Some stations are not even included in the bus lines.

The plans for a high-speed railway line and the associated adaptation of the railway node Bologna have enhanced the interest of all parties involved in public transport in an efficient provincial public-transport system. To the region, an efficient public-transport system means a great step towards the solution of traffic problems. Besides, an efficient connection to the High-Speed Railway network enhances the region's (international) accessibility. That Bologna fulfils a central function in the region for many facilities, including such government services as health care, is another weighty argument. The accessibility of these services largely determines their quality. For the SF, an efficient local network adds much to the appeal of its high-speed service.

These considerations motivated all the parties involved to work together on the realisation of a 'metropolitan railway service' (SFM). In the agreement to that effect, the objective of an efficient public-transport system is the main uniting element. By bringing up the project at the Conferenza Metropolitana, the various regional municipalities have also commited themselves to the project.

Administrative structure

Public transport is currently provided by three different public-controlled parties: the national railway company SF, the Province and the provincial bus company. These companies operate quite independently and separately. Decisions about adaptations of the system always involve several agencies. Moreover, for investments such as the construction of new railway stretches and stations several municipalities always need to be enlisted.

So, to realise the SFM it would be preferable to have one single transport authority for the area. For the time being, there is no legal framework for such an authority. The Metropolitan Area, whose founding is foreseen for 1999, would be a proper legal framework, but as we have seen in the previously, the realisation of that administrative body is still uncertain. Therefore, to accomplish the metropolitan railway service nonetheless, partnership within the existing structure is required.

Strategic networks

For lack of an appropriate administrative structure, recourse had to be taken to the collaboration through public-public networks. The Conferenza Metropolitana presented an opportunity to formalise such collaboration in the shape of a public-public partnership by recognising the project as one of the 25 to be carried out. Besides the parties directly involved in rail transport, the individual municipalities thus have committed themselves to the realisation of the project.

Despite the formalised collaboration and the consensus about the objective of the project, to get the parties aligned on operational decisions tends to be difficult in practice. A formal, distinct structure with short decision procedures is sorely missed.

Leadership

In the development as well as the implementation of the SFM-project, 'pullers' can be clearly identified. The initiative to develop the project was taken by the local parties: the municipality and the province of Bologna, the very ones most confronted with the shortcomings of the existing public-transport system and their effects. They succeeded in convincing the SF and the national government as financier of the railways, that an investment in the connection of Bologna to the high-speed railway system would be more profitable if the local transport system were to be improved at the same time.

The planning and realisation of the SFM-project are strongly bound up with the realisation of the high-speed railway line. So logically, the project management is in the hands of the national railway company, the very party which also renders the greatest financial contribution to the project. Given the need for a formal structure, the question arises whether the SF is the proper locomotive of the project.

Political support

On the local level, the necessity to improve the existing public-transport system was clear. Apart from the direct effects of the greatly increased motorcar traffic, sub-optimum accessibility due to a failing public-transport system also reduces the quality of the public services.

Lack of resources and a hard-to-sway national railway company have held up the solution of the problems. The planned construction of the high-speed railway line and the imminent formation of the partnership Conferenza

100

Metropolitana offered a good opportunity to instill cooperativeness into the parties involved in public transport.

During the execution of the project the fact evolved that the workgroup in its efforts to achieve a technically well-functioning system, is often thwarted by political opposition to operational decisions, although all those involved have committed themselves to the project. To solve such the difficulties within the existing administrative structures often proves laborious.

Spatial economic conditions

Bologna and its surroundings are an important industrial area: in economic terms it is one of the healthiest zones of Italy and even of Europe. Bologna is moreover famous for the organisation of a large number of industrial and commercial annual fairs drawing masses of (international) visitors. Those are aspects that make Bologna interesting for the SF as a high speed rail station. Because moreover the economic activities are not crowded immediately around Bologna but spread across the entire Po-valley, an efficient public-transport connection between Bologna and the industrial areas would enhance the appeal of the high speed rail service. Those circumstances have probably induced the SF's cooperativeness to the SFM-project.

Performance

To improve the public-transport system requires the collaboration of many parties, each with its own orientation: the provincial municipalities to their own territory, the city and the province to the metropolitan area, and the national railway company, naturally, to the entire national railway system. To align these parties is no simple proposition. Nevertheless, the province and the municipality of Bologna have managed to commit these parties to the SFM-project.

Because of the absence of a suitable legal framework to accommodate the parties involved in a formal structure, such as a metropolitan transport authority, the less stringent collaboration in a public-public partnership had to be resorted to. The practical consequence is that the SFM-project is carried out step by step. To operate within existing structures turns out to be laborious. Therefore, adaptation of the administrative structure seems commendable. However, the present process can be seen as an important first step towards a final solution.

Conclusions

The necessity to reform the administrative structure of the Bolognese region is felt in several policy areas. Along with the private sector and various administrative bodies in the region, the national government has become convinced of that necessity. By enacting a new Law in 1990 the government has not only made provision for the reform but actually commanded it. In the top-down approach initially adopted, to visualise the size and competencies of the Metropolitan Area was enjoined upon the local parties. The procedure proved laborious and unsuitable to attain the objective at one go. The Province and the municipality of Bologna then appropriated the initiative, erecting a framework for coordination within the existing legal constellation on the basis of broadly defined objectives.

Public transport within the metropolitan area is one segment which cries out for a new administrative structure. The many parties involved and the existing legal framework forbid an integral approach to the problems. The strong position of the national railway company and its primary interest in long- and medium-distance transport were delaying factors. The conditions changed for the better when the SF decided to connect Bologna to the high speed rail network. Once more, the Province and the municipality of Bologna entered the fray to contrive a solution. They succeeded in convincing the SF and the national government that an integral approach was needed. For this project as well, collaboration in the shape of a public-public partnership appeared the best solution within reach. Although in this case the objectives are more transparent than in that of regional reform, the process is no less laborious.

Both projects are thus conducted under the auspices of a voluntarily institutionalised partnership based on the networks of public bodies. Actually, the Città Metropolitana project is carried out without an integral vision of the social-economic evolution that would be optimum for the metropolitan area. That spells difficulties for any agreements to be concluded among the municipalities involved. With the SFM-project it is not so much the objectives or the lack of them that give problems, but rather the lack of a fixed structure which makes it difficult for the parties not to commit themselves. The SFM-project serves therefore to illustrate the necessity of a metropolitan (transport) authority.

Notes

---

[1]   Co-author: drs. P.W. Poppink
[2]   Les Villes Européennes, DATAR, 1989
[3]   This is based on: Albertini, R (1995), *Windows on Italy - the Constitution,* Istituto Geografico De Agostini
[4]   Accordo per la Città Metropolitana di Bologna

5 Eindhoven

Introduction

Since the mid-1980s the city of Eindhoven has put a lot of effort in renewal of the city and in strengthening its competitive position. The city has acknowledged the fact that it cannot act alone and that the *Greater Eindhoven area* should organise itself to improve and maintain its position in conjunction. For the case study two projects are subject of the analysis. The first project, the Stimulus Programme, is concerned with the region's response to the major problems of two leading companies in the region: Philips and DAF. How has the Eindhoven region coped with the restructuring (Philips) and collapse (DAF) of its two major industrial firms? The second project, 'West Corridor Key Project', is a large-scale urban-renewal scheme to create conditions for sustainable urban development. Next, the chapter sketches the general profile of the region and its economic development followed by a brief discussion of public administration in the Netherlands. After these general topics, the two projects will be addressed. The chapter provides background information and an update on the Stimulus developments up to now, followed by an analysis of the project in the theoretical setting of organising capacity. Next, the 'West Corridor Key Project' is discussed, followed by analysis of the project in the theoretical setting of organising capacity. Finally, the conclusions of the Eindhoven case are presented.

Profile

At the beginning of the twentieth century the city of Eindhoven was no more than a small agricultural town with only 5,000 inhabitants in the rural area of 'Zuidoost-Brabant' (South-East Brabant). From the foundation of the 'Philips Gloeilampen N.V' in 1891, the city of Eindhoven and the area of South-East Brabant have followed in the wake of the electronics pioneer; Philips has developed into a multinational corporation, Eindhoven has become the fifth largest city in the Netherlands with a population of 198,000 and centre of a region of 670,000.

The appearance of the city of Eindhoven is determined by urban design of the twentieth century. Its city centre, buildings and housing estates offer a cross-section of twentieth century (housing) design. Of course the city's fast growth and Eindhoven's preoccupation with technology have also left their mark on the city's appearance. But young as it appears, Eindhoven is actually one of the oldest towns in the Netherlands. It was granted a royal charter as early as 1232. Since then wars, plundering and fires in the centuries that followed, have destroyed almost all early inheritance. So, the rise of the Philips company is the foundation on which Eindhoven as it is today, was built.

Eindhoven may be the fifth largest Dutch city, up to the early 1980s its urban environment did not live up to that status. The town centre looked chaotic, and apart from the Evoluon there were no special attractions vital to the image. Since the early 1980s Eindhoven has put a lot of effort in city renewal. Already a high-quality shopping centre ('Heuvelgalerie') and a concert hall ('muziekcentrum Frits Philips') have been opened, and the city centre is currently under reconstruction. Eindhoven is busy bringing its urban environment in line with its economic, social and cultural position.

Eindhoven is the centre of South-East Brabant. The population of that area has grown explosively along with that of the city. Eindhoven is the largest city in South-East Brabant, which comprises 34 municipalities[1] and a population of more than 670,000. In the 1980s Eindhoven and the region attained 'normal' population growth levels. Nonetheless, the region's growth rate was still higher than the national average: 7.4 versus 6.7 per cent.

The area of South-East Brabant is also referred to as Eindhoven region or the Greater Eindhoven area. It is situated in the southern part of the Netherlands and belongs to the Province of Brabant. The Greater Eindhoven area accounts for 3.3 per cent of Dutch acreage and 4.4 per cent of the Dutch population. Eindhoven (194,000) and Helmond (72,000) are the two urban centres, followed by Veldhoven (40,000). The south-eastern zone of the Eindhoven region is mainly rural. Like elsewhere in Europe, city and hinterland function as one system. The inhabitants of the surrounding municipalities go shopping and often work in Eindhoven or Helmond; vice versa, inhabitants of Eindhoven and Helmond go to the region's country side for leisure activities.

Even though the region is not part of the Randstad[2], the traditional Dutch 'gravity centre', it can hardly be maintained to be peripheral either in a national or a European perspective. It is situated within the rectangle formed by the Randstad, central Germany, the Ruhr area and the Belgian cities of Brussels and Antwerp. Table 1 presents the distances from Eindhoven to other relevant cities. The Dutch government has recognised the (inter)national potential and attributed to Eindhoven the status of 'stedelijk knooppunt ('urban nodal point')[3.]

Table 1
Distances from Eindhoven to nearby international cities
(in kilometres)

City	Distance	City	Distance
Rotterdam	110	Düsseldorf	100
Amsterdam	120	Brussels	140
The Hague	130	Frankfurt	340
Antwerp	100	Paris	450

Source: CBS, *in Feiten en Cijfers Regio Eindhoven,* 1994, N.V. Rede

Economic development

Traditionally the Eindhoven region ranks among the more prosperous in the Netherlands. It prides itself on being, next to the Randstad, the largest centre of employment in the Netherlands with around 246,000 jobs for a population of 670,000 (to compare: the Rotterdam region accounts for 442,000 jobs for a population of nearly 1,200,000). Up to the mid-1980s, Eindhoven region's growth rates had been higher than the national average. The mid-1980s marked a turning point; thereafter the regional employment development has stayed behind the national and provincial development. Table 2 indicates that the Eindhoven region attained only half the growth of the Province of North

Brabant and that of the nation. Between 1986 and 1991 the yearly employment growth rate dropped from 5.3 to 0.9 per cent.

Table 2
Development of the number of jobs in region, province and Netherlands for 1989 - 1993

	1989	index (1989=100)	1993	index
Eindhoven region	237,700	100	246,600	103.7
Province of Northern Brabant	749,700	100	803,400	107.2
The Netherlands	5,139,500	100	5,489,100	106.8

Source: CBS, *in Feiten en Cijfers Regio Eindhoven,* N.V. Rede, 1994.

From 1991 onwards things got worse: on balance the region started to lose jobs. Up to 1994 the regional employment figures continued to drop, as figure 1 reveals. Eindhoven's economic downturn has been largely brought about by the major problems of two leading industrial firms that had dominated the area for years: DAF (international lorry constructors) and Philips (an electronics multinational). In the early 1980s the Philips company employed 35,000 people in the Greater Eindhoven area; in 1993 the figure was down to 21,000. So, in ten years' time, around 14,000 jobs disappeared, 6,000 of which in the late 1980s and early 1990s. In addition, in 1993, the DAF company collapsed and another 2,500 jobs were lost. Moreover, the DAF company used an extensive network of regional suppliers who were also hit by the blow. It became clear that the Eindhoven region had relied too much on its two giants.

Currently the region appears to have crept out of the recession. The region has absorbed the Philips and DAF setbacks. In 1995 the employment figures are expected to recover the level of 1992, as figure 1 demonstrates. The restructuring of Philips - the so-called Centurion operation - is still going on. The company now focuses on its core business. Fortunately the Philips and DAF restructuring seem to have generated spin-off in the form of newly started small businesses.

Not surprisingly with Philips and DAF in the region, industrial and industry-related activities determine the regional economy. However there is more than Philips and DAF. Eindhoven prides itself to be the industrial mainport of the Netherlands, next to Rotterdam (harbour) and Amsterdam (airport). Nationally, there is something to be said for Eindhoven's claim. A diverse range of industrial clusters - in the field of mechatronics, automotive, electronics, environmental and medical technology - clearly puts the region in the front ranks. The dominance of industry-related activities is certainly not due to production facilities only. The region is characterised by a virile concentration of Research and Development activities.

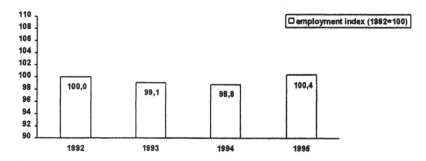

Figure 1   Regional employment development in the Eindhoven region, 1992 - 1995

Together with the bordering North Limburg region, Eindhoven accounts for one half of national R & D expenses, which puts it among the European top three of knowledge-intensive industrial areas. So, industrial and industry-related employment carries much weight in total regional employment. However, in recent years the significance of industry as employer has decreased; not only the volume of industrial employment but also its share in total employment has diminished (see table 3). If the problems of Philips and DAF are taken in consideration that does not come as a surprise.

Private enterprise in Eindhoven is internationally oriented. Not only Philips but also less well known companies trade across the border. On estimation, around one third of the local companies do business internationally, which takes the region's performance clearly above the national average of around one fifth. Furthermore, the interest of foreign businesses in Eindhoven as a possible location confirms the international orientation of the region; over the years the region has welcomed a number of foreign companies. However, the need to reduce the reliance on Philips still more persists. Eindhoven is a region with economic potential, especially in the field of high-technology. It should capitalise on that potential to the full, to strengthen and widen its economic base, the ultimate aim being to reduce the reliance on Philips and DAF and to re-attain the growth levels of previous decades.

Table 3
Employment in the Eindhoven region by sector
for 1992, 1993 and 1994

Sector	1992		1993		1994	
	abs.	rel.(%)	abs	rel.(%)	abs.	rel.(%)
Agriculture	10983	4.5	1091	4.5	10692	4.4
Industry	65608	27.2	6265	26.2	59546	24.9
Public utilities	1405	0.5	144	0.6	1444	0.6
Construction	20100	8.3	1933	8.0	18802	7.8
Trade & repair companies	36710	15.2	3823	15.9	38715	16.2
Hotel & cater. busin.	6381	2.6	660	2.7	6767	2.8
Transport & commun.	10167	4.2	953	3.9	10052	4.2
Financial institutions	7150	2.9	726	3.0	7184	3.0
Business services	23535	9.7	2422	10.1	24649	10.3
Public administration	8873	3.6	897	3.7	9226	3.8
Education	13917	5.7	1386	5.8	14179	5.9
Health care	23348	9.6	2370	9.9	24340	10.2
Other services	5429	2.2	592	2.4	6160	2.5
Temporary employees	7600	3.1	645	2.7	6670	2.8
Total	241206	100.0	23913	100.0	238426	100.0

Source: Arbeidsvoorziening Zuidoost-Brabant (1995)

Administrative structure and regional co-operation

History

The administrative model in the Netherlands dates back from the nineteenth century. The law recognises three governmental institutions: national government, provinces and municipalities. Twelve provinces make up the intermediate level. Initially the provinces had a fairly high degree of autonomy, but from World War II onwards the influence of the national government has increased considerably. The centralisation of tasks at the national level reached its limits some time ago. Especially in the urban areas, administrative reform has become absolutely necessary. Central government has to hand over some tasks and leave more scope for lower levels of government. The Dutch government has recognised the importance of breaking up the urban administrative inertia and has issued a number of documents in which the urgency of reform is acknowledged. Seven urban areas have been selected where revision of the administrative structure is considered essential (Ministry of Foreign Affairs, 1993) and a change of law ('general law') is in preparation.

The Eindhoven region is one of the seven so-called BON areas. These BON-areas are renewing their administrative organisations, at different paces and with varying co-operativeness of municipalities involved. The discrepancy of scale between the functional urban region - city and ring - and the smaller municipalities impedes efficient and effective governance. After all, the future of all municipalities involved depends on the position of the functional region. The road to a regional administrative body will not be the same for all BON-areas. For some the model of the city province ('stadsprovincie') will be the solution, for other areas a redraw of municipal boundaries will be the option selected.

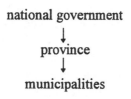

Figure 2   Administrative structure in the Netherlands

The Eindhoven situation

As of yet none of the seven BON areas are governed by a regional administration, although in some areas more progress has been made than in others. In the Eindhoven region -as in some others- a regional co-operative body ('Samenwerkingsverband Regio Eindhoven') has been set up, comprising 32 out of the 34 municipalities. The 'Samenwerkingsverband Regio Eindhoven' (SRE) is a combination of two smaller districts ('gewesten'). The municipalities' participation is voluntary. The objective of SRE is to look after the common interest of participating municipalities in the fields of town planning, public housing, traffic and transport, leisure pursuits, tourism, nature and countryside, environment and waste disposal, health care, social-economic affairs, employment policy, social services and other services such as the fire brigade. Mark that 'looking after the common interest' is not necessarily the same as 'looking after the regional interest'. The former can be conceived of as extended local governance, the latter as regional governance. The present objective severely limits the opportunities for SRE to act. In anticipation of new laws, the next step in the renewal process should be to move the SRE more towards the regional interest. However, a proposal to reform the SRE agreement has been rejected by some municipalities.

Decision power in the SRE lies with the regioraad ('region council') comprising 60 members, representing all participating municipalities. Each municipality is represented by at least two council members; municipalities with a population over 15,000 get one extra seat, and so on. The city of Eindhoven holds 13 seats, Helmond holds five. Decisions are taken by majority of votes and are prepared by the regional board under the chairmanship of the burgomaster of Eindhoven.

N.V. REDE and Milieudienst Regio Eindhoven

However difficult the road to administrative co-operation among the municipalities may be, two agencies are indeed operating successfully on the regional scale. One of them is N.V. REDE, the regional economic development corporation for the Eindhoven region. Its objective is to stimulate regional business companies and strengthen the regional economic structure as well as to improve the region's employment structure. Five 'core activities' make up the development corporation's daily business: business consultancy, finance, business parks, economic promotion and acquisition, and structural reinforcement projects. Formally, N.V. REDE has no administrative power to enforce its decisions. But all municipalities have accepted N.V. REDE and respect its policy decisions.

Very recently a regional department for environmental services was created. The environmental department of the City of Eindhoven was already working together with other departments in the region, fulfilling some tasks for other municipalities. Now, the departments in Eindhoven and Helmond will be absorbed in a new regional body, as one step forward towards regional collaboration.

The Stimulus Programme

Inducement

The rise and prosperity of Eindhoven as an industrial region used to be closely linked up with the presence of a few large multinational and international companies: Philips (electronics), DAF (Trucks) and Nedcar (automotive). These companies, and in particular Philips, used to dominate the region. In the Netherlands and abroad the city of Eindhoven was known first and foremost as the hometown of Philips; many persons were directly employed by the multinational or depended indirectly on the giant. However, that has changed fundamentally in recent years. From the early 1980s on the once inviolate position of Philips deteriorated rapidly. The company 'lost track' of its markets and intensive Japanese competition revealed how costly and inefficient the Philips production process was. In the second half of the 1980s the multinational's bastion balanced on the verge of collapse. A large-scale slimming-down operation and a thorough review of company methods were called for. Under the skilful leadership of a newly appointed president - Jan Timmer - a comprehensive restructuring operation named Centurion was started in 1988 with great impact in the Greater Eindhoven area. Production units were either closed or relocated to areas with low-cost labour, and the company's organisation was modernised. The estimation is that between 1988 and 1991 Centurion eliminated around 10,000 Philips jobs and increased the supply of vacant office space and business premises dramatically. Another important implication of Philips's troubles and company restructuring was that Philips lost its leading position. Today Philips is 'preoccupied' with its own problems and therefore paying less attention to the Greater Eindhoven area.

In the Centurion operation, the discharge of employees had been gradual, based on a solid and fair redundancy scheme. That was not so when another large company, the international lorry manufacturer DAF, fell into trouble. In 1993, to the surprise of many, the DAF company collapsed. Unlike the Philips crisis, the downfall of DAF was unexpected. Of course, like Philips, DAF had for some time been hard put to it to stay competitive, but the firm was generally believed to be in a better position than Philips. Wrongly so, for bankruptcy became inevitable for DAF. On estimate, 2500 employees of the company itself and 2500 employees of suppliers and subcontractors lost their jobs. After liquidation, DAF was restarted with only one third of its former employees.

The Philips and DAF stories are parts of a more general trend of industrial restructuring, but it was the DAF downfall that triggered a debate in the Greater Eindhoven area, resulting in the so-called Stimulus programme. Its aim is to create between 2000 and 3000 new jobs in the region, especially in small and medium-size companies, to compensate for the loss of jobs with Philips and DAF. The focus is on the formation of clusters of business companies alone and clusters of companies together with other (local) knowledge centres. Clustering is put in as an instrument to 'anchor' these businesses in the region.

Starting up the Stimulus programme

Although the DAF downfall can be regarded as part of a more general trend of industrial restructuring, it turned out to be the impetus of change. Not only the actual loss of employment but also the media coverage it received played a role to that effect. The DAF company is well known throughout the Netherlands and its sudden collapse became headline news. The massive employment loss combined with the unexpectedness and DAF's reputation, kept the matter in the regional and national media for weeks on end, and shook up the actors in the Greater Eindhoven area. All regional actors came to realise that something had to be done.

On the initiative of the mayor of Eindhoven and the Governor of the Province of North Brabant a round table was organised with all relevant actors. The Eindhoven Regional Partnership (Samenwerkingsverband Regio Eindhoven, SRE), the Chamber of Commerce, the regional economic development corporation (N.V. REDE), the cities of Eindhoven and Helmond, trade unions, employers' associations, the Province of North Brabant, local knowledge centres and the regional employment office (RBA) attended the meeting, and the national Ministry of Economic Affairs was represented by its state secretary. The main conclusion of the meeting was that to cope with the structural changes, an extra stimulus was needed to rehabilitate the regional economy. Jointly the participants set to work on an economic action plan. The completed plan envisaged structural co-operation of the business community, local government and intermediary organisations to create a milieu in which the private sector can prosper and is stimulated to be innovative. The Greater Eindhoven Area is to strengthen its competitive power and initiate a continuous process of renewal and innovation. The plan suggested five policy areas:

- strengthening of knowledge-intensive high quality production;
- institutions to companies;
- projects especially tailored to small and medium-size firms;
- the labour market and the need for motivated technically skilled manpower;
- opportunities for starting companies.

Implementation of the action plan required financial backing. The SRE, comprising all municipalities, seemed the proper platform to raise the money, but for the fact that co-operation in SRE had not been optimum up till then. The Burgomaster of Eindhoven -as chairman of the SRE- managed to convince the SRE members that the economic position of the region was at stake and that a joint effort was in order. The effort was made and yielded enough funds to start implementing the action; all 32 SRE municipalities contributed 11.50 guilders per inhabitant, resulting in a working capital of around 7 million Dutch guilders.

The Ministry of Economic Affairs followed the Eindhoven discussion actively. It was the Ministry that suggested applying to the European Union for financial support to broaden the financial basis. By the Ministry's judgment, the Eindhoven Region fitted the criteria for the so-called Objective-2 status. Through its Structural Funds, the European Union offers financial aid to regions that find themselves in a difficult predicament through industrial restructuring. Initially the parties involved were in two minds about asking for European support. Some welcomed the idea, others doubted that the financial benefits would outweigh a possible negative effect on Eindhoven's image. For, in spite of serious challenges, the Eindhoven region is by no means a classic example of a 'region in distress', but rather an area improvement of knowledge transmission from the knowledge with potential. Finally the decision was made to apply for the Objective-2 status in order to make capital out of the region's potentiality.

To be eligible for Objective-2 funding, the action plan had to be extended, formalised and made to comply with demands and conditions set for the Union's structural funds. In December 1994, the restructuring programme, henceforth called the Stimulus programme and laid down in the revised action plan ('Enig Programmerings Document' (EPD)), was accepted by the European Commission, initially for three years. For that three-year period the Union has made available 67 million ECU to co-finance projects through the structural funds, namely, two thirds from the European Fund for Regional Development (EFRD) and one third from the European Social Fund (EFS).

Prior to the decision to apply for European support, the region did have an action plan and seven million Dutch guilders to carry the plan out. The acceptance of the revised action plan -now called the Stimulus programme- increased the financial possibilities considerably and gave rise to the creation of an agency responsible for implementing the Stimulus programme. Brussels demands supervision of the Stimulus programme by a 'Comité van Toezicht' ('Supervisory Committee', something like a Board of Commissioners) on which all stakeholders take seats: a representative of DG-16, representatives of the Dutch Ministries of Economic Affairs and Social Affairs, the chairman of the SRE, and representatives of the Province, trade unions, employers' associations, and of the RBA. A Steering group (a kind of Executive) has been formed of second-level representatives of the same institutions, to decide whether the project proposals are in line with the EPD; careful judgment is called for.

To bridge the gap between the Steering Committee and the private sector, a small office has been set up for the so-called 'programme management'. It has no official status, and is primarily concerned with providing information to private actors, and helping them draw up a well-founded application for European funding. The office is temporary. In addition an important contribution by formulating applications, is expected from intermediary organisations such as N.V. REDE, RBA and the regional centre for innovation ('Innovatiecentrum').

At first, the possibility of support from the European Union meant an enormous boost for the project; it induced Dutch public actors to make more generous contributions too. For after all, the European Union provides at most half the costs of each approved project, and expects the other half to be put up by the local, regional or national government, alone or in combination. Nor is that all there is to say about European support. The positive effects were welcome, but the complexity of European regulations has caused much delay. For an action plan drawn up back in 1993, it took

116

until December 1994 for European assistance to be endorsed. That delay had put pressure on the feeling of common responsibility that lay at the heart of the project.

Outline of the programme

The ultimate objective of the Stimulus programme for the restructuring of the regional economy is to reduce unemployment and create two or three thousand new jobs. Three goals tie the programme together: to strengthen the industrial fabric, to stimulate tourism, and to enhance the location climate.

The first priority and main focus of the Single Programming Document (EPD) is the same as that of its predecessor, namely, to initiate new industrial clusters or networks, or, as the European Union formulates it: to strengthen the industrial fabric. The future of industry in the Greater Eindhoven Area depends largely on the introduction of new technologies and new methods of management. The 'environment' of the industrial companies is important in that connection. The best way to strengthen the industrial fabric is to fortify the constellation of small and medium-size companies, using the region's strong points -the knowledge and experience in the field of modern technology and the tradition of co-operation and economic clustering- to offset the region's weakness, which is its vulnerable dependency on a few major industrial companies.

The 'environment' of the industrial companies should not be understood too narrowly. The availability of knowledge and the willingness to co-operate are important elements, but quite as fundamental are the availability and accessibility of adequate business premises. Together these factors make up the 'industrial fabric'. For its enhancement, the Stimulus programme distinguishes five points of action:

- to renovate, improve and re-use industrial estates and buildings and establish new high-quality industrial parks;
- to stimulate and initiate industrial co-operation in order to raise the competitive power of industrial companies, in terms of new technology or new products, waste disposal and recycling, environmental-protective production, etc;
- to fill up lacunas in the regional knowledge structure by extending or rearranging existing centres of technology and training;
- to invest in 'human capital' to adjust and maintain the level of knowledge of the workforce in accordance with the demand of the industrial sector;

117

– social return and knowledge transfer: to involve as many as possible of those laid off by major industrial companies in Stimulus projects, in order to preserve their skills and experience in the region.

The second priority in the programme is to advance tourism and improve the location milieu. Industrial reorganisation has left the city and its surroundings with a legacy of empty office space and other premises. Their redevelopment and alternative employment could add attractions to the already pleasant tourist area of Zuid-Oost Brabant. This would strengthen the region's appeal to holiday makers, excursionists and sojourners, as well as help to safeguard and improve the location climate. More precisely, the objectives are:
– to stimulate day-tripping for a broader target market;
– to redevelop deserted premises in a way to enhance the region's attractiveness;
– to educate and train staff in the relevant sectors in a friendly treatment of clients.

A total investment of around 172 million Ecu is needed, approximately four fifths of the Stimulus resources to be used for the first priority and one fifth for the second. A bit more detail may serve to clarify the picture. Three fifths of the resources are set aside for the direct or indirect benefit of small and medium-size companies. Another fifth will be used for investment in infrastructure. Mark that the European Union's rules do not provide for support to individual companies, with one exception: a subsidy of up to 100,000 Dutch guilders can be granted to a company, under strict rules about the how and when and to whom.

In principle all actors in the region are entitled to submit a proposal or project. But because of the EU ban on individual support, applications for small and medium-size firms have to be made by a group of firms. Although the firms are the most concerned party, different actors can take the lead in developing a project and grouping together interested parties. Of course a company with a good concept may search actively for partners to submit it to the Steering group. But the numerous intermediate organisations can also take the lead and have indeed done so in several instances in their special fields of interest. For instance the RBA has initiated and is managing a new educational programme. Private consultancy firms have also been known to develop an idea which they believed would fit into the Stimulus programme, and to shop around for companies to join them in submitting the project. In

118

such cases the programme management and the intermediary organisations join in to draw up a sound proposal, which is then tested by the Steering Committee in the light of the complex European guidelines, and either accepted or refused.

Some projects and preliminary results

Although it is too early for a proper evaluation, the question is in order whether or not Stimulus has already something to show for its troubles. Early in 1995 the Steering Committee of the Stimulus programme approved the first 14 projects. In December the number had already increased to 90, accounting for half of the EFRO/ESF funds. The projects are concerned with restructuring and revitalising business premises, industrial co-operation, specific training programmes (four of them), increasing the attractiveness and advancing the location climate, and activities of the so-called 'Innovation workshop'. This workshop is connected to the 'Hogeschool Eindhoven' Eindhoven Polytechnic' and offers local businesses a helping hand towards improving their products and production processes or developing a new prototype.

In the first round of the Programme, two-thirds of the resources set aside for infrastructure have been contracted out. The next efforts of the Stimulus programme aim at industrial clustering. In that field much effort is still wanted. An example of a promising project already started is the 'KIC-project', which aims to create the largest national industrial cluster around the multinational Océ, to compete internationally with firms like Kodac and Xerox on the market for copiers. About a hundred suppliers, mainly from Zuid-Oost Brabant and Limburg, have been invited to participate in the development of a new generation of copiers. Stimulus has granted the suppliers a subsidy of nine million Dutch guilders. Instead of simply producing detailed and specified components, the suppliers will be asked to design and construct the components themselves in co-operation with other companies. The multinational, the suppliers and the region benefit from this development: because of the simultaneous development and construction Océ can market its products faster, the suppliers can considerably increase their technological knowledge, and industrial employment in the region is thus safeguarded and a valuable knowledge base established.

Another interesting project is concerned with the collection and reprocessing of electronic equipment for kitchen, living room and office. The Stimulus programme supports this initiative, which promotes the re-use of products, components or material, with a million and a half Dutch guilders. It is a pilot project which by now has entered the phase of logistic and technical design, arrangements for funding and management having been made. The initiative combines environmental and economic goals and involves both the public and the private sector. The recently instituted 'Milieudienst Regio Eindhoven' (Environmental Department for the Eindhoven region) was very helpful getting the project started, raising funds and making potential partners enthusiastic for the project. Together with the Milieudienst, branch organisations have succeeded in getting national recognition for the project. Other participants are the regional waste-disposal service (which collects the discarded electronic equipment) and the companies MIREC and COOLREC (who dismantle the collected equipment and make the parts fit for re-use). The 'sheltered workshops' in the region join in for routine jobs.

Organising capacity and the Stimulus project: analysis

Challenge and need for organising capacity

Until a few years ago the region of Eindhoven depended too much on a few large multinationals in the region. For a long time that was no problem, but when Philips and DAF fell into serious trouble and many thousands of jobs disappeared, the vulnerability became all too clear. The problems with Philips and DAF are not isolated, but part of the industrial restructuring the region is passing through. The challenge for the region is now to broaden and renovate its industrial basis, so as to become less dependent on the major companies and at the same time compensate the loss of employment. Eindhoven cannot accomplish that on its own. The interests of the other municipalities in the region are also at stake. Besides, private companies have to be enlisted, because it is for them to provide the broader industrial basis. And the intermediary organisations are a party too, because of their connections with both the private and the public sector. To be able to collaborate, these parties need to look across the 'borders' of their own organisations, and that is where organising capacity comes in as a decisive factor.

Spatial-economic conditions

After the large-scale restructuring of Philips, a number of complexes and estates, scattered across the region, were left vacant. Some of DAF's suppliers have not survived the failure of that company, and municipalities in the Eindhoven region bacame saddled with idle capacity in the form of empty spaces. That made those municipalities more receptive to plans for joint action. Moreover, the pain of the massive lay-offs from Philips and DAF was felt in the entire region. Many surrounding municipalities were confronted with unemployment on an unprecedented scale. All such developments were an additional impulse towards the success of the Stimulus programme.

Political support

Politically, the light was green. In the region itself, all the large political parties favoured the new approach. The impact of the problem and the necessity to turn the tide was widely recognised among them. The national government also supported the initiative from the start, pointed out the possibility of financial support from the European Union, and played an active part in the procedure. The government's support is indeed an absolute condition for an application to be considered in Brussels. In the event, the region received the Objective-2 status for a period of three years, but it took almost a year and a half before the recognition was a fact. The delay was due to the involved legislation and conditions governing financial support from the structural funds. The enthusiasm and spirit of some of the parties had by then ebbed owing to the long formal procedure and the recurrent red-tape obstacles.

Vision and strategy

The action plan from that preceded the Stimulus programme was broadly supported in the region. All relevant bodies and organisations were involved in the preliminaries to the action plan, and gave their approval. The DAF-failure proved to be the last push needed to get the parties together, all being convinced of the need for action. That consensus was 'translated' into an action plan and later-on into the Single Programming Document (EPD). Two themes were consciously chosen: to favour (clusters in) small and medium-size enterprise (MKB) and to add to, and make better use of, the know-how in the region. All actors were behind that choice: it was a broadly supported vision. Moreover, the EPD formulates objectives and defines -though not always in concrete terms- how they can be attained. Both in the action plan and in the EPD, an important part is allotted to public-private partnership.

Administrative structure

From the beginning it has been evident to everyone involved that the challenge could not be taken up by the public actors alone. Consciously, therefore, they have solicited the help of the private sector. The contacts within the administrative structure are on the whole more difficult. The 'Samenwerkingsverband Regio Eindhoven' (Partnership of the Eindhoven Region), in which the municipalities are united, has not yet been given adequate substance. Admittedly agreements have been made to organise services on the regional scale, but 'combined partial interests' are still taking precedence over true regional interests. The fact is that the smaller municipalities live in dread of domination by Eindhoven and Helmond. However, for the Stimulus programme Eindhoven did find response in the region. The Philips and DAF problems resounded throughout the region and made the other municipalities cooperative. Under pressure of the circumstances, the status quo was broken.

Strategic networks

In drawing up and especially implementing the Stimulus project, collaboration and frequent contact among all actors involved was the first concern. Indeed, they were absolutely vital, for without the formation of a network the project could never have taken off. Around the project an extensive network has developed, in which all the interested parties in the region are taking an active part. The parties needed one another; they were mutually dependent and had a common objective. A helpful circumstance was that the region counted already -and still does- a multitude of networks. The intermediary organisations, in particular the Regional Employment Service (RBA) and N.V. REDE, are frequently in touch with those networks and function as transfer tables on which the appropriate parties can meet. Moreover the whole Stimulus project turns around network formation - clustering- in private enterprise. It strengthens the contacts within the region and opens -once the objectives are attained- perspectives for the future.

Leadership

The city of Eindhoven and the Province of North Brabant were the initiator of the meeting which produced the action plan. All parties concerned have taken their responsibilities. Within their possibilities, resources and expertise, they have launched projects and actively put them in motion. So, the project has been pulled by several actors, both in the preliminary and in the implementation stage. RBA and N.V. REDE fulfil a locomotive function in their relevant policy areas. At the preliminary stage, the burgomaster of Eindhoven as a very important actor. He is also the president of the SRE, and now that the other municipalities were motivated to collaborate, he could at crucial moments pull the cart, lobbying with the national government and gathering a substantial starting capital. To have more than one captain on the bridge is no problem in this case because the parties know one another, get along well, and accept one anothers' input.

Performance

Since the action plan was launched in 1993, quite some time had passed before action was indeed taken. Early in 1995 the first projects were approved by the Steering Group and since then there have been lots of others. That so much time elapsed between the initiative and the first results is due to the long-winded procedure to be gone through with the European Union to become eligible for financial support. By now, the Steering Group can already pride itself on such interesting projects as the supply network around Océ. More of such pure clustering projects should be urgently started. Most of the means for infrastructural elements of the programme have been allocated, but with respect to the clustering there are still opportunities. Moreover, the figures show that the region is emerging from the recession; Stimulus has certainly contributed to that development.

The 'West-corridor' project

Inducement

From the early 1980s, Eindhoven more and more recognised the need to invest much more than before in the future of the city. The region of Eindhoven is one of the most important urban nodal points in the Netherlands. To make future capital out of that fact, Eindhoven had to win more (international) standing. The quality of the urban environment is decisive to that effect.

In the preceding decades, urban development in Eindhoven had been allowed to sprawl discriminately, with the result that its image no longer corresponded to a city that size. Change was imperative, the more so as the Eindhoven's internationally oriented business companies demanded a clear international definition to cope with increasing European competition. The winners in the new Europe will be the cities best able to combine economic growth, accessibility and environmental quality. Especially in the urban nodal points, accessibility and environmental quality are under pressure from worsening congestion[4]. Eindhoven recognised and accepted the challenge, choosing as the proper instrument an appealing and daring metropolitan renovation project. The purpose of 'Sleutelproject Westcorridor' (West-Corridor Key Project) is to give Eindhoven a qualitative injection. This revitalising project envisages high-grade business locations and housing in the western part of Eindhoven, made accessible by excellent public transport.

Much support fell to the West-Corridor ideas as an aftermatch to the problems with DAF and Philips. An urban revitalisation project such as this also opens prospects for spatial-economic renovation. Owing to the contraction of Philips, business buildings in the Philips complexes become vacant in quick succession, causing 'holes' to fall especially in the western part of the city. The municipality and Philips will jointly have to find a solution. The re-use of the idle capacity is another important incentive for the project.

Preparatory phase and context of the project

At the end of the 1980s, several departments of the national government issued their own policy documents. Though coloured by the different policy perspectives of the departments, all these documents clearly reflected a new approach to spatial planning[5]. The approach was stated most clearly in the document issued by the spatial planning department called Vierde Nota Ruimtelijke Ordening (VINO; Fourth Note on Spatial Planning)- , which marked three major changes in Dutch spatial planning:
– a shift from equity to efficiency: no longer is the fair distribution of inhabitants and economic activities across the Dutch territory the primary goal of spatial planning. The national government has recognised the economic and environmental significance of the large Dutch cities, and

pronounced seven urban areas -including the Greater Eindhoven area- to be of paramount importance;
– the conclusion of the national government that spatial planning cannot remain as centrally organised as in previous decades, and that local development of ideas should be stimulated;
– the conviction that to achieve sustainable development, economic growth, accessibility and environmental quality must go hand in hand.

At the same time the city of Eindhoven produced an 'urban development concept' of the future development of the city of Eindhoven[6]. The document (1990) starts from what is called the 'natural development' of the city. In the western part of the city close to rail and road infrastructure and in the vicinity of Eindhoven airport, Eindhoven's economic sector is concentrated, while to the left the green Dommel estuary offers a pleasant and quiet living environment. In principle, the planning concept takes this division for granted, labelling the left-hand side as *activity* zone and the right-hand side as *rest zone*, with the area within Eindhoven's 'ring road' as the centre. That concept was taken over in the town planning for the Eindhoven region ('Regiovisie', 1993) and in the general zoning scheme ('streekplan') drawn up by the province of North Brabant.

In the 1990-document on Eindhoven's urban development, three large-scale projects take pride of place: redevelopment of the city centre, the 'Dommel-Zone project' and 'the West-Corridor Key Project'. In the 1980s, the restructuring and 'enlargement' plans for the city centre were launched. The city centre lacked cohesion and appeal, being too small and one-dimensional. The new stylish shopping centre 'Heuvelgalerie', covering one third of the city-centre acreage, has already given the city centre a positive injection. Even before it was integrated in the town-planning concept, the redevelopment of Eindhoven's city centre had long been on the political agenda. Eindhoven had been aching over its inner city for more than 40 years. The restructuring and renewal of the city centre had been postponed again and again, mostly owing to administrative and financial sluggishness. Actually, the restructuring had started before the town-planning document was drawn up. In 1986, the political and administrative climate had become more favourable to the idea. In the 1980s Eindhoven got a new -more entrepreneurial - 'type' of mayor that contributed to a likewise change in administrative culture. The political circles had The Board of Burgomaster and Aldermen launched the city-centre revitalisation without definite contracts or complete financial security. They felt they had to seize the opportunity to tackle the problems of the city centre with both hands, accepting the financial risks. That decision has been extremely important to Eindhoven. The 'Heuvelgalerie' is a huge success and has changed the attitude to renewal in Eindhoven. The second 'Dommel Zone' project is concerned with the protection of the 'green' and quiet eastern part of Eindhoven and the development of new recreational facilities and additional neighbourhoods.

The present case study focuses on the third project: the 'Sleutelproject Westcorridor' ('West-Corridor Key Project'). The first concern in Eindhoven's policy document was to improve the quality of the urban environment. The national revision of spatial planning policy reinforced Eindhoven's ambitions. Remember that the Greater Eindhoven area ranks among the seven (inter)national urban nodal points. The national recognition had led Eindhoven to count on (financial) support for its initiatives. Responding to the invitation in the VINO document, the city suggested that the 'urban development concept', and more in particular the West-Corridor and Dommel-Zone projects, were in accordance with the outlines of the new national policy. The argument was that for the city to fulfil a nodal function, its role as an economic engine of national importance *and* a (supra-regional) centre in the southern part of the Netherlands should be strengthened. In the 1991 supplement to VINO, 'Vierde Nota Ruimtelijke Ordening Extra' (VINEX), the national government pronounced the West Corridor to be of regional importance and awarded it the status of potential key project ('potentieel sleutelproject'); the Dommel-Zone project was considered to be of local - municipal - significance and therefore did not appear in the VINEX document.

At first the 'potential key project' label worked as a catalyst for the project and a boost to confidence. A project organisation was created, guided by a steering committee of members of the City Councils of Eindhoven and Veldhoven (Veldhoven's territory is involved), representatives of the Ministerie van Verkeer en Waterstaat ('Ministry of Public Works') and the Ministerie van Volkshuisvesting, Ruimtelijke Ordening en Milieu (VROM; Ministry of Housing, Spatial Planning and Environment), and civil servants of Eindhoven, Veldhoven, the Province of Northern Brabant, 'Vervoersregio Eindhoven' (Eindhoven Transport Region) and the Ministry of Public Works. The final report on the development strategy was ready and in the hands of VROM by the end of 1992.

Outline of the development strategy

The 'Sleutelproject Westcorridor' (West-Corridor Key Project) is not so much a strictly defined project as a development *strategy*. The West-Corridor Key Project falls apart into numerous independently conceived or developed sub-projects. From the area around the central station, the 'Key Project' spreads outwards to Eindhoven airport and the city centre of the neighbouring municipality Veldhoven, that is, from the city centre across the western city borders. According to the development strategy, the different locations were to be connected by high-quality public transport. Actually the idea for a high-quality public-transport connection was developed at meetings of the 'Transport Region'. The 'Town Development Department' took it from there and gradually the idea grew out to the large-scale urban-renewal project now known as the Sleutelproject Westcorridor.

As mentioned before, the Sleutelproject Westcorridor fits within a larger framework of town planning. Following on the one hand the logic of Eindhoven development, the West Corridor was also purposely intended to connect three important infrastructure nodes: the central station, the motorway junction called 'Poot van Metz' (Metz's leg), and Eindhoven airport. The West-Corridor area is divided in ten sub-sections. Eindhoven and the famous Dutch architect Teun Koolhaas have developed a master plan to redesign the area of the Central Station, the first sub-section (1), featuring a pleasant urban environment convenient for pedestrians and bicyclists, and high-quality building. Quality is the key word here, for the ultimate aim is to create a top location for business, mainly in the service sector. Simultaneously a thorough reconstruction of the road network is planned. As it is, a portion of through traffic still has to pass through the inner city, spoiling the easy access that is an absolute condition for a top location. Another important stimulus for redevelopment of the western part of Eindhoven derives from Philips's Centurion operation described earlier. Many Philips premises and buildings are no longer used for Philips purposes. The vacancy of these large premises and buildings pose a threat to the local real-estate market and the quality of the urban environment. At the same time the vacancy offers enormous opportunities for redevelopment. The favourably located sites -Emmasingel complex (2) and 'Philips-complex Strijp' (4) close to the city centre- have been chosen to be redesigned in line with the West-Corridor development strategy. Of course those complexes are the property of Philips, who will have the final say in the selection of new users. However, Philips and Eindhoven have a common interest in producing a viable option for their re-use. So the municipality is intimately involved in the decision-making process. In among those Philips complexes, the stadium of local football club PSV Eindhoven and its environment are also part of the scheme (3). Close to the Philips complexes in the 'Strijp' area lies the older characteristic residential area Strijp (10). The 'West-Corridor Project' provides for measures to upgrade the area. The Evoluon (5) is to be connected to the high-quality public-transport line.

The second infrastructure node in the corridor is the 'Poot van Metz' area (6), where the planned corridor is planned to join the highway network. A business location with easy access by cars will be the result. Between the 'Poot van Metz' and the third node, Eindhoven airport (8), lies the Meerhoven area (7). On these grounds - partly on Eindhoven territory and partly on (former) Veldhoven territory - vast new housing estates and new business premises have been planned as part of the VINEX-schemes. Finally, the project stretches to the renewed city centre of neighbour Veldhoven (9).

Progress

The designation of seven (inter)national urban nodal points and the turn-about in national policy raised expectations in the areas concerned as to possible State support for new projects. After a while the initial enthusiasm in Eindhoven faded away. In 1991 the national government attributed to the West-Corridor strategy the status of 'potential key project', suggesting in principle eligibility for national funding. Negotiations between the national and local representatives were to lead to the definite status of key project. Only in the summer of 1995 did Eindhoven and the two ministries involved - VROM and Public Works reach an agreement.

The final agreement is somewhat disappointing from Eindhoven's point of view. On estimation, the project requires public investment of around a thousand million Dutch guilders. From the early stages on the idea had prevailed -based on the message of the VINEX policy document- that the national government would follow their policy outline by granting direct financial support for key projects. That was also what Eindhoven expected. However the negotiations between representatives of either side dragged on for a long time. Moreover, direct financial support for the integral West-Corridor project appears never to have been an option. Four years later, in June 1995, the negotiations resulted in a covenant acknowledging the status of key project. For the Meerhoven housing schemes -fitting ideally in the

VINEX framework- direct financial support has been granted; for the integral West-Corridor project no lump-sum contribution has been promised. Instead, the two Ministries involved provide partial funding for (short-term plans for) infrastructure, soil cleansing and land reclamation. Hence a clear gap remains between the estimated costs of the project and the resources raised up till now.

Why did it take so long? For one thing, the national government had apparently misjudged or overlooked the financial consequences of its policy. But the lack of co-operation of yet another Ministry, that of Defence, complicated the negotiations tremendously. Some of the land that was to be used for the VINEX housing schemes was in the hand of that Ministry, and Eindhoven had to buy it. The Ministry of Defence asked a fancy price for the plot of land and was not inclined to take a more flexible attitude. Thus one Ministry (of Defence) by its stubbornness was at cross-purposes with the other (VROM). It took years for the two ministries to communicate properly and for the Ministry of Defence to moderate its demands.

The project stretches across Eindhoven's and some of Veldhoven's territory. It is also undoubtedly a project of metropolitan scope. Given the scale and extent, it will have an impact not only on Eindhoven but also on the competitive position of the Greater Eindhoven area. A positive factor was been that the two Ministries involved wanted to do business only with the (metropolitan) *region*. Under normal circumstances it would have been virtually impossible for Eindhoven to convince the other municipalities of the advantages of collaboration and to gain wide regional support. However, the financial incentive of the ministerial decision that the profits and losses of new housing developments in the Greater Eindhoven area were to be settled regionally, worked wonders. In fact that decision forced the municipalities to the joint exploitation of new housing developments in the region. The municipalities of the region are 'condemned to one another', being compelled to collaborate as if a regional land-managing department existed. Of the 28,000 new houses to be built in the region, around 7,000 have been planned in the Meerhoven area. The housing estates in the Meerhoven area will be densely populated; the land area per housing unit will be smaller than elsewhere in the region. Had the other municipalities continued to build less economically, in terms of land, then the schemes in the Meerhoven area would have become a financial disaster. The present construction prevents that, since losses in Meerhoven will be shared regionally.

That the West-Corridor project is considered important not only for Eindhoven but also for the region is evident from the financial resources flowing to it from the regional fund. The regional funds holds 145 million guilders, paid in by the ten urban areas in the region in proportion to the number of inhabitants; a portion of it goes to the project. Besides, the project has been included in the regional vision that has been drawn up and approved jointly by the 32 municipalities in the SRE. The support is remarkable in view of the rather awkward relations in the region notably with respect to housing. Even more remarkable is that Veldhoven has actually made land available to Eindhoven. With other small municipalities around the city, such as Nuenen and Best, Eindhoven is at loggerheads. Eindhoven needs space to build houses and to that end requires the cooperation of these suburban municipalities.

The delay of the project is due not only to the attitude of the national government. In the Eindhoven region itself, the start-up was beset with difficulties. Initially the project had its own organisation and manager, but that set-up soon proved unworkable. The West-Corridor Key Project is not really a well-defined project that can be controlled as such; it is a compilation of mostly autonomous parts. Such a structure is hard to control. By now the project organisation has been dissolved, and the steering group mentioned before is now charged with guarding the *cohesion*. Many departments of the Town Development Office are involved in the project. A project bureau has been created to harmonise and coordinate the activities within the Office. Under the project bureau come the municipal project leaders of the sub-projects as far as the municipality has a significant part to play. Sometimes coordination has been accomplished with the most interested parties: Philips for its own complexes, the association of citizens in the residential quarter De Strijp, and for instance the future licensee of the Poortgebouw in the cental station district. The emphasis is still on *municipal* control, however.

Financially, too, the project was divided into parts when a national subsidy for the integral project was late coming off. The funds invested in the project from VINEX, the municipality, the region, and venture capital from private investors, do not yet make up the total amount needed. Therefore an approach has been adopted by which elements of the project are financed successively. There is moderate optimism about closing the gap; there are certainly chances of additional financing, notably for the high-grade public-transport connection, but to delay the start any longer was not deemed justified. The missing amount has to be collected while the scheme is in progress.

The municipal elections of 1994 have slowed down the proceedings as well. After the publication of VINEX, the Town Development Office elaborated the idea of the West-Corridor Project, finishing the final report in December 1992. In the course of 1993 the strategic note was presented to the Municipal Council and unanimously approved. By Eindhoven standards it is a huge project with considerable financial consequences. Therefore, the politicians in Eindhoven took the view that the new municipal council should given the chance to express themselves about the project. Although work on parts was continued, with the Council making the necessary decisions, delay was inevitable. After the new board took office, the project was reconsidered, more attention being given to the social dimensions. In the new board's programme the emphasis is on employment and safety. Those are the very problems that are near to the citizen's heart, so that the board has an interest in enhancing and keeping the support of the citizens by presenting them with immediately visible results. Another important effect of the political reconsideration is that the new board has charged one specific alderman with the West-Corridor project. He will be involved in the project integrally -across the various political portfolios- and from the operational to the strategic level.

Present situation

Most of the project is still at the preparatory stage, but a few sub-projects are more advanced. The financing of housing at Meerhoven has been arranged and in 1997 the first houses are to be completed. A striking fact is that the projects that have entered, or are about to enter, the execution stage, are funded either by private investors or by Stimulus money. The Stimulus programme has certainly acted as a catalyst for the West-Corridor project. The long trajectory of negotiations with the State and the political delay in Eindhoven itself necessitated a phased execution of the West-Corridor strategy, and the contributions from the Stimulus programme helped to make that approach possible. The fact that the European Union makes funds available on the basis of co-financing has incited the central government to greater financial efforts.

The adding of a new wing to the PSV-stadium costs 35 million guilders, a a major portion of which is accounted for by the football club. However, the regional funds has contributed four million (for environmental issues), and funds from the Stimulus programme are also flowing to the project. Furthermore, the reconstruction of the Philips complex on the Emmasingel has come in a decisive phase. The Emmasingel complex is part of Eindhoven's city centre. The buildings of the complex are no longer in use and Philips wanted to take them down and sell the land. Eindhoven preferred to absorb the complex into the city centre. To realise that ambition, the complex should accommodate a mixture of living, working and leisure functions and services. The idea is for the rehabilitation to add to the appeal of the city centre and thus draw more visitors to it. Part of the complex will be demolished to make room for new houses, for which the money (54 million) will be put up by a private investor. The intention is, however, to save some characteristic buildings from demolition and make them ready for new occupation. The plans regarding the so-called 'White Lady' are particularly interesting. By the 'White Lady' are understood the white Philips buildings on the Emmasingel. They date from 1928 and were designed by the Dutch architect Roosenburg. They are so unique and radiate such magic that their re-use would enrich the city centre. The resistance against demolition was initiated by artists. They wanted to reconstruct and reallocate the buildings, with the accent on art and cultural activities. However, the re-usable area would be gigantic: 36,000 square metres. To rehabilitate the complex on such a flimsy basis would be utopian. No investors can be found simply because the concept lacks commercial perspectives. Gradually, more parties got involved in the restauration of the 'White Lady', and the Emmasingel Foundation was created. The foundation has succeeded in drawing up a feasible project proposal. The Eindhoven library, Philips Corporate Design, the European Design Centre of the Eindhoven Academy for Industrial Design and an art and culture center will be the new occupiers. With two-third of the complex in the hands of private investers and developers, the project can be instantly carried out, thanks in particular to the efforts of some inspiring pioneers within the Emmasingel Foundation.

An important element of the 'key project' is the envisaged high-grade public-transport connection that is to link the principal locations in western Eindhoven. The State has promised a subsidy of 60 million guilders, and in the framework of the Stimulus programme several companies have been put in touch with one another to develop an environment-saving bus for the purpose. Whether a bus connection is the obvious choice for the kind of supreme transport envisaged in the concept of the West Corridor, is questionable. The discussions on that point are still going on. At any rate, the political choice is to open up the area by public transport, which is why car access -apart from the 'Poot van Metz'- does not rank high in the West-Corridor concept. The growing of passenger traffic will have to be largely coped with by public transport. Whether that is indeed feasible depends entirely on the quality of the public transport supplied. If that fails, many car owners will refuse to make the transfer, and the pretention of top location prove illusory.

The West-Corridor project claims to offer a sustainable solution for the economic development of Eindhoven. That explains the political preference for a high-grade public-transport connection. However, the idea of sustainability was not given substance from the first. Representatives of the regional environmental department were not among the original discussion partners. Only at the time of reconsideration in 1994/1995 were efforts made to give more substance to the sustainability objective. Especially in relation to the building of houses in Meerhoven and the organisation of public space much has been improved. With a few simple modifications the ambitions with respect to the quality of the environment have been secured.

Organising capacity and the West-corridor project: analysis

Challenge and the need for organising capacity

It has already been pointed out that Eindhoven missed the enchantment and style associated with a city of its size. An important factor in that respect is the quality of the urban environment. Since the mid-1980s, Eindhoven has been making serious efforts to catch up, choosing the further economic development of the western part of the town as the road to that end. It is already the economic gravity centre of Eindhoven, but the conditions are far from optimum. The accessibility leaves much to be desired and Eindhoven runs the risk that the great buildings which Philips has abandoned will offer a dreary spectacle. The challenge for Eindhoven is to make a virtue of necessity, making quality the key word for rehabilitation, and combining accessibility, quality of the environment and economic vitality. A challenge which many cities are facing nowadays. The metropolitan renovation project called the West-Corridor project, is in fact an umbrella covering a large number of sub-projects, involving a variety of knowhow and multiple interested parties. To give substance to the ambition of sustainable renovation, all the forces and all the expertise available in *city and region must be enlisted*; therefore, organising capacity is becoming all-important.

Spatial-economic conditions

The West Corridor aims at the spatial reorganisation and revitalisation of the western part of Eindhoven. The (internal) accessibility of Eindhoven's economic gravity centre falls short in several respects. Not for nothing has the large-scale reconstruction of the city centre already been taken in hand. Eindhoven has consciously opted for economic development in the western zone. To that end, the area needs attractive business locations, good access and a pleasant living environment. To overcome the present bottlenecks - congestion, lack of top locations, quantitative and qualitative shortages on the housing market- *is the first concern* of the West-Corridor concept.

Those who are involved in the West-Corridor project on behalf of the municipality know very well what the project aims for, since it has sprung from a development strategy! Until shortly before the West-Corridor project was launched, Eindhoven's spatial-economic policy gave no evidence of any long-term vision. Halfway the 1980s the policy changed, and the West-Corridor strategy is one effect of that change. Besides, the vision of Eindhoven has been accommodated in the regional plan, to secure support from the region. Efforts to win support among the population and from local private enterprise came later, as did the contacts with N.V. REDE and the Regional Environmental Department. Hence the number of interim adjustments to the concept. In sum, by now there is a vision, for which the Town Development Office is belatedly trying to get the support of the directly interested. Nor has a consensus been achieved about the effectuation of the high-grade public-transport connection.

Administrative structure

Progress was seriously delayed by the attitude taken by the relevant ministries during negotiations. Frankly, Eindhoven had built up too high expectations after the project's acceptation for VINEX. Expectations to which admittedly the central government had given food. In the Dutch situation, support from the central government is indispensable for a project in which so many public investments are involved, so that to a certain degree Eindhoven depends upon the State.

On the other hand, Eindhoven itself has caused some delay as well. For a long time the project remained mostly a municipal undertaking, more in particular an object of the Town Development Office. Other actors -private companies, inhabitants- were enlisted not at all, too little or too late. The sights were set too much inwards, and the project remained too long within

134

the formalised structures. That is also evident from the problems with the organisation initially charged with the control. The variety of actors, interests and sub-projects made central control from the municipality impractical. Although a measure of central control from the City Development Office remains advisable, those interested should have been involved earlier. In the present situation the Development Office still sits at the centre, but it has set its sights outward as well as inward.

Strategic networks

Apparently, the project cannot be re-floated within the 'formalised' structure. The available capacity and competency in the town have to be enlisted to keep the project on the move and complete it successfully. That goes beyond the municipal organisation; indeed, for such a comprehensive revitalisation project, an active search for the qualities needed has to be mounted outside the municipal apparatus. Now that the dialogue with third parties -project developers, building contractors, private companies and citizens- has been opened, the movement seems to be gaining impetus. Clearly, the impulse has to come from outside. Just now, the projects taking off in a promising way seem to be in particular those in which investors, project developers and bodies like the Emmasingel Foundation have taken the lead. Stimulus funds have helped to get some project elements started, and possibly also to bring about the changed attitude of the Town Development Department. Interest from private entrepreneurs appears to develop provided they are taken seriously as discussion partners. For several sub-projects investors have come forward, and involvement is growing in other respects as well.

Political support

The status of potential 'key project' signified a stimulus for the West Corridor. After the recognition by the State, nothing seemed to hinder the speedy realisation of the project. However, the positive effect of that stimulus petered out as the negotiations went on and on. Originally, a covenant between State and region was to confirm the status of 'key project' in 1993; in the event it took to June 1995. Eindhoven received conflicting signals from the Dutch authorities. The VINEX-recognition had given rise to expectations in Eindhoven which the Ministries could not or would not fulfil. Besides, the communication between the Ministries of Housing, Spatial Planning and Environment and of Public Works, and later the Defence

Ministry, appeared to be far from optimum. There were green as well as red lights from The Hague.

Leadership

The West-Corridor project comes under the Town Development Department. Therefore, the project was at first mostly pulled by that department. While logical in itself, the effect was that the project belonged too much too the Department rather than the City or the region of Eindhoven. Apart from that, the success of the project depends on persons of institutions that carry the component parts. A good example is the Emmasingel Foundation. Within the foundation a small group of people has managed to get the White-Lady project ready for take-off. In the new board an experienced aldermen has now been made responsible for the West-Corridor project. He will pull the cart and function as a point of address. Perhaps that set-up will accelerate the procedure. The aldermen is politically answerable and is perhaps better than others able to bridge the gap between officialdom and private sector.

Performance

Although the West Corridor is a long-term project, the conclusion may already be drawn that so far the performance has not been optimum. Naturally, the troublesome negotiations with the State are to blame. However, nor has Eindhoven made optimum use of the potential of the city. There has clearly been a learning effect, both as regards the organisation of the project and in the search for partners. With the signing of the covenant a crucial phase has begun. The phased approach has so far been kept in motion by external impulses. The question is, can the municipality keep up with the movement and jump the wagon itself? There is another serious obstacle: how will the envisaged high-quality public-transport line be realised? The quality of the West-Corridor zone very much depends on it. Concessions as to the quality of the connection could jeopardise the economic vitality of the entire West-Corridor project.

Conclusions

Until the mid-1980s, the prosperous economic development of the Greater Eindhoven area was closely bound up with the success of some major companies in the region: Nedcar, DAF, and most of all, Philips. Philips was not only economically very important, socially too the presence of Philips had clearly put its mark on the region. Its very dependency made the Greater Eindhoven area vulnerable; when Philips and DAF fell in great difficulties, repercussions were immediately felt in city and region. The decline of the great economic propeller firms illustrated once more that the region had to take the initiative and should not just sit and wait for the great motors to pull the economic cart. Eindhoven has potential, but the competition in Europe is not sitting back. It is for (the region of) Eindhoven to use its potential in full. In sum, organising capacity is becoming essential. In the present case study, two projects have been analysed in detail: the Stimulus Programme and the West-Corridor Key Project.

The massive loss of employment with Philips (from the second half of the 1980s onward) and DAF (1993), and the extensive attention paid in all media to the DAF-failure, gave rise to what is now known as the Stimulus Programme. This programme aims at reinforcing the position of small and medium-size companies to create new employment; clustering is the keyword in order to anchor these companies to the region, it is here that prospects open themselves. The shock of the 'unexpected' collapse of DAF created the momentum for government and private enterprise to join forces. Jointly an action plan was drawn up and the regional municipalities donated seven million guilders to forge the plans into actions. Next, the region, at the instigation of the Central Government, succeeded in acquiring European support in the setting of Objective 2. More than a year after the action plan was launched, European approval and financial support had been secured.

The public and private sectors have jointly given substance to the Stimulus programme. The Central government, the SRE and Eindhoven have exerted themselves to bring together sufficient (European) resources, and create the administrative marginal conditions. That task fell to the public parties, because only they were formally entitled to generate the financial means. The Stimulus programme puts its faith in clustering in small-scale enterprise. The public actors -municipalities, region, municipal departments, intermediary (regional) organisations- are predominantly concerned with creating the conditions, but for a large part it is the companies that have to give substance to the clustering. Naturally, the intermediary organisations are in the vanguard for the development of concrete projects, but often the motive force will have to come from private enterprise. It may be a company from the region, or from elsewhere in the country or abroad. The envisaged clustering is meant to enhance the organising capacity in the region. Clustering is most successful when the companies are functionally related and when there is a distinct leader to take care of the orchestration. The network of Eindhoven suppliers to the Limburg company of Océ van der Grinten is illustrative. The envisaged 'horizontal' clustering of companies from clearly different branches is not yet taking shape. Evidently the functional dependency between the network initiator -the orchestrator- and the other players in the network is a condition for the formation of economic clusters.

The implementation of the programme is in full swing. A few appealing short-time results have already been recorded. The success of Stimulus is mainly due to the fact that all those concerned were co-operative and agreed upon the approach. The seriousness of the problems enabled the mayor of Eindhoven and the Governor of the Province of North Brabant to organise the necessary support. The national political interest has worked as a consolidating factor. Moreover, clever use has been made of the momentum -the media attention for DAF. Regrettably, much time was lost in the long-winded bureaucratic treatment of the Stimulus proposal in Brussels. It has caused a partial loss of the momentum. If the European trajectory could have been traversed more speedily, the performance would have been much better. Nevertheless, the collaboration proceeds satisfactorily because the region has a tradition to keep up with respect to the formal and informal contacts between government and private enterprise. That the regional economic development company N.V. REDE is regarded as part of the private sector, which formally it is not, is a good illustration.

With the second project, the West-Corridor Key Project, far more problems have arisen. The West-Corridor Key Project comprises a spatial development strategy for the revitalisation of a large area in the western part of Eindhoven. The project fits into the national policy of spatial planning laid down in the VINO and VINEX. The Central Government is therefore an important party; a large portion of the financing has to come from the State. The metropolitan revitalisation project provides for new housing, business locations and other facilities, to be linked by high-grade public transport. The project requires the investment of more than a thousand million guilders and involves many interested parties. Although the final report was ready by the end of 1992, the majority of project parts are still at the preparation stage. The greatest obstacle has been the attitude of the Central Government. The first recognition of the project in the VINEX (1991) was a tremendous incentive and created expectations of integral financial support from the Central Government. However, the Ministry of VROM was unable or unwilling to meet the expectations, and only in the summer of 1995 could an agreement be signed. For certain elements -housing, cleansing of polluted soil, and infrastructure- the State makes resources available. Integral financial support for the project has never been an option for the Central Government. The conflicting political signals have done the project no good.

The problems arising from the Central Government's attitude towards the West Corridor were largely outside Eindhoven's competency, but they were responsible for the sluggish progress of the project. On the other hand, in Eindhoven itself there were difficulties as well. Initially the project found insufficient support among other significant players in Eindhoven, so that the project was carried mainly by the Department of Town Development. With a project of such magnitude, those directly interested should function as serious discussion partners and be invited to help with the thinking. For the West-Corridor project, efforts to span a bridge between public and private actors were made belatedly. A third negative point is the poor cooperation from municipalities in the region, despite the presence of the SRE. That the Ministry of VROM wanted to do business only with the region has been very important for the envisaged house building in the West Corridor. Only after the Ministry had inserted a financial incentive 'enjoining' upon the municipalities to work together were they prepared to take up the housing problem. In that way, demolition of the West Corridor was avoided.

After the revision in 1994 and above all the cross-pollination with Stimulus funds, the project now seems to be taking off. Very importantly, an experienced aldermen has been made politically responsible for the entire project, right across the different portfolios. The aldermen can function as locomotive and point of address and put the project definitely on the rails. That is a good and crucial development because there are still important challenges to be met. The financing of the entire project is not yet arranged and the high-grade public-transport connection still has to be given shape. Now that there is a distinct leader, he can take care to put quality first in the final choice on that score. Too many concessions with respect to quality could jeopardise the viability of the entire project.

From the case study, a lot has changed in the Eindhoven region since the early 1980s. Both government and business companies are actively working towards revitalisation. Since the impasse around the reconstruction and qualitative enhancement of the city centre in 1986 (after a 40-year tug-of-war) was broken, a climate has developed in which belief in the region's own capacity is the primary factor. To ensure its competitive position, Eindhoven certainly cannot sit back and rest, but town and region have clearly gained in energy and decisiveness.

Abbreviations used

BON	Besturen op Niveau (Administration at the proper level)
SRE	Co-operative Body for the Eindhoven metropolitan region
RBA	Regional Employment Service
EPD	Single Programming Document
VINO	Fourth Policy Report on Physical Planning in the Netherlands
VINEX	Fourth Policy Report on Physical Planning Extra
VROM	Ministry of Spatial Planning and Environment

Notes

---

[1] In alphabetical order: Aarle-Rixtel, Asten, Bakel en Milheeze, Beek en Donk, Bergeyk, Best, Bladel en Netersel, Budel, Deurne, Eersel, Eindhoven, Geldrop, Gemert, Heeze, Helmond, Hoogeloon C.A., Leende, Lieshout, Luyksgestel, Maarlheeze, Mierlo, Nuenen C.A., Oirschot, Reusel, Riethoven, Someren, Son en Breugel, Valkenswaard, Veldhoven, Vessem C.A., Waalre and Westerhoven.

[2] The Randstad is the name commonly given to the densely populated urban area in the western part of the Netherlands with in the four largest cities: Amsterdam, Rotterdam, The Hague and Utrecht.

[3] See: Ministerie van VROM, *Vierde Nota Ruimtelijke Ordening*, 1991.

[4] See, for example:European Commission, *Europe 2000+*, 1995.

[5] *Vierde Nota Ruimtelijke Ordening and Vierde Nota Ruimtelijke Ordening Extra, Nationaal Milieu Beleidsplan* (Ministry of VROM) and *Structuurschema Verkeer en Vervoer* (Ministry of Verkeer en Waterstaat).

[6] Dienst Stadsontwikkeling, *Structuurschets Eindhoven binnen de ring*, 1990.

6 Lisbon

Introduction

Lisbon, together with Porto, is the principal city of Portugal. It is the capital and the country's administrative centre. But Lisbon, or better: the Greater Lisbon area, is also Portugal's economic centre. Continuous investment to keep that function is a national concern. In the 1980s and before that has not always been respected. By now, investment to enhance Lisbon's competitive position has high priority; both the national and the local authorities try to give substance to the revitalisation of the city. In 1998, the EXPO is coming to Lisbon and that event will be put in as an instrument to revitalise a part of Lisbon. A gigantic operation involving much organising capacity. Therefore, EXPO '98 is central to this chapter. First, the chapter sketches a profile of the Greater Lisbon area, followed by a description of its economic development. Next, the chapter outlines the administrative structure in the Greater Lisbon area. The chapter then extensively deals with the EXPO and its impact on Lisbon, followed by an analysis of the project on the basis of the theory of organising capacity presented in chapter 1. Finally the chapter finishes off with the conclusions of the Lisbon case.

Profile[1]

The city of Lisbon, capital of Portugal, covers an area of 83.8 square km and has a population of 660,000 (1991); the population density is nearly 8,000 inhabitants/square km. The traditional function of Lisbon as the administrative centre of Portugal is still reflected in the stately buildings in the old city centre. Today, Lisbon is still a government city, and the presence of Central Government clearly marks the city as a centre of employment as well as culture. Most important Ministries are located in the city centre. Naturally, the vestiges of the rich Portuguese maritime history can still be found there. They add to the magic of the town.

What is considered to be the metropolitan area of Lisbon (AML) consists of the capital city and 17 other municipalities, along the two river banks of the Tagus, with a total population of about 2.5 million people and an area of more than 3,000 square km (see table 1). That extensive area accommodates more than a quarter of the Portuguese population and confirms the status of Lisbon as *the* centre of Portugal.

Table 1
Basic data on Lisbon and the Metropolitan Area

	Lisbon	Metropolitan Area
Square km	83.8	3,121.6
Population (1991)	663,394	2,551,750
% population of the country	7.1	25.4

From the Second World War until 1974, Portugal was governed by dictators, first Salazar, and next his successor. In those and subsequent years, the investment level trailed behind that of the important European countries. That changed in the 1980s, but in consequence of the 'old' policy Lisbon is confronted by two serious problems: on the one hand the concentration of some problem groups in the city centre, and on the other poor accessibility. That the Greater Lisbon area was assigned the status of Objective-1 region by the European guidelines was therefore no surprise.

Social segregation and demographic development

The first problem, social segregation, is closely bound up with the demographic development and unfavourable migration patterns. Between 1981 and 1991 the capital city lost about 17 per cent of its population, owing to death rates (15.9 per thousand) dramatically surpassing birth rates (9.6 per thousand) and the voluminous migration of mainly the middle classes to the suburbs of the metropolitan area and even beyond (see figure 1).

142

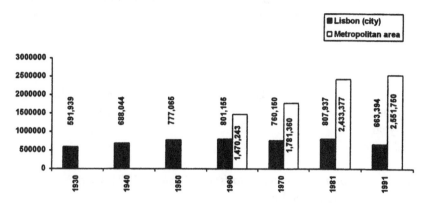

Figure 1   Population development for the city and the metropolitan
            area for 1981-1991

That demographic phenomenon has had a major impact on the city centre,
which gets progressively emptier, only the people in poor socio-economic
conditions remaining in the area. This tends to consolidate areas of urban
poverty in downtown neighbourhoods.

One result of the migratory process is that the population in the city of
Lisbon ages: while children account for 14.2 no more than per cent, the
elderly over 64 represent up to 18.8 per cent (see table 2). Meanwhile the
population of the metropolitan area increased to 2.1 per cent between 1981
and 1991. This represents near-stabilisation of growth in contrast to the high
growth rates during the 1960s and 1970s. The metropolitan population is
younger than that of the central city, with only 13.1 per cent elderly persons
and 19.2 per cent children.

This crooked demographic growth is attended by serious social problems.
Indicators of the social situation of Lisbon show that the city ranks above the
average of the country, but is also the spot in which the most acute problems
of exclusion are concentrated. Spatially the social problems are found mainly
in the historical centre of the city, which has an aged population,
downgraded housing, and mobility difficulties due to the steep inclining
streets.

The quantity as well as the quality of the housing is inadequate. There is a
great shortage of housing. Furthermore, there are still many people living in
shanty towns or in provisional dwelling units. In the historical city, the

houses are old and out of repair. There is little economic activity and the population has a low level of education, relatively to the Lisbon average.

Table 2
Age Structure (%, 1991)

	Lisbon (city)	Metropolitan Area
0-15 years	14.2	19.2
15-64 years	67.0	74.3
65 and over	18.8	13.1

Source: *Lisboa. Elementos Estatísticos Básicos,* 1994. Cámara Municipal de Lisboa

Despite the efforts of authorities, the need to relocate the population continues to be pressing: the estimate is that 11,000 dwelling units are needed until 2001 in the framework of the Programa Especial de Realojamento (Special Relocation Programme, PER).

The inadequate quality of the housing stock and the concentration of elderly people is a legacy of the rent-control law. The law protected the interests of tenants by fixing the rents. Since the oil crisis of 1972, inflation eroded the real income of landlords and took away the incentive to invest in their housing stock. Now that the law has been changed, the allocation through market forces is restored.

Besides these territorial situations, there are several points of acute exclusion in the city, such as the neighbourhood de Casal Ventoso, where an URBAN-initiative project will be implemented, and various groups in marginal conditions owing to drug dependency, homelessness, mental illness, sensorial and physical deficiencies, etc.

Illiteracy is another serious problem in the Metropolitan Area of Lisbon. The average rate of illiteracy is 8.2 per cent, but this figure hides wide differences among municipalities, as some of them count 15 per cent of illiterate persons. The City of Lisbon itself scores better with an illiteracy rate of 5.7 per cent. Raising the educational level is a hot item of most development programmes.

Mobility and traffic

The second great problem of Lisbon is its bad accessibility. Traffic congestion is normal in Lisbon. The road and rail structure is strongly radial.

Frequently improved new access roads have negative impacts on the links with the existing urban fabric. Movement and traffic flows are intense in Lisbon. Estimates show that about 700,000 vehicles circulate daily in Lisbon, with 300,000 incoming cars from the metropolitan area. In the centre there is a lack of parking space for cars. As a consequence, the parking system is chaotic and authorities estimate that half of the vehicles are illegally parked.

The public transportation system takes care of part of the commuting flows. The city has 19 km of metropolitan rail (25 stations), which transported 144 million passengers in 1992; there are 570 km of bus routes in 92 lines with a total of 388 million passengers; 92 km of tramway lines (10 lines) and four lifts. The railway network transports about 270,000 passengers daily. The public transportation system is completed with the river boats across the estuary of the Tagus, which carry about 46 million passengers a year. However, the public transportation system is not efficient and effective enough; there are serious deficits and the different modal systems are not integrated.

The Lisbon airport accommodates 235 daily flights (1990) with a total of 5.4 million passengers. The port of Lisbon counted of 4,446 ships in 1992 with a merchandise volume of 17.7 million tons.

Economic aspects[2]

The activity rate of the AML is 51.1 per cent (1991), that of the males (55.9 per cent) surpassing that of females by ten points (see table 3). Unemployment rates in the metropolitan area are relatively moderate at 7.7 per cent of the economically active population in 1991[3]. Lately, unemployment has increased slightly. Even if on the whole the unemployment rates are moderate, in some metropolitan municipalities large groups of unemployed are concentrated.

Seven out of ten of the employed population in the metropolitan area work in the tertiary sector, which in the city of Lisbon reaches the peak of four fifths of the employed, the industrial sector occupying about one fifth of the population. It is worth mentioning that in six out of the 18 metropolitan municipalities, between one tenth and one fifth of the population is still agrarian.

The city of Lisbon is still the main work place of the metropolitan area. On estimation, about 600,000 jobs are located within the city limits, half of them covered by city residents. The commuting flows are very important, averaging 300,000 daily trips, to which we should add the trips for shopping and studying. Overall commuting flows are increasing in the metropolitan area.

Table 3
Economically active population

	Lisbon		Metrop. Area	
	abs.	%	abs.	%
Men	161,737	55.3	679,374	55.9
Women	141,439	46.7	535,796	44.1
Total	303,176	100.0	1,215,170	100.0
Activity rate		45,7		51.1

Source: Lisboa. Elementos Estatísticos Básicos, 1994. Cám. Municip.Lisboa

The largest employment sectors in Lisbon are the personal, community and public administration services accounting for 35 per cent of total jobs. These types of activity are related to the capital function of Lisbon city. Retail and restaurant businesses account for one fifth of employment. At a greater distance, we find such sectors as manufacturing industries, financial and business services, and the sector of communications and transport (see table 4).

The industrial sector of the city is formed mainly by the production of metallurgy and transportation materials, publishing and graphical arts, chemistry and oil, food processing and finally textiles and apparel. Between 1981 and 1991 the business and financial sector were the ones that grew most dramatically, while losses of employment were experienced mainly in the manufacturing industries.

Table 4
Job distribution by branch of activity (thousands) for Lisbon

	1981	1991
Industry	97	66
Construction and public works	33	24
Retail and Restaurants	115	116
Transportation and communication	61	54
Finances, Insurance and Business services	47	71
Public Administration, Community services	194	184
Other activities	8	7
Total	555	522

Source: Lisboa. Elementos Estatísticos Básicos, 1994. Cám. Municip.Lisboa

Administrative structure[4]

Portugal has inherited from the past a highly centralist regime. Decisions are made on the national level and knowledge also resides on that level. Lower levels of government sometimes have difficulty obtaining the right information and the necessary knowledge. In theory public administration in Portugal comprises three layers of government see figure 1): national government, seven regions and the municipalities. In practice there are two independent public actors: state and municipality. The regions are intermediary between the State and the municipalities. However, these bodies do not operate autonomously, but as regional departments of the state government ('extended state administration'). Their task is to co-ordinate and implement, or cause to be implemented, measures necessary for the development of the region involved.

State

↓

(regions)

↓

Municipalities

Figure 2   **Administrative structure in Portugal**

Within their legal responsibilities the municipalities are autonomous. The present tasks and responsibilities of the municipalities are laid down in a municipal law of 1984. In that same year an Act came into force to regulate the municipal finances. Municipalities obtain their income from two main sources: their own taxes and transfer payments from the State. By law Portuguese municipalities are relatively large, and therefore less than the smaller communities in other countries need to enter into partnerships because of a too narrow (financial) support of their own. Recently a slight change has become apparent. A few municipalities in the metropolitan area of Lisbon have recognised the need for co-operation. Nonetheless the State (still) has much influence on the lower administrative tiers and on many public services. A large part of public transport, for instance, comes directly under the Ministry of Transport.

Finally, another characteristic of the administrative culture in Portugal is the prevalence political parties give to ideologistic principles. That can work out negatively for their co-operativeness. The tendency to leave no doubt where a party stands is one reason why political coalitions of parties are rare in the public administration of Portugal. Only since the last elections has the city of Lisbon been governed by a coalition of the communists and the socialists.

The EXPO '98 and EXPO URBE Project

The challenge

In 1998 Portugal, and in particular Lisbon, will host the world exhibition. The EXPO will draw many visitors from at home and abroad, and put Portugal and Lisbon in the international limelight. Lisbon and also Portugal very much want to burnish their image. Until 1974, Portugal was governed by one Marcelo Caetano, the successor of Salazar who had been in the saddle for forty years. In 1974 the dictatorship came to an end. While it lasted, Portugal hardly communicated with the world outside; its sights were mostly set inwards. The current governors experience that legacy as a disadvantage to be overcome. Therefore, Portugal values every opportunity to manifest itself internationally. The EXPO in 1998 in the Portuguese capital Lisbon gives focus to that ambition.

However, international promotion is not the only objective. Lisbon's ambitions reach much further. The EXPO is put in as a lever for the sustainable revitalisation of a deprived part of Lisbon. The company that has been founded to organise the EXPO '98 thus has a twofold objective: to organise the world exhibition as such, and to revitalise that urban zone concerned. That zone is on record as a bad, polluted area. To stage the EXPO in that very zone and transform it into a pleasant residential, working and living environment that will renew its drive and status and become a second centre of Lisbon, is an awesome undertaking.

The EXPO is a national project, and naturally the national government has a lead role in it. However, the Portuguese government cannot do it all on its own. It needs the collaboration of market parties and lower governments as well as the support of the population. In sum, to perform the great job in good time, organising capacity is indispensable.

The strategy

The organisers of the EXPO '98 in Lisbon have tried to learn from the positive and negative experiences of the EXPO in Seville in 1992. A delegation of EXPO '98 has followed on the spot the whole trajectory from six months before the world exhibition. The world exhibition in Seville could not complain about lack of interest from the international media, although the number of visitors was disappointing. The greatest setback in Seville is, however, the failing of long-term profit for the city. The town had failed to make good capital of the event. Many of the constructions erected especially for the world exhibition, among them a great exhibition hall, are no longer in use. The sites for the EXPO have cost a great deal, and to invest so much in provisions used once for the one event has not been efficient. As a result the Seville EXPO organisation is wrestling with enormous financial deficits. The Lisbon company also visited Barcelona, the site of the 1992 Olympic Games. Those responsible in Barcelona were more attentive to the long-term advantages to be gained for the city. Besides a terrific amount of publicity they have succeeded in hauling in at least some long-term profits from the Olympic Games. The idea was that any services produced specifically for the Games would go on being used afterwards. That idea has not materialised in full. One aspect not sufficiently taken into account was that future residents and the services available should match; a certain volume of population calls for an adequate level of services, and the other way round.

The lessons from Barcelona and Seville have been taken as point of departure for the EXPO '98 in Lisbon. Neither Portugal nor Lisbon can afford to make the same mistakes. Right from the start the fact was realised that the EXPO '98 would simultaneously have to serve two different purposes. The world exhibition is supposed to be an original, sparkling event with international appeal, but first and foremost the EXPO is to become the driving wheel of a metropolitan regeneration project of a magnitude unprecedented in Portugal. An old industrial area in the Oriental zone in the eastern part of Lisbon, on record as one of the most deprived town quarters, has been chosen as object. In that sense EXPO '98 is to become more than a unique event putting Portugal, and Lisbon in particular, in the limelight. The industrial area will be transformed into a new high quality urban area; EXPO '98 is regarded as an exceptional chance -a catalyst- to revitalise a deprived Lisbon neighbourhood.

To achieve the two goals, the Portuguese government has floated a joint-stock company with public capital - *Parque EXPO '98*. That company has two tasks:

-       to develop the selected 330 industrial acres into a new high quality urban area.
-       to conceive, design, prepare, construct and manage the world exhibition on 60 acres within this intervention zone;

Henceforth we will therefore distinguish EXPO URBE (the regeneration project) and EXPO '98 (the exhibition). The combination of the two goals is hoped to ensure lasting profit to Lisbon. No doubt, the EXPO will considerably enhance Lisbon's image, but image building is a continuous process, needing follow-ups to confirm and retain the positive image. Without an explicit policy in that sense, the effect will soon peter out. The successful revitalisation of a 'bad area' will also have a long-term effect on Lisbon's image and reinforce its competitive position. An effect, moreover, that will be clearly visible to the private sector and the citizens.

Besides the twofold objective, the financing merits due attention. Both Barcelona and Seville were left with a considerable deficit, constituting a drag on the further development of the cities. In Lisbon, the EXPO has to be self-supporting. The visitors are expected to pay towards the running costs. The principal source of funds, however, will be EXPO URBE. Parque EXPO '98 is selling the facilities built for the EXPO for other uses after the event. The serviced land is to be sold to investors and project developers. Only with respect to the facilities needed for the world exhibition will Parque EXPO '98 intervene as project developer should that be necessary to meet the deadline of 1998. The market is expected to assume a major part of the risks of EXPO URBE. The overall financing is provided by a consortium of the principal Portuguese banks.

History and background

There was a plausible reason to choose the year 1998 for the Lisbon EXPO. In 1998 it will be exactly 500 years ago that Vasco da Gama -the famous Portuguese explorer- undertook his first voyage to India. A century of scientific preparation under five different kings had preceded the voyage. Vasco da Gama's ship sailed to the East in May 1498. His voyage marked the beginning of merchant shipping to India and neighbouring countries. Portugal was soon followed by other countries, notably the Netherlands and Great Britain. Portugal celebrates Vasco da Gama's undertaking with various festivities. Formally, the EXPO is no part of Portugal's official programme of celebrations to the honour of Vasco da Gama, but undoubtedly takes its inspiration from the explorations of 500 years ago.

The theme of the EXPO '98 fits jointlessly in with the festivities around the historical exploratory voyage. Oceans are its central theme. The motto reads: 'The Oceans, Heritage for the Future'. Portugal has about eight hundred kilometres of coastline, so that the future of the oceans is a fitting theme for the Lisbon EXPO. Portugal has invited all UN countries to make a contribution to the EXPO by each giving their own vision of the future of the oceans. Moreover Portugal has proposed -also in the setting of the UN- to proclaim 1998 as 'year of the oceans'.

The EXPO-grounds

In 1992, Portugal and the city of Lisbon were assigned the organisation of the EXPO '98. After lengthy and intensive discussions, the decision was taken to locate the EXPO partly in the Oriental zone of Lisbon and partly on territory of neighbouring municipality Loures. The Oriental zone is situated in the eastern part of the city, close to Lisbon Airport; its name is due to the merchantmen from or destined to Africa that used to call at the local port until the early 1950s. Obsolete industries and social housing are currently the dominating aspects of that zone. Given the theme of the EXPO -the future of the oceans- a strip of land five kilometres long along the River Tagus has been selected. The intervention area of Parque EXPO'98 is a territory of some 330 hectares. Within that intervention zone, about 60 hectares concern the design, construction and management of the world exhibition itself.

The chosen zone is peripheral and divided between Lisbon and Loures territory. However, from a metropolitan perspective, it is centrally located and that was one of the reasons to select that area. While the whole environment of the EXPO-zone is not exactly appealing, the strip along the

RIVER TAGUS within the Oriental zone is particularly depressing. Before the activities were started, it was undeniably one of the most impoverished, polluted and degenerated areas of the metropolitan Lisbon. The small port in the middle of the strip was in use in the 1940s, mostly for sea-planes from and to England and the Azores. The harbour became obsolete with the replacement of sea-planes by modern aircraft. Today the main port activities are located in Sebutal, 25 miles from Lisbon where car producers Renault and a consortium of Ford and Volkswagen make use of the port facilities. Near the abandoned port there was an obsolete oil refinery dating from the 1930s, still going at full blast, surrounded by storage tanks. The land beneath the petro-chemical installation is heavily polluted by oil rests and other refinery waste. Because of EXPO the oil refinery industry has moved to the ports of Sines, 100 miles away from Lisbon. Not only the oil industry but also other establishments with strongly polluting and obsolete installations have polluted the soil. The position and prospects of the local activities were marginal. With a few exceptions, they were hardly competitive. An outsider is the storage of the Portuguese army, but even that is no great shakes. The Army used the area mostly as a cemetery for old and dejected weaponry. The northern part of the 330 hectares, near the mouth of the River Trancão, has for decades been the location of Lisbon's municipal dump and a waste-disposal installation. At first sight, little credit is to be gained for Lisbon from this area.

To select precisely this 'worst' part of Lisbon has been selected as the site for the EXPO, was an act of valour. The choice means a terrific challenge and a heavy task.

EXPO '98: the exhibition

Around the ancient port -central to the EXPO URBE zone- about sixty hectares are being serviced for the world exhibition. The theme of the world exhibition is the future of the oceans. The EXPO '98 counts five pavilions which will express the theme in different ways. The first, the Pavilion of the Oceans ('Pavilhão dos Oceanos') is to become the greatest and most modern Oceanarium of Europe. It will be located in the water in the middle of the port. The Oceanarium consists of a central aquarium surrounded by four smaller tanks representing the sub-aquatic life in different parts of the globe. The second pavilion, named Pavilion of Portugal ('Pavilhão de Portugal') illustrates the history of Portuguese shipping. For indeed, the Portuguese have a rich history on that score. The third Pavilion, Utopia, exhibits (future) multi-media applications. With much pomp and circumstance the visitor is invited to explore the multi-media world. The fourth 'Pavilhão do Conhecimento dos Mares' pays attention to the history of the oceans, from their first development until the present. In the fifth 'Pavilhão do Futuro' the attention is directed to the future of the Oceans. Here, much will be asked from the visitors themselves. The fifth pavilion is to be a 'parliament' for the future of the oceans, where the participation of the public is given priority. Finally, the stands of the participating countries will be accommodated in the new Lisbon Exhibition Hall. This new 'Centro de Exposições de Lisboa' in the EXPO area will take over the function of the existing one form the 1950s that is to be transformed in a new congress centre.

EXPO URBE

The revitalisation project is referred to as EXPO URBE. The showpiece and central link in the new zone is to become the new east station ('Estação do Oriente'), built to the design of a famous architect. The station complex will be a high-quality interchange for several means of transport, where trains, underground trains and coaches meet. The train stop links EXPO URBE to the suburban, national and international rail networks. There is a modest stopping place now, but Estação do Oriente is scheduled to become the new central station of Lisbon. The underground railway will connect it to the present Central Business District (to get to the historic inner-city one has to change subway lines), and the new station is also to serve as a node of regional coach traffic. Lisbon has great hopes from the direct connection with the nearby airport. Travellers will be able to check in for the airport at the station, from where a luxurious fast public-transport connection is to take the passengers directly to the Departures hall of Lisbon Airport. Moreover, about six thousand parking slots will be constructed in the vicinity of the station (at three minutes' walking distance)

On both sides of the new station, a business district of high standing is planned. The business district will be constructed on unique raised platforms spanning the two main avenues of the site, and will be enriched by a first-class hotel. The lower levels of the platform will provide ample room for carparks and shops. The business district of EXPO URBE is to become *the* new business centre of Lisbon. Investment in an adequate and high-grade telecommunication infrastructure has absolute priority. Moreover, the business district will have to provide a variety of locations for the various market segments.

The situation of EXPO URBE along the River Tagus is also capitalised in the project. The waterfront will be completely revised and enriched with, among other things, a leisure port accommodating 500 small boats. Along the waterside, restaurants, bars and speciality retail outlets will front a tree-lined promenade. A residential area has been planned which offers a variety of styles, sizes and habitats. EXPO URBE will guarantee a sizeable supply of houses (for about thirty thousand inhabitants), addressed in particular to the medium and higher income brackets. EXPO village, where the guests from the participating countries will be accommodated, will afterwards go on serving residential purposes. Near EXPO village an urban park of about 80 hectares is projected, with tennis courts, a sports centre, and golf links.

The facilities built specifically for the exhibition will also serve new functions after the EXPO. Only the Pavilhão do Futuro will be demolished after the world exhibition. The Oceanarium remains intact, and Parque EXPO '98 is negotiating with Seaworld about its exploitation in the future. The Portuguese Pavilion is to be used by a government agency. A said earlier, the complex accommodating the booths of the participating countries is going to be the new exhibition centre of Lisbon and thus the property of the agency in charge. Not less than 60,000 square metres of exhibition room will be created. The Utopia Pavilion will become the Lisbon Sports and multipurpose arena. The hall will be made suitable for indoor sports, pop concerts and other manifestations. The Pavilhão do Conhecimento dos Mares is supposed to become a new museum concerning the oceans. Finally, the intention is to create all manner of services in or close to the area: shops, schools, hotels, etc.

A critical factor is the relation between EXPO URBE and the surrounding Oriental zone. Will it be possible to connect the two, to ensure that the zone profits from the revitalisation, so that EXPO URBE becomes an integral part of it? The urban-planning department of Lisbon has drawn up a master zoning plan which gives attention to the potential threat of a divided town quarter. Money is being invested in the upgrading of the surrounding dwellings. The expectation is that the developments in the EXPO-grounds will revive the interest for the neighbouring locations.

The organisation

Pressed for time, and for the sake of decisiveness, the Portuguese government has decided to found the Parque EXPO '98 Limited Liability Company, entrusting it with the realisation of the twofold objective. That is possible only if Parque EXPO '98 has special competencies. Parque EXPO '98 combines the qualities of a normal business company and a government agency. Basically it resembles any other company, nine-tenths state-owned and one-tenth owned by Lisbon. The company can wield extensive power within the selected 330 hectares: 'it is a city in its own right'. Thus Parque EXPO '98 is able to forego long-winded decision procedures and keep the project going fast ahead. Parque EXPO '98 is first and foremost a land developer. Only with regard to the exhibition is the company acting as a project developer engaged specifically to get the preparations for the world exhibition completed in time.

Naturally, Parque EXPO '98 cannot entirely avoid government intervention, but a special legal framework has been drawn up to accelerate the procedures. Parque EXPO '98 has developed the masterplan for EXPO URBE, outlining zones for business activity, housing, amenities, and the infrastructure needed. In 1994 the plan was approved by a committee of representatives of the ministries of Environment and Natural Resources, Public Works, Planning, Finance, and Seas, as well as delegates from the municipalities Lisbon and Loures and a few regional bodies. The approval opened the way for more detailed schemes; six similarly composed workgroups have taken them in hand. Meanwhile the first two detailed plans have been approved, two more have nearly passed through the approval trajectory, and the last two still have to be submitted. The municipal council of Lisbon and a representative of Parque EXPO '98 must also give their consent. Once that trajectory is past, the road for Parque EXPO '98 is free. Nevertheless, concrete proposals still have to be submitted to the board of Parque EXPO '98 and to the mayor, who issues the permits. The decision-making process has been somewhat delayed after all by occasional long discussions in the six workgroups.

Parque EXPO '98 is a holding sprouting different elements, among which participations in other related companies. Figure 1 shows how the elements hang together. The holding controls four elements. The firm of Parque itself, the EXPO division arranging everything to do with the exhibition, a section occupying itself with the infrastructure and co-ordinating the works, and the financial section. An extensive urban-planning unit counsels and supports the Board. It works out the designs for the EXPO '98 and EXPO URBE fit for implementation. The EXPO Sociedade Gestora Parcipacipaçois Sociais (SGPS) controls the participations of Parque EXPO '98. Valorsul is a company that organises the dismantling of the municipal dump, still in operation, and of the waste-processing installation, and is also responsible for the construction of a new waste-processing installation elsewhere in the metropolitan area. Parque EXPO '98 takes part in the development of the Oceanarium. The multi-modal station to be built comes under the responsibility of Gare Intermodale Lisboa (GIL), in which besides Parque EXPO '98, the national railways ('Caminhos de ferro Portugal'; CP) has an interest. EXPO URBE finally, accounts for selling and marketing in the framework of the project of the same name. The total holding is controlled by a board chaired by a former European Commissioner, a strong personality who moreover enjoys the confidence of all parties concerned.

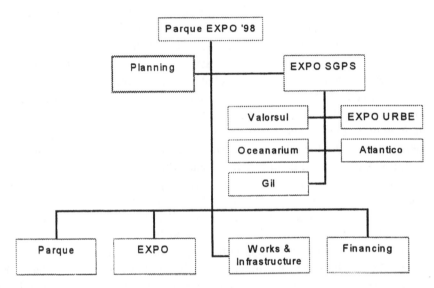

Figure 3   Parque EXPO organisation chart

The financing

EXPO '98 and EXPO URBE are pre-financed by a consortium of banks. Parque EXPO '98 is spending a total of 1.3 billion dollars in the cleaning of the grounds and the demolition of the obsolete installations, and buying out the residents and companies that used to be located there, and investing in new infrastructure and the multi-modal new station. Mark that the business location and housing are not included in that sum; project developers and other market parties will have to generate the resources for that purpose. Parque EXPO '98 was made a present of a starting capital of 3.5 million US dollars from the national government, as well as 50 million dollars' worth of land. Most of the land used to be the property of the national harbour authority, which conceded its rights under pressure of the government. The remainder comes from commercial loans, the government standing security for 300 million US dollars.

Together, EXPO URBE and EXPO '98 will have to generate sufficient revenues to pay back the loans. The sales of sites are supposed to yield some 600 million US dollars (over half the total revenues). The world exhibition itself will also generate income.

Table 5
EXPO financing in percentages

Sales of the sites	53
World exhibition revenues	30
Value of participation in EXPO sub-projects	7
Contributions from the European Union	4
Value of the shares in Parque EXPO '98	6
Total	100

Besides ticket sales, about 30 per cent of the total revenue are counted on from catering, merchandising etc. From an estimated eight million visitors that share can hopefully be received. The expectation is that of those eight million, three fifths will be come from Portugal itself. Half of the remaining two fifths will probably be Spaniards. Elements for which Parque EXPO occasionally puts up venture capital, also represent a certain value (about 7 per cent). The European Union makes a contribution towards the cleansing of the River Trancão, of which a small part will be channelled to Parque EXPO '98 to clean up the river bed near the exhibition. The value of the shares in Parque EXPO is estimated at six or seven per cent of the total sum involved in the EXPO (see table 5)

EXPO '98: accessibility

The traffic situation in and around Lisbon is frankly worrisome. Much through traffic still has to pass through the city, and the bridge over the Tagus is every day packed with hooting motorists. The revitalised urban zone will generate additional transport flows, which without an altered policy will make the access roads into and the main roads of Lisbon burst even more at the seams. Lisbon is one of the most congested cities in Europe. With a view to the EXPO '98 and EXPO URBE, some infrastructural improvements are carried through which are meant to assure access to the area and relieve the traffic conditions in Lisbon. Even before the EXPO actually came into view, there had been discussions whether, and if so, where, to build another bridge across the River Tagus. The present single bridge can no longer cope with the flow of commuters. The EXPO has accelerated these discussions, and the Ministry of Public Works, Transportation and Communications has invited market parties to make a bid for the construction and exploitation of the new bridge across the Tagus. The cost of the 18-km-long bridge has to be recouped by toll collection. In April 1994 a British-French-Portuguese consortium received the concession to build a bridge and exploit it for 33 years. The bridge will close as it were the ring around the city, reducing through traffic through the ancient city centre, and forms an adequate connection between north and south. One third of the construction costs of the bridge will be taken care of by a contribution from the European Cohesion Fund (EFRO).

North of the EXPO-grounds runs the vital Northern motorway. At present, motorists cannot yet enter the eastern part of Lisbon from the motorway direct and without hindrance; they have to take the long way through the city centre. Along the motorway a new interchange point is being constructed at the point where the bridge, the Northern motorway and a new road to the EXPO-area meet. Parque EXPO '98 is working closely together here with the responsible Ministry. Parque EXPO '98 also takes care of the improvement and construction of further supply roads to the area.

Public transport has been enlisted in the fight against congestion. The new station will also serve as a stopping place for the metropolitan railway. To that end the existing line is extended to the Oriental zone, with the station as new terminal. The underground line offers a direct connection with the centre.

EXPO spin-off: cleansing of the River Trancão

The EXPO-grounds cover five kilometres of Lisbon's waterfront along the River Tagus. The Tagus is in direct contact with the Atlantic Ocean. Besides the Tagus, the EXPO-organisation has to do with another river, the Trancão river, which flows into the Tagus at the northernmost point of the EXPO-grounds. The Trancão has a catchment area of 300 square kilometres inland. It is beset with two grave evils: it is one of Europe's most polluted rivers, and its catchment area has been repeatedly upset in the past by serious floods.

In the catchment area there are many outdated and highly polluting industries which discharge their waste material into the river. In the past these industries could settle there freely to profit from whatever the delta offered: cheap land -because of the peripheral situation-, no environmental rules, and running water to get rid of their waste. Nor is it only the industries that have polluted the river. The area is densely populated and the households also use the Trancão as a sewer. Much used -polluted- water from the households is discharged directly into the river. The bad situation of the Trancão is for the most part due to the lack of any form of spatial planning in the municipalities concerned. Portugal has a limited tradition of spatial planning. Only in 1990 was a law introduced obliging municipalities to draw up a plan regulating the land-use.

In the past, the area has repeatedly suffered from quite heavy floods. In 1967 the floods took many lives and in 1983 the area was once more under water. The floods are due to sudden tidal waves -from the sea- which raise the water level of the Trancão very fast. Because the Trancão cannot cope with such a surfeit of water, the delta is flooded, with a ready chance of victims given the dense population in the area. Plans to protect the delta from sudden rises of the water level sorely lacked, just as for the fight against pollution.

The floods have been an object of discussion for twenty years, and pollution has also been on the political agenda for quite some time. With the 1990 amendment of the law, the Ministry of Environment and Natural Resources took the initiative to activate the municipalities and actually to proceed to spatial planning. Moreover, the Ministry has developed a masterplan for the entire estuary, proposing measures to fight pollution as well as flooding. The plan provides for the building of three water-purification plants (one is already in use in the future urban park), the construction or raising of dykes, the planting of greenery, the broadening and deepening of the river, and the digging off of polluted sediment.

The EXPO has worked as a catalyst for the implementation of the masterplan. Without the EXPO the plan would have had to be carried out anyway, but the EXPO has set an absolute deadline: 1998. With respect to the world exhibition, three matters count. For one thing, the progressive pollution of the water has to be stopped and the highly tainted water purified. The theme of the EXPO '98 is the future of the oceans, and badly polluted river flowing along the EXPO-site would be very awkward. Moreover, the fact that purification is taken in hand shows that the organisation takes the future of the waters serious. For another, pollution has clearly advanced very near to the EXPO-grounds. In the estuary of the Trancão the sediments are tainted down to a depth of 50 metres. Soil, water and river bed are black as coal and malodorous from the badly polluted sediment. That, too, will have to be remedied before the EXPO is opened. Third, the river estuary needs widening to cope with a possible flood. Moreover, the intention is to accelerate the raising of the river dykes in the section near the EXPO, and protect the area of the EXPO itself. To that end, the area will be covered with sand-and-water slurry, to secure the urban park by the waterfront close to the river mouth. Although the exhibition itself will cover only about 60 hectares, for the solution of the problems just mentioned it depends on measures in the entire catchment area.

The gigantic environmental and flood problems will take many years to overcome. However, the EXPO is scheduled for 1998, and by that time the measures directly related to the EXPO must be complete. To that end, the Ministry has empowered Parque EXPO to carry through the necessary measures under its own steam, as far as the EXPO-grounds are involved. The situation is unique for Portugal.

Meanwhile, one water-purification plant is in use and the other two are imminent.

EXPO spin-off: solid-waste treatment

In the area where the world exhibition is to be held, a waste-treatment plant and a municipal dump are still established. The household dirt of about one fifth of the inhabitants of the metropolitan region is carried to the dump. The obsolete plant has to make way for the EXPO '98. To find an alternative location will not be easy.

Even before the ideas about the EXPO had solidified, the waste problem was urgent in the Greater Lisbon area. By using the present installations to capacity, 660,000 tons of waste can be processed. However, the waste mountain keeps growing and will presently exceed the present capacity, so that a solution must be found at short delay. Already in 1987 seven municipalities, among them Lisbon, got together to look for a collective solution for the waste problem. They decided to appoint a workgroup of experts, which in an extensive study tried to find a structural solution for the household-waste problem of the seven municipalities. The study was completed in 1990; the workgroup's advice for optimum functioning was to replace the present constellation with a new system of three centres for waste treatment: a dump and treatment plant in the EXPO-area, a dump and treatment plant in Oeiras, and a waste incinerator in Loures. Three of the seven municipalities were not pleased with the result of the study; they wanted an incinerator within their own jurisdiction to remain independent. Therewith, the association of seven municipalities was dissolved. In the end Lisbon, Loures, Villa Franca de Xira and Amadora have continued in the chosen direction. Unfortunately, at the time they lacked the means to finance the entire operation.

The plans for the EXPO put paid to the reckonings of the workgroup. No longer was replacement of the waste-treatment plant and maintaining the dump in the EXPO-area a feasible proposition, because to continue trading waste in that area would spoil the attractiveness of the urban area. EXPO '98 has committed itself to help solve the matter. The dismantling of the present plant, the cleansing of the soil and the realisation of a new incinerator have thus been related to one another. To keep everything under control, a firm was founded in 1994 under the name of Valorsul, in which the four municipalities and Parque EXPO '98 are partners. Valorsul comes under the umbrella of the Parque EXPO firm. The EXPO pays for the dismantling and the cleansing of the soil. The new plant is financed with European support (50 per cent) and contributions from the partners (the other half). Any deficits will be paid up by the partners. The European support is indeed separate from the EXPO. Valorsul is in search of a new location for the facilities now present in the EXPO-area. In 1997 the dismantling operation in the EXPO-area must be complete, and in 1998 the new installation must come into use. Valorsul will control the plant for the first 25 years; afterwards the entire installation will become the property of the Portuguese government.

In the new situation the total capacity will hardly increase. On environmental considerations the conscious choice was not to respond to the predicted growth by extending the capacity. Valorsul is at the moment working out a large-scale recycling and collecting programme which is supposed to prevent the quantities of waste from reaching the predicted volume. Whether the programme is really adequate remains to be seen.

State of the art

Parque EXPO '98 has made good progress with the preliminaries for the world exhibition. The military depot, the oil tanks and the refinery have been removed as well as other industrial buildings and houses. The soil of the refinery is being cleansed. The building of the Oceanarium and the pavilions is in full swing, and the first pile for the EXPO-village has been driven into the ground. The municipal dump and the associated waste-treatment plants are still operational, but as soon as a suitable temporary location has been found, the operations will be moved there, of course in consultation with the new treatment plant to be erected in Loures. The situation around the River Trancão continues to be under study. Experts from Parque EXPO '98 and the Ministry of Environment and Natural Resources still do not see eye to eye about the overall approach. The matter has to be treated discreetly, since the urban park is projected on the very site of the present municipal dump. EXPO URBE has a far longer time horizon, but the new station, the bridge and the new road connection must be ready in time for the flows of visitors to EXPO to be channelled properly. To get the world exhibition ready before 1998 is a gigantic task. Any delay of some duration can spoil the cake. for rate there is hardly a margin to compensate unforeseen delays. Whether all sites can be sold in the future is very much a matter of speculation. Parque EXPO '98 claims to be ahead of schedule. EXPO village has already been sold to a development company in which Parque EXPO'98 is also shareholder. The planning is to have everything sold by 2010.

The EXPO Project and organising capacity

Spatial-economic conditions

Lisbon is troubled by some serious problems. For one thing there is the worsening congestion of the (inter)local road network. Accessibility is under pressure. For another, the city's demographic balance is upset. Many employed people, especially from the middle classes, have left Lisbon for the surrounding municipalities, because the present housing supply does not meet their quality requirements. Investment in residential property has hardly been profitable for some decades now, and a considerable lag on that score has developed. Now that the rent-control law is changed, investment in residential property is gradually increasing. Besides, To make good its pretension to be the Atlantic capital of Europe, Lisbon will have ensure a good supply of high-grade business locations and in the near future. That condition cannot be met without a change of policy. The three problems are an additional stimulus to start EXPO '98 and EXPO URBE.

Political support

On the national level the desire to put Portugal, and thus the capital Lisbon, in the international limelights, has distinct priority. Politically the signs are green for EXPO '98 as well as EXPO URBE. The financial scope of the government and certainly of Lisbon is not particularly great. The project has to be self-supporting. The combination of (inter)national promotion and revitalisation of Lisbon through EXPO URBE, coupled to the sale of facilities and sites, can considerably reinforce the financial basis. A fortuitous circumstance is that now, for the first time in 16 years, the government, the municipal board of Lisbon an the President of the Republic profess the same political colour since the elections of January 1996.

Vision and strategy

The project is clearly the product of a well-considered vision. The combination of international promotion and metropolitan revitalisation in a concept that regards accessibility and environmental quality as conditions for successful economic development, appeals to the imagination. A strategic aspect is that EXPO '98 and EXPO URBE have to be supported first and foremost by the market. Up to now, the impression is that the market parties have been insufficiently involved in the conception and elaboration of the ideas. A chance has thus been missed to win broad support of the plan early and thus enhance the chance of success. However, Parque EXPO has attracted personnel out of the commercial world to work on the project, so already there is expertise on the market conditions.

Leadership

The national government not only creates the conditions for the project, it is also its initiator and orchestrator. Admittedly the exhibition will be held in Lisbon and the revitalisation concerns parts of Lisbon and Loures. Therefore alongside the national government the municipality of Lisbon plays an important role. Although EXPO '98 and EXPO URBE are *national* projects, the city of Lisbon is also a partner in Parque EXPO '98 and certainly has a say in the decision making process and has been closely involved in the elaboration of the concept. The *primacy* lies with the Ministries, however. The ministries concerned created Parque EXPO '98 and equipped it with special powers. From that moment, Parque EXPO '98 has directed the show.

Parque EXPO '98 is governed by a prominent and decisive politician who used to defend Portugal's interests as European Commissioner in Brussels.

Given the extent of the project, the hierarchy in the Portuguese regime, and the inordinate time pressure, government orchestration may well be an absolute necessity. Moreover, as spin-off from the EXPO some problems are being taken in hand some of which were anyhow the responsibility of the national government: the new station, the doubling of the railway tracks, the new motorway interchange point, the new bridge and the cleansing of the Trancão. Since these crucial elements are decided on the national level, government leadership seems inevitable. Any other agency acting as locomotive would constantly have to go knocking at ministerial doors, which would meeting the deadline of May 1998 highly improbable.

Administrative structure

Several government levels and also municipalities are -directly or indirectly- involved in EXPO '98 and EXPO URBE. The EXPO is in part projected within the jurisdiction of Loures, and some other municipalities are committed to projects counting as spin-off from the EXPO. The EXPO is a project directed from above, on the national level. Nonetheless a prominent part has been put aside for Lisbon as partner in Parque EXPO '98. The company Parque EXPO '98 is a unique creation, temporarily endowed with competencies normally reserved to the authorities. A 'city in its own right', so to speak, has been created.

Strategic networks

Five ministries, two municipalities and some regional bodies are parties in the EXPO-process. Despite the central directorship of the national government, mutual adjustment is important called for, and Parque EXPO '98 has been founded as the means to that end. The collaboration has thus been given a formal, well-defined basis for consultation. Parque EXPO '98 sits like a spider in its web, keeping in touch with all parties involved.

An important task has been assigned to EXPO URBE, namely, to persuade market parties to buy and develop EXPO-sites and exploit EXPO-facilities once the event is over. The project has to recoup its own investment. Therefore it is very important to involve 'the market' in the elaboration of the concept. The masterplan for EXPO URBE is based primarily on the vision of the public bodies involved. Perhaps the initiators would have done better to reckon with the attitude of important market parties at an earlier stage.

However, the delay need not be disastrous because for the final specification and implementations, developers are given a free hand. Nor could it be otherwise, for from now onwards the market has to give shape to EXPO URBE. Remember that Parque EXPO '98 is in essence not a project developer, but an agency that sells land to project developers who see good prospects in the development of a specific piece of land.

Performance

The time horizon of the world exhibition stretches to 1998, and that of EXPO URBE to the year 2010. To try and give a considered judgement already now of the performance of the projects would be premature. The time pressure for the world exhibition is enormous. The cleansing of polluted soil demands much time. Nevertheless, Parque EXPO '98 has succeeded in retaining the project's momentum. To say the least, Parque EXPO '98 is showing itself a particularly decisive and efficient organisation, with a structure that is probably unique in Europe. The preliminary activities are in full swing. That in itself is an achievement, because so many things are happening at the same time; hundreds of people are working in the EXPO-grounds and the EXPO has many connections with other policy areas. The question remains, however, whether the deadline of May 1998 can be met: the least delay brings the planning in jeopardy. The organisation claims to be ahead of schedule. The sale of premises and EXPO-facilities is the decisive factor and the yardstick of success. So far things go better than expected, but there is still a long way to go. How the market will react is still obscure: the future will show.

Conclusions

In the 1970s and 1980s too little was invested in renovation, not only of Lisbon but throughout Portugal. One results is the unsatisfactory traffic situation in Lisbon. The infrastructure cannot cope with the considerable flow of commuters blocking up the road network day by day. The massive departure from the city to surrounding municipalities started as early as the 1960s, but the infrastructure still has not been adjusted to it. The same is true of the quality of the housing stock. The rents have consciously been kept so low that neither private nor public houseowners were inclined any more to invest in their property. However, a distinct turnabout seems in sight. In Lisbon the two matters, infrastructure and housing, now have high priority.

In the late 1980s and early 1990s the Portuguese government made efforts to get the EXPO to Lisbon. The world exhibition is hoped to put Lisbon and Portugal in the limelight, but is at the same time a lever for the revitalisation of a deprived quarter of Lisbon. The zone in question is a strip of five km length along the River Tagus (with an abandoned port, an oil refinery dating from the 1930s, and heavily polluted soil). That legacy from the past has by now been all but cleared and the building of the exhibition facilities has already started. Some 60 hectares are serviced for the EXPO; a total area of 330 hectares is taken in hand. A new urban area with a high-grade housing, living and working environment is hoped to wipe out the old misery. The parties are also willing to make the necessary investments in accessibility and environmental quality: tainted soil is dug off, the Trancão, one of Europe's worst polluted rivers, is cleansed, a new bridge links the location with the opposite bank, and the access to the motorway is profoundly renovated.

The national government is undeniably the director -the leader- of the project. The holding Parque EXPO '98 has been created to formalise the leader's function. The city of Lisbon is also partner within Parque EXPO '98 and is closely involved with the project. The chairman of the Board of Governors is appointed by the national government. For the time being, EXPO '98 and EXPO URBE are first and foremost public projects. Parque EXPO '98 brings all the public agencies concerned together. Parque EXPO '98 sits as a spider in a predominantly public-public web. The organisation has proved itself capable of putting the project on the rails in a very short time. The 'firm with extensive planning powers' which Parque EXPO '98 in fact is, shows itself very decisive and efficient. Conducive to the progress so far has been the political support enjoyed by EXPO. The bottlenecks -traffic situation, social imbalance- in Lisbon have also clearly inspired to prompt acting so far. The process remains a race against the clock, however, with hardly any flexibility built in to cope with possible delays.

The ultimate success of the project depends on two factors. Will the EXPO draw enough visitors, and will they spend enough to generate the revenues estimated? And will EXPO URBE succeed in selling all its sites before 2010? So far the signals are that the EXPO as a lever of metropolitan renovation has good prospects. An accurate judgement cannot be given, however, until after the year 2000. The persuasion of the market and the collaboration with market parties will largely decide between failure and success. That has been one good reason to recruit from the private sector some associates of EXPO URBE, the agency charged with the important task of working the market. It is for them to bridge the gap between conception and commercial reality.

At any rate, the EXPO-project generates positive spin-off to other policy fields. The collective approach to the disposal of waste, the cleansing of the Trancão and the construction of water-purification plants has been enormously accelerated by the EXPO. The impact of EXPO as an instrument of revitalisation does not stop at the pales of the EXPO URBE zone.

Strikingly, Lisbon (and Loures to a lesser degree) derive much profit from the EXPO '98 and EXPO URBE but have precious little voice in it. Lisbon is 'only' one discussion partner in a project initiated by the national government. Many supporting elements of the two undertakings come under the responsibility of the national governments, and perhaps for that reason the national leadership was inevitable. Another reason for state leadership may be found in the relations prevailing in the administrative system of Portugal. In Lisbon itself the fact is admitted that the city could never alone carry such an extensive project. The lead part played by the national government does not count, therefore, as a sign of Lisbon's inability, but it does give a hefty impetus to its sustainable development. And that is what counts, also with the city council.

Notes

[1] The information is based on: Van den Berg et al (1995), *Audit of European Policies on Metropolitan Cities' Stage II*, chapter 9, *Euricur,Rotterdam.*

[2] The information is based on: Van den Berg et al (1995), *Audit of European Policies on Metropolitan Cities Stage II*, chapter 9, *Euricur, Rotterdam.*

[3] The figure shows only the officially registered unemployed people. 'Unemployed' comprises all persons who are not in paid jobs or self employed, are available for paid jobs and have taken specific steps to find employment. The Strategic Development Department of the City Council thinks that this underestimates the real unemployment of the city which they reckon is between 9 and 10 per cent.

[4] The contents of this part is based on Berg, L van den, H.A. van Klink, J. van der Meer (1993), *Governing Metropolitan Regions*, chapter 6.

7 Munich

Introduction

Munich region is well known for its high living standards and solid economic performance; it is counted among the most successful regions of Europe. But even a region as affluent as the Munich region has to organise itself to sustain its positive development in the future. The next part sketches the general profile of the region and describes its economic development. Next, some features of public administration in Germany are briefly discussed. After the 'general' information, the case study focuses on two themes: the reorganisation of the Munich transport region, and the possible creation of an economic development agency for the Munich region. The chapter describes the progress in reorganising the transport region up till now, followed by an analysis in the theoretical setting of organising capacity. After that, the chapter considers the co-ordination of regional economic development, followed by an analysis in the light of organising capacity. Finally, the conclusion ties together all the central aspects in the Munich case.

Profile

Urban structure in Germany is not dominated by one central city, as France is by Paris. Cities of international standing are distributed across the German territory. In Southern Germany three urban regions can be regarded as of international or inter-regional importance: Stuttgart, Nürnberg and Munich. The latter, metropolitan Munich, stands out: in economic terms but also because of its high living standard and pleasant living environment. The city of Munich is an excellent illustration of the vitality of Southern Germany in today's Europe. At the heart of this area, metropolitan Munich is favourably situated in the centre of Europe.

Munich is the capital of the Freestate of Bavaria ('Freistaat Bayern'). The area of Bavaria takes up 70,554 square kilometres with a population of nearly 12,000,000, and is the second largest state ('Bundesland') after North-Rhine Westphalia ('Nord Rhein Westfalen'). Its capital Munich covers 310 square kilometres and with almost 1,300,000 inhabitants it is the third largest city of Germany. After World War II Munich's population grew rapidly and already in the nineteen-fifties Munich welcomed its millionth inhabitant. Growth continued into the early 1970s. From then on the population figures more or less stabilised with a slight drawback in the early 1980s. From 1987 onward the city started to grow again, though not at the pace of earlier decades. The new growth is primarily due to immigration.

The city itself is relatively spacious; Munich's city council has forbidden high-rise buildings in the city centre. The river Isar runs through the city from south-eastern to north-eastern part. This river determines largely Munich's aspect. Although a densily populated modern city, Munich has always preserved its 'green' character. Moreover, it is surrounded by a lovely green countryside: an undulating landscape with numerous lakes, forested hills and even glacial moraines, ideal for popular leisure pursuits.

Unlike the city, its surroundings have grown tremendously in population in the last two decades. Since the 1960s the share of the 'Umland' in total regional population has increased from around 37 per cent to 44 per cent in the early 1980s, and to almost 48 per cent in 1993. The city of Munich has developed into the centre of an urban region with a population of nearly 2,400,000. Apart from the city of Munich ('Landeshauptstadt München'), the metropolitan area of Munich, the so-called Munich region[1] (Region 14), consists of eight counties ('Landkreisen') surrounding the city, varying in size from 97,000 to 278,000. These counties comprise numerous relatively small but powerful municipalities ('Kommunen'). Remarkably, the second largest municipality in Region 14 after the city of Munich counts only 38,000 inhabitants.

Though the city resumed its population growth in 1987, the combined population of the counties has grown much faster, as said earlier. Between 1987 and 1993 the city's population increased by 4.5 per cent, the counties' population by 10.8 per cent. As a consequence of the rapid population growth in the counties, commuter traffic has risen by 140 per cent since 1970 and commuters travelling more than 35 kilometres by 164 per cent (to compare: city traffic has increased only by 34 per cent). This is no surprise because the spread of jobs over the region has not fully followed on that of the population. Two out of every three jobs are still found in the city of Munich, but only half the region's population resides there. However since the mid 1980s the number of jobs outside the city has been growing rapidly. Besides commuter traffic to Munich, other intra-regional traffic flows have grown as well.

Economic development

From the early 1980s on Munich's economy has been growing constantly. Between 1980 and 1990 Gross National Product (GNP) for Munich almost doubled from 56,100,000,000 DM to 92,350,000,000 DM (see table 1). This clearly illustrates Munich's economic dynamism and economic importance; with only 11 per cent of the Bavarian population its share in Bavarian GNP amounts to more than one fifth; the Munich region accounts for 35 per cent of GNP with only one fifth of the population. In the 1980s *Munich's* share in Bavarian GNP diminished slightly: from 22.3 to 21.1 per cent; however, the share of the *Munich region* stayed on the same level. So, the economic importance of Munich's hinterland is increasing. The Munich region is still one of the prosperous regions in Germany. Nonetheless there are signals that also in the Munich region the growth figures will go down as a consequence of the general economic development.

The unemployment rate in Munich has increased from 5.9 per cent in 1993 to 7.2 per cent in 1996. Still, in the German perspective, Munich's unemployment rate is relatively low. Most of the major German cities score higher unemployment rates. Nevertheless, the increase shows that also Munich needs to monitor unemployment development carefully.

Munich's modern and balanced economic structure is commonly referred to as the 'Münchner Mischung' (Munich mix). A wide range of economic activities are to be found in the area, but the economic image of Munich derives from high-technology activities and the service sector. The patterns in city and surrounding area do not differ substantially; only the service sector clearly favours the city as location (see table 2). The economy of Munich can be called 'balanced' on three counts: the range of economic activities, firm size, and presence of innovative and 'entrepreneurial' firms. The numerous small-scale innovative private research institutions and companies secure the Mischung in the coming years.

171

Table 1
GNP for Munich

	1980	1986	1990
GNP at market prices	56,100,000,000	76,180,000,000	92,350,000,000
Proportion of Bavarian GNP	22.3	22.	21.
GNP per capita	43,190	59,240	72,640
Share of sectors in GNP:			
Agriculture	0.1	0.1	0.1
Manufacturing	34.9	34.3	31.0
Commerce, transport, communications	14.7	13.6	13.5
Services	50.3	52.0	55.4
Total	100.0	100.0	100.0

Source: *Munich - the city and its economy*, Referat für Arbeit und Wirtschaft, 1994

To say that the service sector is an important aspect of Munich is somewhat of an understatement. Actually in the last two decades Munich has developed into a service city in the broadest sense. Practically all service activities have grown considerably as table 3 clearly indicates. On average employment in the service sector increased by one fifth between 1979 and 1993. Together with employment growth in technology (21 per cent) the service sector made up for job losses in manufacturing (- 26 per cent).

To understand more the favourable position of Munich today, we have to go back in history to just after the ending of the Second World War, when Germany was divided. German territory held by American, British and French forces became West-Germany and territory held by the Russians became East-Germany. The prospect of a communist society in Eastern-Germany induced a mass departure of companies and capital to the West. Some of these companies, including Siemens, settled in the Munich region. A lot of refugees from East-Germany also came to the area, among them many entrepreneurs. Several reasons for choosing Munich have been put forward. Certainly there was an element of chance involved.

Table 2
**Employment by sector in the Munich region, city and surrounding area
for 1995**

Sectors	Planungsregion 14	Munich	Surrounding area
Agriculture	6,187	2,120	4,067
Energy & water supply	10,096	7,454	2,642
Manufacturing	240,183	139,843	100,340
Building, construction	56,115	30,058	26,057
Retail and wholesale trade	149,277	91,708	57,569
Transport and communications	58,568	36,566	22,002
Banking and Insurance	73,702	63,379	10,323
Other services	314,374	221,095	93,279
Non profit organisations, private households	33,387	28,311	5,076
Regional public authorities & social security	55,620	33,670	21,950
Secondary sector	25,1%	22,5%	30,0%
Tertiary sector	68,7%	72,6%	61,2%
Total	997,509	654,204	343,305

Source: Referat für Arbeit und Wirtschaft, Landeshauptstadt München

Numerous places were eligible for the fleeing companies and people to go to. A strong appeal was the relatively underdeveloped local, mainly rural, economy. There was no existing industrial structure, so Siemens could start form scratch. The settlement of Siemens in the region induced other (associated) companies to follow suit.

Munich has clearly made capital out of that positive post-war development. Munich thanks its economic verve of today to the combination of the right 'hardware' and 'software' location factors. For one thing, Munich boasts a wealth of knowledge centres: a public university and quite a lot of high-quality private research institutions, as well as a well-educated workforce and specialised high-tech staff. Even now, the Munich region attracts higher educated people from other regions and also first-class educational facilities in the region and famous research institutions such as the Max Planck institute (which like Siemens had come over from Berlin shortly after the Second World War) strengthen the knowledge base from within.

Table 3
Employment growth and growth rates
in selected service sectors 1979-1993

Sectors	Absolute growth (x1000)	Growth rate (%)
Legal and Economic Consultancy	-0.4	-0.4
Health care and	2.5	6.4
Science and art	13.3	26.5
Hygiene and personal care	8.6	37.0
Retail and wholesale	2.0	17.1
Banking and insurance	11.0	26.0
Transport and communication	13.0	47.0
Other services	33.1	101.0
Total	83.1	

Source: *Analysen zur Stadentwicklung*, Landeshauptstadt München
Referat für Stadplanung und Bauordnung

The region's modern and balanced economic structure is another factor in its favour, as is the extensive transport infrastructure covering the territory. The living climate is pleasant. The green countryside surrounding the city, not yet spoilt by encroaching economic activities, offers ample scope for leisure pursuits.

Administrative structure

The decentralised public administration in Germany dates back to the period before the founding of one German state in the second half of the nineteenth century. Back in those days, the Germany territory was divided among separate kingdoms.The unification of these little kingdoms into one nation state could be achieved only if local autonomy could be preserved in some way. So, Germany became a federation of states, with the Federal Government leaving much to the states to decide.

Especially in the Freestate of Bavaria that mentality prevailed. Within Bavaria decentralisation is extended to the municipal level: Bavarian law gives much weight to autonomous municipal planning. Administratively, a strong state government on the one hand and fairly autonomous municipalities on the other do not leave much room for intermediate levels of government. Less so if the counties are taken into consideration. The municipalities are grouped together in a county, mainly to provide services that cannot be supplied by the relatively small municipalities themselves. In Munich region however, the counties serve a political goal as well. Traditionally the political colour of the state and the numerous small municipalities in the surrounding area of Munich is that of the Christian democrats, whereas the city is mostly governed by the social democrats. Combined municipal forces in counties creates a stronger position relative to the city.

As briefly touched upon before, the city is large compared to the surrounding municipalities. The population of Munich makes up more than half that of the Munich region. With the next smaller municipality accounting for only 38,000 inhabitants and the remaining ones for even less, the condition is created for the municipalities to fear dominance by the big city. That imbalance in size complicates regional matters considerably and impedes co-operation. That situation is aggravated by political fear of losing out on the next elections. In Germany, mayors are elected directly every four years and governors (of the counties) every six years. Given the imbalance in size and municipal autonomy, the threat of losing office makes co-operation towards regional settlement of *positive* and *negative* aspects extremely difficult. For instance, for the sake of efficient waste disposal on the regional scale, some districts and municipalities do not accept the location of facilities on their territory. Not surprisingly, local inhabitants would not be too happy with such developments and might present the mayor or governor with the bill in the next election.

The territorial structure of the administrative units is another subject. As said earlier, in the Munich region all municipalities except Munich are grouped in counties[2]. Munich, a so-called 'Kreisfreie Stadt', is encircled by the counties. Space in the city of Munich has become a scarce good; for future development the city needs the co-operation of the counties. In practice this concerns Landkreis München, whose territory encompasses the city almost completely. The peculiar shape of this Landkreis as a necklace around the city puts it in a position to block city development. Therefore, good relations with Landkreis München are essential.

Reorganising Munich's transport region

The first theme to address is the reorganisation of public transport in the Munich region. Until recently, the *Münchner Verkehrs- und Tarifsverbund* (MVV) co-ordinated regional public transport to good effect. Institutional changes made adjustment of the MVV necessary. This part of the chapter analyses the process of change. A brief introduction to Munich's transport *system* is followed by an overview of background and present functioning of the MVV. Next, the challenge to MVV's functioning by institutional change and by the limits to the transport system is described. This is followed by a sketch of the present situation.

The Munich transport system

Most of today's public transport infrastructure dates from the early 1970s. In 1972 Munich hosted the Olympic games, which was a good opportunity to improve the public transport facilities in the Greater Munich area. In the city of Munich passengers can make use of subway ('U-bahn'), tram ('Straßenbahn') and bus ('Stadtbus'); for travelling into and out of the city, fast railway connections ('S-Bahn') with the counties are at their disposal, as well as regional bus services ('Regionalbus') for transport to the S-Bahn tracks.

Public transport infrastructure in the region has been constructed with the city of Munich as the centre. S-Bahn and U-bahn come together in the centre of the city. S-Bahn railway connects each county to Munich and the region's railway network can be characterised as extensive: its lines disperse up to 50 kilometres from the centre into the region.

MVV

Up to 1972 the Greater Munich area was served by three different and independent public transport carriers: Munich municipal public transport authority (bus, tram), the German Federal Railroad (railway) and the German Federal Post (regional buses). Each of these carriers had its own service network, its own tariffs and its own timetable. Given the need for better and attractive public transport this arrangement was no longer satisfactory. In 1972 MVV was founded by the city of Munich and the national railway company - now *Deutsche Bahn AG*, at the time *Deutsche Bundesbahn*. The two partners ('Gesellschafter') set up a private limited company ('Gesellschaft mit beschränkter Haftung') whose field of activity initially consisted of the Munich city territory and the S-Bahn tracks. The state of Bavaria and the Federal Government took seat on the board of governors. Each partner was responsible for its own 'product': the city for its public-transport facilities - subway, tram and buses - and the former national railway company for the S-Bahn in city und surrounding area. Their responsibility comprises managing and operating their transport services as well as bearing the costs involved and covering any deficits. Clearly the merit of MVV lies in its co-ordinative activities. MVV co-ordinates the different modes of public transport, plans overall regional transport activities and combines all services into one joint timetable. Another primary objective of MVV and in fact the reason for its establishment, is the introduction of one tariff for different services. Up to 1971 each supplier had set his own fare and consequently travellers had to buy different tickets for their services. From its establishment, MVV has negotiated, calculated and imposed one fee for public transport. And because of that MVV also takes responsibility for the distribution and division of the returns.

Until 1978 only the city of Munich and the national railway company had co-operated in MVV; regional buses had been provided by various mostly private companies with their own pricing system and hardly any co-ordination. Recognising that this was an undesirable situation for its citizens, the Munich county ('Landkreis München') decided to work with MVV, albeit not as a partner. Another seven surrounding counties followed suit, none of them becoming partners. For the S-Bahn another county is involved as well (Wolfratshausen).The participation of the nine counties (one more than in Planungsregion 14) is laid down in separate covenants ('Verkehrsdurchführungsverträge') between each county and MVV. Those arrangements state that the county in co-operation with MVV become responsible for regional bus services within county borders. The county states what level of supply of regional bus services it wants and MVV negotiates a contract with a public or private bus company on behalf of the county. Regional bus lines are integrated in the overall schedule and bus companies have to settle for the unified transportation fee. The costs of these services, principally the payments to the bus company, are carried by the county alone. This arrangement is unique in Germany; the 'Verkehrsverbund' in München region is the only one where the counties have not joined as partners.

Up to now MVV has functioned satisfactorily from the points of view of the partners as well as the counties. All partners and counties are individually responsible for any deficit related to their product. In 1993 the city of

Munich as well as the railway company had to cover a deficit of around 300,000,000 Deutsch Mark (DM). The counties jointly had to put up 29,000,000 DM to balance their budgets. Understandably, the distinct difference in deficits between counties and city has been criticised by the latter. A high proportion of the county population uses Munich's transport services. Of course Munich gets its share of the ticket sales but for the Greater Munich area, ticket sales cover only half the costs.

Institutional changes

Recently it has become clear that MVV can not continue in its present form because of two major changes. For one thing, efforts are made in Germany, in compliance with European guidelines, to open the way for competition in public transport. For another, the Federal Government has decided to privatise the national railway company, and on top of that to decentralise responsibility for intra-regional transport to the German states ('Länder'). Obviously, these changes present a major challenge to Greater Munich public transport.

Competition implies a clear division between 'demand' and 'supply'. The present organisation of MVV does not meet at this criterion; MVV 'demands' railway transport, but the supplier, Deutsche Bahn AG, is also a partner in MVV. In a competitive environment this will not do and in the new MVV there can be no place for Deutsche Bahn AG. Privatisation of the national railway company upsets the present financial arrangements. In MVV, both partners were responsible for their own deficits. In practice this meant that the deficit of the railway company ended up on the plate of the Federal Government. Privatisation of the railway company puts an end to that situation. The Federal Government will no longer balance the budget of intra-regional public transport. In case of the Munich region, from 1996 onwards the Freestate of Bavaria will carry that responsibility. The Federal Government distributes financial means among the states and it is up to the state to allocate these funds.

The limits of Munich's transport system

MVV is currently under outside pressure; the transport *system* itself experiences pressure from within the region. The limits of the region's public transport system will soon be reached. Up till now the system has functioned satisfactorily but with the ongoing economic and demographic development in the surrounding area of the city, the system will become inadequate. At the time of construction it was self-evident that all transport services were directed to the centre, Munich. However the structure of the Greater Munich Area has changed considerably. The central orientation is increasingly becoming an obstacle given the prosperous economic development and population growth in the region outside the city of Munich itself. All S-bahn tracks come together in the city of Munich without any cross-region links between the tracks. In the present situation and certainly in the near future - given the outlook of further economic and population growth in the area - a network connecting existing S-bahn tracks corresponds better with the present regional situation. In addition cross-regional links will also take the pressure from the heart of the present system, the so-called 'Stammstrecke': a railway track in the city centre used by all S-Bahn lines. This track is becoming more and more a bottleneck in the present community. The Stammstrecke allows only a limiting number of trains on the track at the same time. Therefore, the current frequency of departure of S-Bahn trains, one every 20 minutes, can hardly be increased. The problem has developed for some time now; since 1983 no substantial investments have been made, because the railway company was not allowed to spending that would enlarge the deficit even further.

Not only has intra-regional commuting put pressure on the system, but the scale of the transport region is also changing. Munich's transport region has been developed according to the functional 'economic' region ('Wirtschaftsraum') of the early 1970s. By now the economic region has become considerably larger; commuter traffic flows go over far longer distances these days.

The present situation

At the moment a basic agreement seems to have been concluded regarding the new MVV. After a year of debate, Deutsche Bahn AG is going to leave - unenthusiastically - MVV to open the way for a clear distinction between demand and supply in public transport. From 1996 onwards, Deutsche Bahn AG will have to negotiate its price with the Freestate of Bavaria. With AG leaving, direct financial backing by Federal Government will also end.

Given the changes described above, the renewal of MVV is a good moment to involve the counties. Their direct participation relieves the task of MVV and enlarges regional support of MVV. However, at first some counties were hesitant to do so because they feared to be dominated by the city of Munich. The counties do not yet fully recognise, or are unable to (for political or financial reasons), the necessity of high-standard public transport in the Greater Munich Area. On average there is no co-ordination of public transport between 'Stadt' und 'Umland' other than through MVV. There is no 'regional awareness' in the counties, mainly because most counties do not yet experience the same pressures on their relatively simple public transport infrastructure. The implication is that the initiative to break up the status quo had to come from the Freestate of Bavaria. In the new constellation, Bavaria controls the railway tracks as a consequence of the planned decentralisation. Thus, the future of MVV lay in the hands of the state of Bavaria. Finally Bavaria decided to enter MVV which made renewal of MVV possible. The participation of Bavaria constituted a strong, persuasive argument for the counties to join in as well. In principle all parties involved, decided to stay in or enter MVV and the precise role of each participant has been laid down. Participants of the 'Betreiberverbund' are: the city of Munich (tram, U- Bahn and busses), counties (busses), Freestate of Bavaria (all railway tracks: S-Bahn and Nahverkehrszüge). Especially the role of the state deserves attention. Not only does it control the railway tracks but it is also responsible for the distribution of financial means for public transport across the region. Ideally the state should distribute funds in proportion to traffic flows. However, more rural parts of Bavaria have to be served as well. Public transport in those areas involves high costs and relatively low benefits and therefore the state has not yet committed itself to a percentage of overall means for the Munich region. Clearly the state is in a position to increase regional awareness by means of its distributive task. The creation of one budget for all regional transport in MVV could lead to better co-operation and do justice to the interwovenness of Stadt and Umland.

It appears that the Munich region has successfully responded to the challenge of preserving an effective organisation of regional public transport in MVV. Whether it has also safeguarded high standards remains to be seen. The system is in need of constructive adjustment and other counties should join in to once again adjust the transport region to the functional economic region. Whether this will happen is still unclear. The renewal of MVV is an excellent moment to consider this properly. Much will depend on the Freestate of Bavaria and the financial means available for improvement of the system.

MVV reorganisation and organising capacity: analysis

Munich's public transport region is facing two challenges simultaneously at the moment. Firstly the region's institution for co-ordination of intra-regional public transport, the *Münchner Verkehrs- und Tarifverbund* (MVV) can no longer continue in its present form. Secondly, Munich region's public rail system is in need of infrastructural improvement. Here we will analyse both challenges by the theory of organising capacity.

Challenges and the need for organising capacity

The need to reorganise the MVV is due to the decisions of the Federal Government. One decision was that the Federal Government was to hand over its responsibility for intra-regional public rail transport to the Länder, and other were that, to comply with European guidelines, conditions for competition in public transport were to be created. Furthermore, one of the partners in MVV, the national railway company, had been privatised. All this made reorganisation of MVV necessary. Previously, it became clear that reorganisation of MVV involves various public actors: the Freestate of Bavaria, the city of Munich, the nine counties (directly), national government (indirectly), and also the recently privatised national railway company. MVV's organisation changes fundamentally and in that process the interests of all administratively independent public actors have to be brought in line.

The second challenge concerns Munich's public transport *system*. Munich's current public transport infrastructure dates back to the Olympic games of 1972. That event meant an enormous boost to public transport in the area. Since then the spatial pattern of working, living and commuter traffic has become more complex however, with rapid population and economic growth in the city's hinterland. The system was designed with Munich as the indisputable centre in the S-Bahn network. Today the centre-orientation has become a bottleneck to efficient and effective intra-regional public transport. The system is under pressure not only from changing spatial patterns within Munich's transport region -shaped according to the so-called 'Wirtschaftsraum' of 1972 and never updated since - but also from Munich's economic hinterland being much larger now than at the start of MVV in 1972. The need to extend MVV's working area to other counties has to be taken seriously.

Both challenges need to be met in order to safeguard the high quality and accessibility of the Munich public transport system in a sustainable way. Effective and high-quality public transport will keep the utilisation rate of public transport high and incite still more car travellers to switch to the more environmental-friendly public transport, pushing back congestion and reducing environmental pollution. Needless to say that these are vital issues in the modern economy of Munich. Given the spatial scale, the actors and complex challenges, organising capacity becomes increasingly important. Reasons enough to discuss the organising capacity of Munich's transport region.

Vision and strategy

The reorganisation of the MVV is not part of a wider strategic metropolitan framework guiding the change process and setting goals. Instructions to reorganise had come from higher layers of government and all parties in Munich region had to act upon them. However from the beginning there has been 'common consent' among the relevant regional actors that MVV as an instrument for effective co-ordination of all regional public transport should be preserved. Despite differences in attitude to and possible solutions for MVV reorganisation, this consensus proved to be strong enough to bind all actors together. So all actors knew what they wanted; in that sense they shared the same vision and goals.

The consensus does not stretch to the second challenge. Previously the national railway company, and thus indirectly the Federal Government, had been responsible for infrastructural investments in the S-Bahn network. From 1983 on, the Federal Government had prohibited investments that would add to the deficits of the national railway company, reducing infrastructural investment to the minimum. With a privatised railway company and the state taking the place of Federal Government, a totally new situation has been created. The state of Bavaria gets a fixed amount from the Federal Government and has been made responsible for its allocation. All actors need time to adjust to the changed circumstances and still have to grow into their new role. Once the new MVV has taken shape and the roles of the state of Bavaria, the city and the counties have become clear, the second challenge can be taken up. In the present constellation there is no shared vision - 'common consent' - of future development of the public transport system. That does not imply that there are no solutions or valuable ideas. For instance MVV staff had recognised the problem long before and developed some solutions but is neither equipped nor empowered to act upon them. It is clear that the impact of the reorganisation of MVV will not be limited to

MVV but extend to the second challenge, perhaps with new opportunities for breaking up the status quo.

Administrative structure

Apart from the privatised railway company, reorganisation of MVV is mainly concerned with different layers of public administration. The federal government pulled the trigger, and state, districts and city were forced to reconsider the functioning of MVV. MVV had performed satisfactorily up to that moment but the reorganisation of MVV revealed the unspoken tension between the city and the counties, making collaboration difficult. The debate centred around the deficits of public transport. In 1993 the city had to put up 300 million DM, the counties jointly 29 million. Munich's strong argument is that the counties' population make extensive use of public transport services on city territory, with the city and (previously) the railway company taking the financial burden. True, MVV distributes ticket sales according to passenger flows, but these sales cover only half of the cost involved. However the financial position of the counties is much weaker than that of the city, which narrows the margin for stronger financial participation. Both city and counties had to be careful lest this dispute become an obstacle in the process of redesigning MVV.

Another main problem within the administrative structure is to redefine the role of the state of Bavaria. By shifting the responsibility for intra-regional transport to the state level, the Federal Government has put Bavaria in the key position. Because of this new role it had become inevitable for Bavaria to participate in the new MVV. Hesitant and rather passive at first, Bavaria recently decided to enter the renewed MVV. Despite the state's initial hesitance this can be regarded as an important decision. Because of the state's decision to join, the counties have decided to become full partners in MVV. For fear of losing out if not represented adequately and on the consideration that the main obstacle in their view - the threat of being dominated by the city in MVV - had disappeared. This speeded negotiations up and made a general agreement on a new MVV possible, with still much remaining to be settled, however.

Of course, participation of the state in MVV does not solve the more general lack of co-ordination and co-operativenesss between different administrative layers and actors. The region still lacks a mechanism to put matters in a wider regional perspective.

Leadership

An important question is: who will take up the challenges, who will be the leader? So far, none of the actors has clearly taken the lead; none of them has tried to bring together the relevant actors and keep track of progress. The city of Munich is willing to but unable, being too 'big' in the eyes of counties; while the counties have little inclination to do so. In the new situation, where the state has become 'owner' of the most important asset: the S-Bahn tracks, the region tends to look at the state for direction. The new circumstances demanded an initiative from the state of Bavaria; no one else could be the leader. Some problems are not yet solved: Will the state perhaps put the matter of accessibility in a wider regional perspective? That is uncertain. The undeniable fact is that for this matter active inspiring leadership is lacking. The solution is the result of the severe pressure of the problem.

Spatial-economic conditions

It became clear that future accessibility will be eroded unless the transport system is modernised. However that fact has not been recognised by all relevant regional actors, let alone given priority, because the generally favourable spatial-economic conditions have sofar obscured any negative effects in terms of economic development and environmental quality. Accessibility aside, Munich's strong position in the region is for the moment safeguarded by qualities that are decisive in the (international) market arena nowadays: a strong, diversified modern economic structure - known as the Münchner Mischung - and a pleasant, high-quality living environment. The signals of deteriorating accessibility are not strong enough to be heard by all actors involved; today's economic success is blurring possible negative effects in the future. In addition, the direct pressure of congestion is mostly concentrated in the city of Munich and in Landkreis München. The other counties are not yet seriously congested overall, the region is not yet suffering enough on that count to make a short-term regional solution imperative. In the long run, however, without infrastructural improvement to safeguard accessibilty, the spatial-economic conditions are bound to deteriorate

Political support

The need to reorganise the MVV is due directly to the Federal Government's changing the institutional setting for regional transport. On the national level the conditions were not merely favourable to reorganisation, actually they have made reorganisation necessary. Besides, the withdrawal of the Federal Government has made the state and region the relevant policy context. This has considerable financial consequences. The Federal Government no longer balances the budget for regional public transport. This is expected to tighten the financial margins for adjusting the transport system and in particular the S-Bahn network. In addition the state of Bavaria has been made responsible for allocation of funds across the state territory, which means another constraint on additional financial efforts in the Munich region. Although a large part of commuter traffic goes over MVV territory, it remains to be seen whether a proportional part of the budget will go to MVV as well. Bavaria is also responsible for public transport in the more rural areas of the state, where costs are high and revenues scarce. This is an important political aspect, possibly restricting regional possibilities.

On the local level the political conditions are unfavourable because of the somewhat awkward relationship between the city on the one hand and counties and municipalities on the other hand. Party-political differences make the problems worse.

Strategic networks

Apparently, strategic networks and certainly interaction between the public and private sector do not seem to have a fundamental role. Redesigning of MVV has been performed mainly within the administrative structure through the formal channels. Mainly, not entirely: other, more informal, channels have also been involved. That networks have not played a decisive or even full complementary role in the process, is nonetheless true.

Performance

It is rather early to judge the performance of Munich region with respect to challenges in public transport. The actors have jointly succeeded in preserving MVV. In that they have been successful, but there is still enough to do. Detailed elaboration of the agreement is still in progress, and much depends on the financial means to be made available by the state to MVV.

MVV lacks the financial resources to do a proper job, nor can it count on widespread, especially financial, support in the region. Securing accessibility implies more than reorganising MVV alone.

Co-ordination of regional economic development

The need for better co-ordination

The second theme is the need for better co-ordinated economic policy on the regional scale. Satisfactory as its economic performance of today may be, to keep it so in the future the Munich region must be careful to preserve and create the conditions. Given the economic interweaving of city and surrounding area, the two should be considered in conjunction. The very success of the region has made space scarce and costly. The growing population needs housing, and to keep pace with present and future economic development, business premises have to be built. To deal with this matter properly, a strategic concept on the scale of the region is called for. Some have suggested to establish a regional economic development agency which, starting from a strategic framework, could be developed jointly by actors in the region.

The problem elaborated

To keep the balance in the region's economic structure requires the collective development of business premises. As a result of the economic success and the high living standards all over the region, many manufacturing and transport activities have been driven out of it. But even the present information society still needs such activities: though basic with low value added, they are useful and necessary to the functioning of the regional economy. The economic success has pushed up land prices tremendously both in the city and in the surrounding area. For most of the basic activities the city of Munich has become far too expensive, by now already 69 per cent of the city's employment is in the service sector. Even when companies can afford the price of some premises in the region, municipalities in the 'green' attractive 'Umland' tend to keep out these less popular activities, for fear that they will degrade the quality of the local living environment.

The role of present regional planning institutions

The Munich region is already equipped with a regional planning institution. Bavarian law stipulates that for spatial-planning purposes the state is divided into regions. Munich is the centre of region 14, in which the municipalities and the counties have to co-operate in matters of spatial planning. For this planning task, a regional planning authority ('Regionaler Planungsverband'

186

(RPV)) has been created. The organisation is built around two institutions within the jurisdiction. In the first the city of Munich, eight counties and all other municipalities (185) each send one representative to the planning assembly ('Verbandversammlung').The second is the planning committee ('Planungsausschuß'). The representation is based on the number of inhabitants, but that of Munich is restricted to 40 per cent - otherwise the city would hold a majority position. According to Bavarian Law RPV:

- is responsible for regional planning in its territory;
- decides on the regional plan and possible amendments and incorporates and attunes the interest of all members within the framework of regional planning;
- formulates and works out objectives for spatial development and planning;
- gives its opinion on zoning schemes and development plans and examines, if they are in line with the objectives of the regional-plan (all development plans run through the office of RPV);
- is responsible for attuning of separately developed spatial plans;
- organises and executes spatial planning;
- develops solutions to regional development problems (for example: the improvement of regional tracks)

In addition it judges infrastructure planning (Raumordnungsverfahren) on behalf of the Bavarian state.

Actually there is yet another institution in the Munich region. In 1972 before the RPV was founded, a co-operative body ('Äußerer Wirtschaftsraum München' (PVAWM)) had been created voluntarily with the city, the nine counties (one more than RPV) and 145 of the counties' municipalities covering nine tenths of the region's population. Its objective was to better co-ordinate the new settlement in the region. Two independent planning bodies is obviously too much and they cannot possibly function side by side without co-ordination, so the two institutions co-operate intensively. In practice the staff of the Äußerer Wirtschaftsraum München and of the Regionaler Planungsverband jointly develop the spatial planning concept for the region.

Regional planning as realised by RPV has to jump numerous hurdles before policy is implemented. RPV is only an instrument for the highest common denominator, that is, all municipalities have to be heaped together in order to get things from the ground. Therefore, the main contribution of RPV is to secure the green countryside from being absorbed. The sluggish decision procedures influence the possibilities of the jointly accepted spatial plan. This regional plan is fairly general in its prescriptions with considerable room left to the individual municipalities to do as they please. Though the plan has its merits it can hardly be regarded as a widely supported strategic spatial concept that brings the settlement and establishment aspirations of all municipalities in line. The same applies to matters of transport, housing and business premises and waste-disposal. Not because the RPV staff is incapable but because it is not possible to reinforce the members to accomodate less popular tasks like a waste disposal centre. As depicted earlier municipal autonomy is deeply rooted in Bavarian law and culture and the mayor of the municipalities as well as the governor of the counties are elected directly; co-operation could confront them with unacceptable electoral losses. In theory, RPV could decide by majority of votes, but in practice the search for a widely acceptable compromise has priority.

Present situation and prospects

RPV and PVÄWM, in their present form, have proved not to be the proper vehicle to co-ordinate economic policy on a regional scale. The problem is clear but how to solve it? For some years now the idea of a new organisation to co-ordinate location has been considered. Because an additional body is politically out of the question, therefore the creation of a holding specially equipped for this task has been suggested. But such a construction is not widely supported either. Even if there would be support for the idea, the fact that land prices are extremely high and most land is in private hands, is no help. Developers of premises have to guard carefully against speculation. Any advance communication about possible land use, any interest openly expressed, instantly drive the prices up. Therefore the region will have to start from scratch buying land in order to create a stepping stone for future development. Lacking the financial means to do so, the municipalities need to seek the support of financial institutions. The present constellation in the region does not give much scope for renewal. To stimulate new initiatives, in imitation of the succesfull example in the Ruhr area, a platform ('Initiativ Kreis') was mounted to bring all vital public and private decision makers together. However after a hopeful start the momentum has petered out, and various participants have delegated the Initiativ Kreis to deputies.

The idea to start up a regional economic development agency has not yet gained enough ground to become a viable option. Several initiatives to gain support for the idea have been launched, but sofar without concrete results. The matter has been discussed in the 'Initiativ Kreis' but the priority of participants has shifted. The greatest obstacle is the municipalities unwillingness of the municipalities to give up some of their autonomy. The Chamber of Commerce ('Industrie und Handelskammer' (IHK)) has asked municipalities to propose sites on which to locate the threatened basic economic activities. However, the sites suggested by the municipalities did not meet the IHK's criteria or the planning critera of RPV. Recently, the State of Bavaria discusses the effect of the use of financial incentives to stimulate co-operativeness.

Planungsregion 14 no longer corresponds to the functional economic region of today. A positive step to overcome that drawback is the recently concluded partnership between Ingolstadt, Munich and Augsburg (MAI). It puts things in a wider, more appropriate perspective. Unlike in Planungsregion 14, there is more understanding that the partners are in the 'same boat'. Gradually, their faith in co-operation as a means to make better use of their potentialities is increasing. The objective of the partnership is to produce a 'Leitbild' for future development and collectively meet European competition. The partnership is young and the partners have to become used to one and other. For the present it is concentrating on marketing the region internationally. It is too early to deal with more difficult issues, where both positive and negative effects have to be taken into account. In that case, MAI also runs the risk to meet similar problems as in Planungsregion 14. However, it is a first step towards the ultimate goal. As of yet, an association has been established with public and private participants. The number of the members (communities, counties, Chambers of Commerce, Regionale Planungsverbände and private firms) is increasing.

Organising capacity and economic development co-ordination: analysis

The challenge and the need for organising capacity

There is a reverse side to the economic success of the Munich region: the tendency to drive necessary but unattractive distribution and transport activities from the area. High land prices in the Munich area limit the number of possible locations for these activities, but a more important reason is that many communities in the region are explicitly excluding such 'inconvenient' activities from their spatial planning. The tendency has two clear negative effects. For one thing, it jeopardises the optimum functioning of the regional economy; for another, the location of distribution centres at some distance makes for longer distances and thus extra environmental costs. As in the matter of public transport, all public actors in the region are directly or indirectly involved: state, counties, city and municipality. The Chamber of Commerce has also shown itself interested. In addition, some representatives of the private sector have a seat on the InitiativKreis München, where the matter has also been a point of discussion. To cope with the reverse side of economic success, a well-co-ordinated economic policy is called for, able to keep the economic balance intact and to ensure that Munich remains a competitive location for business. To meet the challenge, the idea of an economic development agency for the area has been launched. To protect Munich's favourable diversified economic structure - a great asset in a competitive Europe - all relevant actors should support the idea and be willing to work towards a collective solution. To reach a solution on the adequate spatial scale subscribed to by all relevant actors, organising capacity once more is of the essence.

Spatial-economic conditions

Actually, the challenge springs from the spatial-economic conditions as described previously. But the signals are not loud enough to be widely recognised. In the last years, the disproportional displacement of basic economic activities had been obscured by the overall prosperous development of the region. In that ambiguous situation no clear undeniable signal is sounded to all relevant actors.

Political support

Politically, the idea of an economic development agency has not been given the green light either. Even with matters of strategic economic importance at stake, an additional institution could not function properly alongside the existing ones: 'Regionaler Planungsverband' and 'Äußerer Wirtschaftsraum München', the state, the city, the counties and the municipalities. A considerable rearrangement of the institutional framework would be necessary, but the will to achieve it is lacking, certainly among the municipalities. On that consideration the form of a holding company was suggested for the purpose. But even for a non-institutional holding company the climate is unfavourable, because most of the actors would still have to hand over some autonomy regarding their economic and spatial development planning, and few are willing to do so.They do not see the necessity to change the situation.

Vision and strategy

Whereas with reference to the MVV reorganisation all actors shared to some degree the same vision and objective, no common consent has yet been reached in the area of regional economic policy. The concept of an economic development agency for the region promises a better co-ordinated development and a halt to the ousting of basic economic activities. The city of Munich launched the idea from fear for its long-term competitive position. The support is poor and its campaign for better economic co-ordination in the Greater Munich area found little support among the region's municipalities. Although some have recognised the problem as well. In Landkreis Dachau, the 'Landrat' initiated a small-scale agency to deal with the issue locally. Simultaneously, the negative economic side-effects of success had also been recognised within the 'Industrie und Handelskammer' (IHK) (Chamber of Commerce). But the Chamber of Commerce stresses that its limited resources and lack of formal competence hinder the Chamber to play a leading role in communicating the problem regionally. The state of Bavaria has created the 'Regionaler Planungsverband' (RPV) which finds its base in Bavarian law. RPV is responsible for spatial planning and for drawing up a strategic spatial plan for the region. Given that responsibility, it can hardly be expected to give instant support to, and advocate the creation of a new agency for strategic economic development. Nevertheless, the RPV, too, is aware of the problem. However, they lack sufficient financial resources.

Administrative structure

The proposed economic development agency should work from an economic development strategy with clear-cut priorities. Of course such a strategy has spatial consequences, and therefore needs the co-operation of all administrative actors involved: RPV city, counties and municipalities. Within the administrative structure, the gravity centre of spatial planning is on the municipal level, with RPV taking care of spatial planning on the regional level. Although RPV's spatial-planning schemes narrow to some extent the municipal margin for independent spatial planning, they leave most of the municipal autonomy intact, and few municipalities will voluntarily give up some of that without unequivocal and clear direct benefits in return. Municipal autonomy is deep-rooted in German and certainly Bavarian tradition, so any drastic change on that score is unlikely. RPV decision procedures aggravate the problem: to carry any decision with the RPV council, municipal support is indispensable.

Leadership

Although it is one of the initiators of an economic development agency for City and surroundings, the city of Munich has very little scope to fulfil a pioneering role. In the eyes of the municipalities and counties Munich is too much 'the big one' in its region, and they tend to be wary of any idea promoted by the city. As things are at present, the Chamber of Commerce, as supporter and co-initiator, might assume the leadership. The trouble is that the Chamber of Commerce lacks the 'formal power' needed to achieve efficient co-operation, and is therefore highly dependent on the willingness of the public actors. However it could play a major role in communicating the problem regionally. For the time being, no more than for the reorganisation and improvement of regional public transport are the preconditions for clear and entrepreneurial leadership in matters of economic development, fulfilled.

Strategic networks

Unlike the reorganisation of the MVV, the idea of an economic development agency was launched not only within the administrative structure but also on more informal platforms, in an effort to bring relevant public and private actors together. For example, the subject was brought up for discussion in the 'InitiativKreis München'. Unfortunately, the momentum in this InitiativKreis had already dwindled, and by now the decision makers themselves no longer attend the meetings. IHK's request to municipalities to suggest suitable land sites was another positive initiative towards better co-ordination. However, the premises suggested so far are not really 'suitable'. An inauspicious sign, for should this initiative also get stuck, opponents to the idea would be provided with an additional argument.

Apparently, then, despite the efforts of the city and the Chamber of Commerce, the Munich region has not enough 'channels' to launch successful initiatives for better co-ordination.

The Chamber of Commerce has tried to initiate change, but the private sector itself -apart from participation in the InitiativKreis- has not really become involved. A partial explanation is that some of the most important businesses in the Munich region have their roots elsewhere; a company like Siemens is less 'associated' with Munich than, say, Philips with Eindhoven. The ties between public administrators and the business community are thus less sturdy than elsewhere. As an illustration, public-private partnerships as an effective vehicle for revitalisation projects have not gained such a firm footing in the Munich region as in some other towns.

Performance

Perhaps the best result of the suggestion of an economic development agency is that it may have initiated a constructive discussion of regional economic development. It is early days yet to judge the performance, because the project is still in the pipeline. From the foregoing, at any rate, many obstacles have to be overcome before the idea can be elaborated and the envisaged holding company actually founded. Without sufficient support, the idea appears unfeasible. And if in the end the development agency can be successfully launched, its performance will depend on its concrete specification: what competencies will the agency have and how will it be financed,? Unless such matters are settled to satisfaction, the whole project may yet founder on the conflicts in the region.

Conclusion

The Munich region is one of the most successful regions in Europe, with healthy economic growth, a still low unemployment rate- compared with other metropolitan regions- (about 7 per cent), a high quality of life and a strong, diversified economic structure. However, to maintain its position and stay competitive in Europe, the Greater Munich area has to prepare itself for the future.

The fact is, however, that past prosperity had not induced the Munich region to organise itself for the future. It had not experienced the urge or need actively to create conditions for future sustainable development; Munich's prosperity had come to be taken for granted. Today the Munich region still performs well, but the notion of making ready for the future is slowly gaining ground. The city of Munich, for one, has acknowledged the need, and moreover indicated that it cannot act alone in this. It will need the help of others to put development in a wider, metropolitan perspective.

The first challenge

In the field of public transport, co-operation between state, city and counties will be intensified within the renewed *Münchner Verkehrs- und Tarifsverbund* (MVV). Recognising the direct challenges to MVV, all actors found that the regional interest was mostly their own, and their joint objective became to keep MVV at work. In that sense the actors had a vision in common. However, the events were dictated by circumstances rather than guided by an undoubted 'leader'.

The reform of MVV has not been the only challenge to Munich's public-transport region; indeed, it comes under the broader heading of accessibility. Without specific measures, the public-transport system will be 'flooded' and the region become less accessible by public transport. But, while the reorganisation of MVV was clearly inevitable and all actors had perforce to co-operate, the need to tackle some major bottlenecks in the public transport system is not yet generally recognised. There is not really a shared vision of the system's future operation and the division of costs among participants, nor is there a stimulating leadership to push matters forward. In addition, the Munich region does not seem to have developed the right 'channels' - strategic networks - to generate new ideas and obtain support for these ideas. Mostly the formal channels of public administration have been involved.

The second challenge

Leadership and the 'right' channels are also the key notions in the question of a regional economic development agency. Up till now, none of the institutions involved -state, city, counties, municipalities, and Regionaler Planungsverband- have clearly taken the lead. Again the complementary role of strategic networks is not played to the full. All too readily, new ideas and initiatives become a toy in the conflict between city and counties and between city and municipalities. Of course, to start up the InitiativKreis was a step in the right direction, even if its momentum has already failed. The InitiativKreis may not have brought what some had hoped for or expected, but indeed, it was hardly likely to have the same effect as the forum in the Ruhr area that served as model. The Greater Munich Area lacks tradition and experience with this form of public-private interaction. Nor did the somewhat awkward relationship between city and ring make things easier. To maintain a structurally based, constructive partnership between the public and private actors costs much time and effort.

Clearly, then, there is much to do for the city and its hinterland. Things are changing but still Munich region does not meet all criteria -as put forward in our theoretical outline- of organising capacity to meet either challenge. In general, four factors can be said to be relevant to both themes.

Firstly, constructive regional co-operativeness, apart from compulsory co-operation in the Planungsverband, is lacking. Munich's domination of the region makes the counties and municipalities wary of co-operation. What the region needs is a *mechanism* to take away this pressure.

Secondly, because of the lack of co-operativeness within the administrative structure, the role of networks becomes increasingly important. In the Munich region these networks and the 'channels' connecting the public and private sector appear to be insufficiently developed. Therefore, every opportunity to establish better relations between public and private actors should be grasped. Perhaps the Chamber of Commerce, being relatively independent, could extend its role to organising structural contact between both public and private actors.

Thirdly, there is no clear and widely-supported, regional vision of regional public transport and of regional economic development. A broadly-supported vision could unite the actors and bring efficient co-operation within reach.

Fourthly, another lacking element is a distinct pull factor -leadership- in matters involving several -public or private- actors. With respect to regional public transport the state of Bavaria holds an important trump card: the S-Bahn network. With the state as new owner of the railway network and the counties as full participants, the reorganisation seemed to be a good opportunity to carry through the necessary changes, but so far the opportunity has not been taken up. Much will depend on the financial means provided to Bavaria by the Federal Government, and on Bavaria's willingness to take the lead within MVV, initiating improvement by *financial incentives*. Bavaria seems to be in a position to develop the necessary co-operative instruments. It is not unthinkable - if highly speculative - that the state could stimulate co-operation in the field of regional economic development as well.

An initiative that opens perspectives is the recent establishment of the MAI-partnership between München, Augsburg and Ingolstadt. Despite its non-committed character, it is of strategic importance. MAI sets out to market the MAI region (inter)nationally. However, it also offers an opportunity to the city of Munich to prove its good intentions to its surrounding area and take away the anxiety of the smaller counties and municipalities. Scale-enlargement as a consequence of the partnership could expand the horizon of other regional actors and remove the barrier for some counties to co-operation, as they come to realise that they must either catch up or lose out. However, the MAI-partnership is still young. Topics where both positive and negative aspects have to be settled, have not been touched upon yet. In MAI problems may also arise if more difficult issues are at stake. Of course, MAI is not *the solution* to all Munich region's problems.

Nonetheless, investment by the city of Munich in this partnership could yield more than the direct benefits of the partnership itself.

Notes

---

[1] Here Munich region corresponds with the 'Planungsregion 14',related to the 'Regionaler Planungsverband'. It is also possible to define the region differently. But statistically 'Planungsregion 14' is well documented.

[2] Landkreis Dachau, Landkreis Ebersberg, Landkreis Erding, Landkreis Freising, Landkreis Fürstenfeldbruck, Landkreis Landsberg am Lech, Landkreis München and Landkreis Starnberg.

8 Rotterdam[1]

Introduction

Rotterdam is best known for its harbour, which counts as the world's greatest. In spite of the growing harbour activities, the position of Rotterdam as a mainport is not unchallenged. In several important sectors, such as the container trade, Rotterdam experiences increasing competition from other European ports. The harbour activities have in the course of time encroached upon the territory of other communities. Problems such as environmental pollution and increasing traffic congestion can no longer be solved by Rotterdam alone. Apart from harbour-related problems, Rotterdam is confronted by such urban problems as unemployment, social exclusion, shortage of housing space, etcetera. In recent years Rotterdam has developed numerous initiatives to cope with these problems. This chapter will discuss two such initiatives. After a general outline of the Rotterdam region and a brief discussion of the administrative structure in the Netherlands, the ROM-Rijnmond[2] project will be described in more detail. This project aims at simultaneously strengthening the mainport function of Rotterdam and improving the living environment. Next, the chapter analyses the 'Kop-van-Zuid' (southern-headland) project, a large-scale scheme to develop deserted harbour grounds opposite the city centre, as an illustration of a new urban policy which was adopted in the second half of the 1980s. In the conclusions the main elements of the Rotterdam case will be discussed.

Profile

Population

Rotterdam is a characteristic example of a city at the 'reurbanisation' stage. After years of population losses, lately the records have shown a slight growth. Since the end of the 19th century, when its economy was flourishing, Rotterdam had experienced a strong population growth culminating in a (record) population of 732,000 in 1965. From the 1970s onward, the rising prosperity and in its wake greater mobility, changing residential preferences and decreasing average dwelling occupancy led to a net population loss of about 160,000 inhabitants in twenty years. That very selective deconcentration ('suburbanisation') resulted, in combination with the effects of the 1973 and 1978 energy crises, in grave socio-economic problems. On the waves of the international economic recovery, rigorous policy changes on the national as well as the local level[3] helped to stem the tide: by 1985 the decay of the city of Rotterdam had come to an end. At that moment the city counted 573,000 inhabitants. Since then the population has grown slightly, to 596,000 in 1993. The other municipalities in the region had profited from the suburbanisation. Their total population increased from some 275,000 inhabitants in 1960 to about 530,000 in 1993. Their development has now also stabilised to slight growth. At present, the Rotterdam region counts 1.1 million residents.

Spatial situation

The Rotterdam region belongs to the 'Randstad', one of the largest metropolitan areas of Europe. The Randstad, which has no formal status as a statistical, administrative or planning unit, extends across three provinces and a large number of independent municipalities. Rotterdam is situated in the province of Zuid-Holland. Although there is no clear delimitation, the Randstad can be said to cover about one fourth of Dutch territory, accommodates about two fifths of the Dutch population (that is, six million people) and holds a dominant position in the economy, in particular in the tertiary sector.

Economy

The economy of the Rotterdam region is dominated by the harbour, which counts as the world's greatest. The area serves as an important international logistic node and centre of trade and is regarded by the Dutch government as a cornerstone of the national economy. The port zone also houses Europe's largest petrochemical complex. The transport, industry and trade functions of the area flourished from the end of the 19th century. Strong growth was experienced after the second world war until far into the 1960s. The westward extension of the port area towards the North Sea has facilitated the growth of harbour-linked activities.

From the mid-1960s, industrial development stagnated. Ship building and repair, once a flourishing sector, ran into difficulties and the tertiarisation was slow. Moreover, the new industrial growth sectors were poorly represented in the production structure. The production environment appeared strongly oriented to the transportation sector and the more traditional industries and services. Moreover, as people became conscious of the environment, Rotterdam gained a bad reputation in terms of the quality of the living environment.

The Rotterdam economy, vulnerable as it was, suffered badly under the economic recession of the early 1980s. Unemployment in the city itself rose to over one fifth of the labour force. Nevertheless, in the 1970s an extensive programme of city renovation, almost entirely public-funded, was initiated and largely carried out. The harbour activities were energetically stimulated by the deepening of the channel to the North Sea, the construction of extensive port and distribution estates, container terminals, and a telematics system to automatise the exchange of information controlling the transport flows. In that way, the port of Rotterdam managed to consolidate its position as the European mainport.

From the mid-1980s onward, there were important changes. The economy was once more growing, and Rotterdam shared in the renewed interest for major cities as locations for business services and as residences for certain segments of the higher income brackets. Rotterdam companies not directly related to the port began to invest on a large scale in new office premises, especially in the city centre, which thus acquired more and more an international air. Other high-quality office locations were realised on the outskirts of the city for activities preferring good accessibility by motorcar. In that way, Rotterdam has considerably reduced its arrears as an 'office city' in relation to the promenent Dutch office cities Amsterdam and The Hague. The stock of office floor area increased from 2.5 million (1986) to 3.2 million (1993)[4]. Various Rotterdam headquarters of major companies such as Unilever, the Internationale Nederlanden Groep (banking and insurance), Stad Rotterdam (insurance), Robeco Group (investment funds),

NedLloyd (transport), Mees & Hope (banking) and Crédit Lyonnais (banking) moved to new office buildings in the city centre, joining the headquarters of Shell, ABN/AMRO (banking) and some others already established there. A new World Trade Centre was also completed. The wave of new building, including the now dominant highest office building of the Netherlands, the 150 metre high ING head office, a new casino, a new theatre, and some exclusive residential towers, have given the city's heart a modern air.

Although this development is positive in various respects, the economic structure of Rotterdam obviously remains vulnerable. That is evident, among other things, from the fact that the growth of employment lags behind that of the nation (5 versus 10 per cent between 1987 and 1991). The average growth of Gross Regional Product was in the same period 5 per cent against 5.4 per cent nationally (Rotterdam Development Corporation, 1993). Since 1991, Rotterdam, like other regions, has been up against a stagnating economy. Unemployment is persistent, especially among people of foreign extraction, who represent about one fifth of the population. Table 11.1 reproduces the production structures of the city of Rotterdam.

Table 1
Persons employed in the city of Rotterdam (1977-1992)

Sector	Employed persons (x1000)					
	1977		1985		1992	
	abs.	perc.	abs.	perc.	abs.	perc.
Agriculture	0,6	0,2	0,6	0,2	0,6	0,2
Industry	58,0	19,7	42,6	15,9	40,8	15,1
Public utilities	3,6	1,2	3,5	1,3	2,3	0,8
Construction	18,8	6,4	15,4	5,8	13,6	5,0
Trade	61,1	20,7	47,5	17,8	46,7	17,3
Transport/ communication	58,1	19,7	53,2	19,9	45,7	16,9
Banking/insur-ance/bus.services	33,4	11,3	34,9	13,0	42,1	15,6
Public/non-profit services	61,3	20,8	69,9	26,0	78,0	28,9
Total	295,0	100,0	267,3	100,0	269,8	99,8

Source: COS, 1993

Administrative structure[5]

Since the 19th century the administrative structure of the Netherlands has had three tiers: the national government, 12 provinces and over 650 municipalities. The organisation, tasks and responsibilities have been laid down by the national Legislator and are essentially the same for all provinces and all municipalities. While the provinces and municipalities initially enjoyed policy freedom in many areas, public administration was increasingly centralised. The national government now lays down rules and provides the financial means for the implementation of the government policy. Besides municipalities and provinces, a number of functional administrative bodies have evolved, in many cases of regional scope, ranking between municipalities and provinces. Regional partnerships of municipalities have been formed to undertake, sometimes jointly with the province or the national government, such public tasks as city or regional transport, policing, employment measures, ambulance transport and contingency plans.

The administrative culture in the Netherlands has several distinctive characteristics. In the first place, there is a strong tradition of 'unified thinking', a tendency to develop or organise the same structures everywhere in the country and to eliminate differences. This preference for equality largely governs the financing of local and regional governments by the central government. Local taxes are in that respect insignificant: target payments with limited spending freedom constitute the principal revenues of municipalities. In the second place, great importance is attached to pre-decision involvement and consultation. Decision making often means trying for consensus and the avoidance of painful choices. Attempts are often made to unite all those concerned in new administrative structures. Finally, democratic validity of administrators and separation and clarification of responsibilities are considered important. Dual functions are therefore rare.

The city of Rotterdam is administratively divided into nine boroughs, which are increasingly responsible for such local matters as well-being, sports, leisure activities and street maintenance. The boroughs have budgets to finance activities and to set priorities. The Rotterdam region encompasses 17 municipalities, varying in population from just under 10,000 to about 80,000. These municipalities vary much in character. Some are quite ancient cities and have problems comparable to those of Rotterdam. Others are typical suburbs, absorbing settlers from Rotterdam.

Regional administration in and around Rotterdam has always been related to the development of the harbour, which has a habit of reaching beyond city boundaries. In the past, smaller neighbouring communities were from time to time incorporated by the city of Rotterdam. After the Second World War, it became clear that such incorporations were inadequate and that a regional administration ranking above the municipalities surrounding the port was needed. In 1964 the 'Openbaar Lichaam Rijnmond' (Rhine Estuary Public Body) was created by way of experiment to coordinate activities in a number of policy fields. This body proved to be ineffective, for one thing because it was assigned an incomplete load of tasks and because it was jammed between the powerful and influential bodies of the city of Rotterdam and the Province of Zuid-Holland. In 1986 the body was dissolved.

The need for a platform for consultation and adjustment in the area remained, however. The initiative was therefore taken to establish a 'loose partnership', the 'Overleg Orgaan Rijnmond' (OOR). The activities of the OOR soon went beyond mere consultation to get to grips with spatial-economic problems in the region. The OOR developed a strategic spatial-economic vision which recognised the necessity of a strong regional administrative structure. In 1991 the OOR presented a proposal for a new structure of its own design. The municipalities in the area and the national government gave their support to this proposal. However, in a referendum held in 1995, the citizens of Rotterdam voted against a new administrative structure, probably mostly because they were loath have their city sub-divided into nine separate communities. That subdivision, which would reduce the present domination of Rotterdam, had been a condition for the other communities to join in.

ROM-Rijnmond: the balancing of economic growth and improvement of the environment

Introduction

In the late 1980s, the national and provincial governments issued policy documents whose aim was to change the approach to spatial planning. In the national spatial-planning document VINEX, three major shifts are apparent. The authorities now recognised that spatial planning had become too much centrally controlled, that local development initiatives should be stimulated, and that for a sustainable development, economic growth, accessibility and environmental quality should go hand in hand.

The Rotterdam metropolitan region, usually indicated as the Rijnmond region, was designated as one of eleven areas in which the new spatial policy was to take shape. The Rijnmond area is at the same time one of the most densely populated regions and the most industrialised area of the Netherlands. That causes friction between mainport development on the one hand and the quality of the living environment on the other. In the past, various policy initiatives have been developed to diminish the tension. Because they were all taken independently, overall they proved ineffective. Policy makers now realised that a more integrated approach was needed. To that end, the ROM[6]-Rijnmond project was initiated.

Towards ROM-Rijnmond

The Rijnmond area covers about 60,000 hectares and the territories of 15 communities. It comprises the sea port of Rotterdam, which has the ambition to become a 'mainport'. This ambition is recognised in the governmental policy documents VINO, VINEX and SVV. Its achievement cannot be taken for granted, however, for Rotterdam experiences increasing competition of other European ports. To strengthen the mainport function is therefore considered an essential element of national and local government policy. Environmental problems in the Rijnmond region demand constant attention, as the quality of the living environment is becoming a location factor of increasing importance. The national government recognised the need to take up these matters in an integrate manner, without knowing exactly how to go about it.

Starting up ROM-Rijnmond

Early in 1989 the Ministry for Spatial Planning and the Environment (VROM) initiated talks with the Province of Zuid-Holland and the City of Rotterdam with a view to mounting the ROM-Rijnmond project. No other parties were involved at that stage. It soon became apparent that there was no sufficient basis for the project. An important reason appears to have been that both the Province and the City considered themselves quite capable of handling their own affairs. Another reason appears to have been that the Rotterdam Municipal Port Management (RMPM), an important party in port development, was at the time working on its own strategy for future developments, to which it gave priority. Furthermore, there was some confusion with regard to the goals of the project. These factors obstructed a fundamental discussion of the problems in the Rijnmond area.

The Province took a positive attitude towards ROM-Rijnmond, but felt that the project should focus more on the short-term removal of bottlenecks in the area. This was contrary to the ideas of VROM, which were based on a long-term approach. The two bodies also disagreed on who should assume the role of leader in the project. Another problem was the involvement of the 14 other Rijnmond communities. These communities traditionally have a somewhat awkward relationship with the city of Rotterdam, due to the difference in magnitude[7]. The fact that they had not been contacted initially made them hesitant towards the ROM-Rijnmond project.

The period of disagreements on project leadership and planning horizon lasted until late 1991. By that time two events had taken place. The first was the presentation of the Havenplan (Port Plan) 2010, which contained the strategic vision of the RMPM, and the second was the presentation of the report 'De regio in nieuw perspectief' (The region in a new perspective), which was produced by the 15 Rijnmond communities, including Rotterdam, united in the new Rijnmond Consultative Body (OOR). This report contained a shared and integral vision of the future of the Rijnmond region. It was the result of efforts to establish constructive cooperation among all the Rijnmond communities, a process parallel to the ROM-Rijnmond process.

The starting covenant

Both developments led to a more constructive attitude of parties and made it possible to 'relaunch' the project, and concretely to the signing of the Starting Covenant early in 1992 by the Ministry of Economic Affairs, the Ministry of Spatial Planning and the Environment, the Ministry of Transport, the Province of Zuid-Holland, the city of Rotterdam and the 14 other Rijnmond communities, the OOR consultative body, and three regional organisations for trade and industry. The organisations representing the regional business community had followed the previous discussions mainly from the sideline. The inhabitants of the Rijnmond region were not represented directly; broad support of the harbour and its related activities was assumed.

The covenant was to lead to a 'Masterplan ROM-Rijnmond', aimed at strengthening the port and industry area as mainport and improving the living environment (quality of life). Short-term bottlenecks were envisaged to be dealt with integrally in the framework of a development strategy for the long-term. The agreement was to make use of existing and recently developed plans, such as the Port Plan 2010, rather than develop a new integral vision of the area. Research was to be carried out to take stock of existing plans and goals of actors involved, existing barriers to mainport development, spatial planning and the environment in the Rijnmond region. The intention was not so much to produce a detailed blueprint but rather to create a context for future development. A new external programme manager was appointed to guide the planning process.

During the discussions that followed, different focuses of interest emerged. One group of parties focused strongly on the strengthening of the mainport function, while another stressed the importance of improving the living environment. In the ensuing process of negotiations the regional parties, especially the Province and the City of Rotterdam, kept in close touch to make themselves strong vis-à-vis the central government parties. One reason was that the environmental directives laid down by the central government in the national environmental-policy document NMP[8] did not cater for the regional differentiation of policy. The regional parties argued that since the Rotterdam region was assigned an important function in transport and industry, higher pollution values should be permissible in the area than elsewhere. Other points of discussion were the land-reclamation scheme at the mouth of the Nieuwe Waterweg and the financing of the various projects.

Initially, the organisations for trade and industry were rather sceptical about the feasibility of both the economical and the environmental goals. Gradually, however, they began to see the ROM-Rijnmond project as a means of exercising influence on the development of the region. The business community indicated that tougher environmental standards were acceptable provided that, first, they were not too far out of line with international practice, and second, if environmental regulations became clearer and more consistent, and the procedures shorter. Furthermore, in return for considerable environmental investments the business community demanded that the realisation of several important infrastructural projects, such as a new tunnel across the Caland Canal and further development of the A15 highway, be given a higher priority. These demands were met and the business community committed itself to the project and to the financing of the various sub-projects.

During the negotiations, the traditional separation between harbour and non-harbour matters within the City of Rotterdam surfaced. Harbour matters are dealt with by the Rotterdam Municipal Port Management (RMPM) and non-harbour matters by the Rotterdam Development Company (OBR), and intercourse between them is traditionally relatively scarce. The ROM-

Rijnmond process, however, required the policies of the two bodies to be geared to each other. During the process this appears to have been achieved quite well.

The discussions and negotiations finally produced the Masterplan ROM-Rijnmond, which was approved by the signing, in December 1993, of the Policy Covenant ROM-Rijnmond by all parties involved; a covenant between the private and the public sector, established within the exisiting legal and administrative framework.

The ROM-Rijnmond Masterplan

The Masterplan defined 47 specific projects to be carried out. The projects refer to four main themes: (1) Space for mainport development; (2) comprehensive approach to traffic and transport problems; (3) restructuring of port and industry areas; and (4) reconciling the creation of space for the mainport with the reinforcement of nature and leisure pursuits. The projects were designed for policy consistency and functional coherence. The starting phase ended by the establishment of the masterplan ROM-Rijnmond, which was confirmed by the signing of the formal policy covenant in December 1993.

ROM-Rijnmond comprises such projects as the development of a new distribution estate (Distripark), a land-reclamation scheme at the mouth of the Nieuwe Waterweg, the reduction of traffic speeds and the planting of trees. For every project, the actors involved, the project leadership, the costs incurred, and the time frame were determined. The time frame of the entire ROM-Rijnmond programme ranges from December 1993 until the year 2010. The starts and finishes of the various projects have been fitted in this period. The covenant also contains agreements on:
–   the organisational structure;
–   the monitoring of developments in economy, environment, spatial quality and accessibility;
–   an annual progress report; and
–   a reconsideration of objectives and methods once every four years.

The organisation consists of several bodies with the various actors represented at different levels. At the highest level functions the 'bestuurlijk overleg' (administrative consultative body), composed of administrators. This body supervises the progress of the entire project and decides financial matters. At a lower level the coordination group ('coordinatiegroep') is active, in which the actors are represented at directors' level. This body functions as the primary point of address for the project manager. Its task is to find solutions for any bottlenecks and differences of opinion among parties.

The two bodies meet only a few times a year. For day-to-day matching of activities a third body, the consultation group ('overleggroep') has been installed. The control of progress of the various projects is entrusted to the programme manager. He is appointed by, and answers to, the 'bestuurlijk overleg' body.

The parties involved regarded the masterplan as satisfactory in three respects. In the perspective of mainport development the plan provided for an integral vision of port development, based largely on the Port Plan 2010 produced by the RMPM. In the perspective of spatial planning, the plan would lead to the restructuring of such obsolete harbour areas as Vlaardingen and Schiedam. And, finally, in an environmental perspective the plan provided for a regional differentiation in environmental standards and would in general lead to improved environmental quality.

Realisation

By the signing of the Policy Covenant the project entered the realisation phase, which is to last to the year 2010. Until now, only a few projects has been completed. Most projects are still under study, according to schedule. Several projects have been held up by either financing problems or change of project leader. Besides, in the theatre of national politics the decision making concerning a few major infrastructural projects, which are not part of ROM-Rijnmond, has slowed down. This, in turn, has affected the progress of several ROM-Rijnmond projects which were connected to them. During the first year of ROM-Rijnmond, a system was developed to monitor whether things were actually proceeding according to plan. In several respects the quality of the environment had improved. Furthermore, the cooperation between parties is reported to be satisfactory[9].

However, several problems are emerging. Since the beginning of the ROM-Rijnmond project, several persons who had proved important to the process have changed their positions, among other reasons as a result of elections at both the national and the community level. New personalities with different attitudes towards ROM-Rijnmond have appeared. Personal contacts between representatives of the different parties involved have to be built anew. Moreover, the coordination of the project at the level of the central government has moved from VROM, one of the initiators, to the

207

Ministry of Transport (V&W). As a result, relations among the government bodies and between them and the business community have changed as well. The "ROM-Rijnmond-feeling", or at least the enthusiasm for the project, seems to have diminished somewhat. The personal commitment to the ROM-Rijnmond project threatens to change accordingly.

The programme manager is one of those who directly experience the consequences of these developments. In his function of controlling the progress of the various projects he frequently has to remind parties of the agreements made. A helpful argument to offer when some party is reluctant to live up to its promises concerning a project low on its priority list, is to point out that another project, considered of higher priority, falls also in jeopardy. However, in spite of this argument it has proved difficult to secure financial commitment from the business community for such environmental projects as a forestation scheme.

The programme manager holds no direct competencies over the various project leaders. In some cases this may make it difficult for him to acquire the information he needs for coordination purposes. Because the programme manager may only test decisions made by project leaders against the agreements made, he is sometimes confronted with accomplished facts. Such problems can be solved only through the intermediary of the project leaders' superiors involved.

Decisions with regard to ROM-Rijnmond projects are made along the usual lines within the various municipal and other governmental services involved. The process is thus slow, giving the entire ROM-Rijnmond project a somewhat bureaucratic image. Much of the activity in the first year was devoted to the development of a proper set of control instruments. The attention given to details and methods added to the bureaucratic image.

Finally, the parties involved find it difficult to project ROM-Rijnmond to the public. That is partially due to the fact that most sub-projects are still under study and have not yet produced visible results. Another factor is that participants are uncertain how to present programme: as one integral programme, or through some of the more appealing sub-projects? It is also felt that the financial means are insufficient for extensive communication.

The policy covenant provides for reverifying the agreements made once in four years. At the recently held reverification round, the participants, aware of the problems, reconfirmed their commitment to the project and decided on several organisational changes. The most prominent changes regard the replacement of the coordination group and the 'bestuurlijk-overleg group' by one 'directors' council' in which high-level representatives of the various parties take seats and which meets quite regularly. This council is assisted by an advisory body without decision-making competencies. A recognised disadvantage of these propositions is that by skipping several links the chances of conflict increase. Another change regards the programme management. The function of the programme manager has been split into two new functions: one for daily, operational, management, and one aimed at external relations in the networks in which ROM-Rijnmond operates. Also, a new communication committee is installed, which is to develop a coherent communication strategy towards administrators and the public.

ROM-Rijnmond and organising capacity: analysis

Vision and strategy

At the time the initiative to start up ROM-Rijnmond was taken, a vision of the region's future development had been defined only in broad terms in several policy documents: VINO, NMP and Provinciaal Milieuplan Zuid-Holland. These documents illuminated different aspects and varied in spatial scope. However, a vision of developments in and around the harbour and of a proper administrative structure for the region had not yet taken shape. Although it was clear that the ROM-Rijnmond project was to lead to an integral vision in terms of economics, spatial planning and the environment, there was uncertainty with regard to how detailed it should be and to what the objectives of the project should be. This uncertainty, combined with the desire of one of the most important parties, the RMPM, to develop its own strategic plan prior to committing itself to ROM-Rijnmond impeded constructive dialogue between parties.

The development of vision and strategy for both the port area and the region followed separate tracks for quite some time. When, finally, all parties had determined their own position they adopted a more constructive attitude. The vision and strategy incorporated in the policy covenant are the result of confrontation of and negotiations about the various existing plans. An important factor in the determination and acceptance of the goals, especially with regard to the environment, seems to have been the wish not to let them diverge too much from international practice.

Administrative structure

At the time when ROM-Rijnmond was started up, the project could not easily be fitted into the 'basket' of a proper administrative structure. In the Rijnmond region, a multitude of authorities played a role: the 15 local communities, the Province of Zuid-Holland and the central government. On the local level there was the somewhat awkward relation between the relatively large City of Rotterdam and the other small communities. That Rotterdam was involved in ROM-Rijnmond at an earlier stage than the other communities, did not help matters in that regard. Great effort was needed to bring about constructive cooperation in the region.

In the City of Rotterdam, harbour matters and non-harbour matters were traditionally detached. The RMPM was not used to involving other parties in decisions of port development. Because the ROM-Rijnmond project involves economic, environmental and spatial-planning aspects, cooperation had to be brought about also on the level of the central government. Harbour matters belong to the activity sphere of V&W, while environmental and spatial planning affairs come under the authority of VROM.

Apart from coordination problems *within* the various government levels, there were also problems *between* the different levels. The Province and the City of Rotterdam were hesitant about extensive involvement of the central government in regional matters. The picture was further complicated by different views of the proper approach. The central government favoured a long-term approach, while Rotterdam and the Province preferred a short- and medium-term approach. Gradually the different parties came to realise that a regional approach was required, and assumed a cooperative attitude towards the project.

Strategic networks

Although ideas to develop a formal administrative structure for the Rijnmond region coincided with the development of the ROM-Rijnmond project, such a structure had not yet come about. ROM-Rijnmond emerged from a series of mainly informal contacts among the various government bodies as well as between these bodies and the business community. An important factor was that the project gradually acquired the support of persons in key functions with all parties involved. A prominent role was played by the administrative actors. The initiation and realisation of the project as well as financial commitment was predominantly a matter of the administrative bodies. In their interaction the desire of the regional parties to limit the involvement of and control by the central government was an important factor. The government part in the network is not confined to ROM-Rijnmond. Parallel to that project an important network emerged among the 15 Rijnmond communities: the OOR consultative body, with a wider scope than ROM-Rijnmond.

An important fact in the interaction of network parties has been the coherence of the sub-projects. It has motivated parties to carry out even projects which they might consider of less importance for the sake of the realisation of projects considered of greater importance. This mechanism seems to secure interaction to a significant extent.

A problem that emerged while the networks required for ROM-Rijnmond were being constructed, is how to involve the business community. The bodies representing the business community have no formal power over their members. Compliance by individual companies with agreements made by the representative bodies is not guaranteed. This problem is apparent among other things in the relatively limited financial commitment of the business community to ROM-Rijnmond and its reluctance to finance general environmental sub-projects. There seems to be no clear solution to this problem.

At the beginning of the realisation phase of ROM-Rijnmond, the dependency of the networks established on the persons involved became very clear. As people change their position, the network needs maintenance. Communication appears to be an important instrument for that purpose.

Leadership

To identify one clearly leading party throughout the ROM-Rijnmond process is not easy. In the initial phase VROM took the initiative, but soon found out that especially the Province and the City of Rotterdam did not accept the ministry as leader. They seem gradually to have taken over the initiative from VROM.

To keep the process going within the various parties appeared to be mainly the work of a few individuals. In the longer term that makes the process vulnerable to the turnover of people, as was mentioned above.

Now that the programme is in the realisation phase the discussions about the leadership are restarted. However, this time the central government wants the region to take lead, while the region fears that this would mean a diminished involvement of the central government. This is a remarkable change, given the desire of the regional parties to limit the influence of the

211

national government in the initial phase of the project. After long discussion the City of Rotterdam has taken the lead as the representative for the regional government. The Ministry for Transport now coordinates the activities at the level of the national government.

Political support

Political conditions have on the whole been favourable to the ROM-Rijnmond project. On the national level the fact was realised that projects on the scale of ROM-Rijnmond should no longer be realised in isolation. External integration began to be considered essential. Indeed, the policy documents VINO, SVV and VINEX expressed that a regional approach in different policy areas was necessary.

On the local level the idea gained ground that various problems, such as economic, transport and environmental questions, could no longer be dealt with municipally but should be referred to the regional level. This was an important motivation to establish the OOR consultative body and to lay an administrative foundation for a new regional administrative structure.

Performance

Probably the most important result of the ROM-Rijnmond project is that the various actors have committed themselves to the region. The questions with regard to the regional economy, spatial planning and the environment have been clarified and cooperation has been improved, both *at* the various administrative levels, as well as *between* these levels. Also, the project seems to have worked as a catalyst for the development of other projects such as the business development area Hoekse Waard and the OOR consultative body.

The procedures for a number of infrastructural projects, such as a new tunnel across the Caland Canal and further development of the A15 highway, may well have been speeded up by the ROM-Rijnmond process. Environmental regulation and procedures for pollution permits have been simplified. The project has also led to a new set of instruments to monitor economic, spatial and environmental developments in the region.

Now that the project is in the realisation phase, a problem emerges which could be called that of maintaining momentum. The drive the project possessed between the signing of the starting covenant and the policy covenant proves difficult to keep up. Several factors are involved. First, the project seems to have slipped from the political agenda since it was put on track. Second, some people in key positions have changed positions, and their successors have a different attitude towards ROM-Rijnmond. Third place, there is no well-designed strategy for communication towards administrators, inhabitants and individual companies in the region. Combined with the lack of visible successes such as the completion of appealing projects, ROM-Rijnmond is developing a bureaucratic image. Furthermore, the project manager is not provided with sufficient competence to secure the speedy realisation of the various sub-projects. The recently proposed organisational changes to cope with these problems still have to prove their worth.

Kop van Zuid

Introduction

As described earlier, the employment situation in Rotterdam deteriorated significantly during the 1970s and early 1980s, especially in the sectors trade and industry. The Rotterdam economy was strongly oriented to the harbour and its related activities, while growing sectors like the service industry and high-grade industrial activities were relatively weakly represented. Rotterdam found itself in a difficult position and recognised the need for a new policy approach aimed at broadening its economic basis.

In the second half of the 1980s, a new policy was formulated based on an integral approach to urban development. Key concepts of this policy were quality, competitive power and collaboration. The new policy was to be established with the undertaking of several large-scale projects such as the development schemes for the city centre and the northern perimeter of the city, and the Kop-van-Zuid project. The development of the latter, a 'Waterfront project' projected on the left bank of the Maas river and comprising a mixture of high-grade offices, shops and houses, is described below to illustrate how the new policy approach was developed and put into practice.

Towards a new vision of urban development

During the 1970s Rotterdam pursued an urban policy with a strong social orientation. Attention was directed at restricting polluting activities on the one hand and initiating large-scale town rehabilitation on the other. An extensive programme of town renovation was launched, which provided for the rehabilitation of poor residential quarters on behalf of the original, financially weak citizens. Neighbourhood organisations were quite influential in the determination of the contents of the programme, which was strongly concentrated on the individual town quarters. The dramatic effects of the energy crises during the mid- and late 1970s put an end to the sustainability of the strongly social-oriented policy. Rotterdam, like other traditional European harbour and industrial cities, threatened to fall into a serious socio-economic crisis unless the negative trends were energetically opposed.

Both administrators and neighbourhood organisations became aware of this and were ready to broaden their scope and accept the new ideas which started to arise. The Town Planning Department (TPD), emerged as an important source of new ideas. Halfway the 1980s this department found itself in a difficult position. The TPD was managed on an *ad hoc*-basis; the policy focus was directed mainly at the short term and a vision and strategy with respect to future developments in the city were virtually absent. This situation changed drastically with the appointment of a new director in 1986. One of her first actions was to determine the strengths and weaknesses of Rotterdam as a whole and define possible actions to create new opportunities. A new vision was established based on an integral view of urban development: the focus was to shift from policy directed at separate areas within the city to policy directed at the city as a whole. To attract new economic activities to the city, the location environment of Rotterdam was to change in social and administrative terms as well as in terms of adequate provision of housing, office and business space and facilities.

Concurrently, the municipality realised, as described above, that the difficult social-economic situation in which the city found itself required a new policy approach. Led by the necessity of an integral approach, the city council formed three 'sub-councils' around the themes of spatial-economic renewal, social renewal and administrative renewal. The sub-councils were to mobilise the various municipal services into achieving renewal in the respective areas. The ideas developed by the Town Planning Department thus found fertile soil. A change in administrative culture came about; henceforth wisdom was considered better than strength. Furthermore, the city council also appointed a committee of external experts representing various social groupings to advise on tackling the persisting unemployment in the city. These events led to the presentation of the policy document 'Renewal in Rotterdam' (Vernieuwing in Rotterdam) by the Municipality and the report 'New Rotterdam' by the committee of experts in 1987. Both documents contain a new integral vision of future developments. Important goals are improved accessibility, the construction of high-grade business locations, the building of exclusive houses to draw the more affluent citizens back to the city, and the enhancement of the metropolitan ambience and atmosphere by stimulating art, culture and spatial quality. To that end a more entrepreneurial attitude was introduced based on modern urban management, a streamlined, more market-oriented municipal organisation, and closer collaboration with the market parties and the other municipalities in the region.

The national government was also changing its ideas, giving increasing attention to the problems and possibilities of large urban areas. The importance of the quality of the living environment to attract new companies and the related need for integrated planning of houses, offices, industrial areas, recreational areas and infrastructure were recognised and later on incorporated in the policy documents VINO (1988) and VINEX (1989). Willingness to provide the (financial) means necessary to realise projects aimed at solving problems of the large urban areas was shown.

Although the climate at the various administrative levels changed in favour of revitalisation, concrete commitments were not instantly made. To that end, the support had to be broadened. An extensive communication campaign was launched by the Town Planning Department, together with the Rotterdam City Development Corporation (RCDC), to make people aware of the necessity to attract new businesses, more education, a greater variety in housing stock and high-quality leisure and shopping services. The campaign was addressed to a great many organisations, such as shopkeepers' associations, residents' organisations, the Rotary and Lions, politicians, etcetera. The communication campaign proved effective: the new vision received broad support. The TPD was then given the go-ahead to select some projects for realisation. Significant financial means were made available for this. The Dienst selected six development projects, among which two large-scale ones, namely, the Kop-van-Zuid and the North Rim Development Scheme (IPNR).

The Kop-van-Zuid scheme

In the early 1980s several plans had been developed for the restructuring of the deserted harbour grounds known as "the Kop van Zuid". The area is situated opposite the city centre, on the south bank of the river Maas, which cuts through the city in an east-westerly direction. The early development plans for the area mainly envisaged the construction of housing affordable to the socially weaker groups, and were projected as part of the extensive town renovation programme started in the 1970s. However, because of financial problems and disagreements among municipal services regarding the destination of the area, these plans did not come off.

Desirous to provide the city with a broader and more varied supply of housing and office space and in view of the location of the Kop-van-Zuid, the TPD recognised the high potential of the area: an ideal location for large-scale development based on the concept of Waterfront development as realised in London, Baltimore and other towns. A mixture of high-grade offices, houses and shops was envisaged. However, the idea met with wide-spread scepticism. It was projected in a part of town which was generally considered unattractive, with its deserted harbour grounds, social problems and awkward access due to the River Maas, a significant natural barrier. In the neighbourhood itself people were also doubtful how far such a large-scale project would be feasible on the projected location. Nevertheless, the TPD was commissioned to elaborate the plan, with the clear proviso of great caution.

First priority was therefore given to the design of a plan of solid content. For the town-planning aspects an external specialist was hired, who drew up a masterplan that was not only well thought out but also very presentable. Key elements were quality, accessibility and an integrated set-up. On an area of 125 hectares 5,300 houses have been projected as well as 400,000 m^2 of office space, 35,000 m^2 for businesses, 30,000 m^2 for education facilities and 30,000 m^2 for leisure and other facilities. A major part of the housing is intended for the higher end of the market, although cheaper houses are also provided for. An essential element of the plan is the new direct connection with the city centre in the form of a new bridge across the Maas river. This way the area is to offer opportunities for an extension of the city centre on the South Bank, so that the historical division of the city can be ended. Other infrastructural facilities include new roads and connections to both the subway and the tram-rail system. In the realisation of the scheme, major attention is to be paid to functional, visual and spatial quality aspects, both on the level of the plans for the various parts of the Kop-van-Zuid area as on more detailed levels. The total investment in the project is estimated at more than 4,500 million guilders.

Obviously, an investment of this magnitude could not be borne by the Rotterdam municipality alone. Therefore, the involvement of the private sector was foreseen in the form of a public private partnership. The community was to develop the collective elements of the scheme, such as infrastructural facilities, and private parties were to take care of creating the buildings. For the construction of the new bridge the Community counted on a substantial contribution from the national government. To make the entire project attractive for private investors, quality should be the central theme. Flexibility in the allocation of specific grounds as well as the period of development, was regarded as another essential element; changes in the realisation of the various parts should remain possible.

Creating societal support

At this stage, the Kop-van-Zuid scheme was carried by a limited number of people in the TPD, the RCDC and on the city council. To them, to bring together all the different public and private parties whose involvement in developing and realising the project was required, and to secure their commitment, represented a formidable challenge. Communication, applied in a controlled way, was regarded as the most important instrument. High-quality presentations were prepared and given to carefully selected companies of politicians, citizens, opinion leaders, market parties, etcetera. In that way enthusiasm for the project grew steadily, both in administrative and in societal circles.

On the local level there was some anxiety that the project would be regarded first and foremost as a prestige object and realised at the expense of other social programmes. At an early stage residents' organisations from the surrounding neighbourhoods demanded participation, arguing that the project should provide benefits for their troubled town quarters. These neighbour-hoods suffer from much unemployment and accommodate high concentra-tions of foreign citizens with relatively low levels of education. The city council, mindful of problems in other countries with similar schemes when carried out in isolation from their surroundings (notably the London Docklands), credited the arguments. The programme Social Return was therefore created, based on the necessity of an integral vision of the development potential of the entire area, in the perspective of the surrounding town quarters as well as the Kop-van-Zuid project. The aim was to stimulate employment, education and business activities. To secure support from inhabitants and neighbourhood organisations in the southern part of the city was also important for political reasons. A significant portion of the electorate of the political party which traditionally dominated local politics, the social democrats, resided south of the river.

With the gradually obtained support from the public, it became easier to get the required support on local administrative levels. The local administrative culture at the time seems to have facilitated the process. The period has been typified by those involved as one of 'good-fellowship'; informal contacts were important, councillors were relatively easily accessible to directors of municipal services as well as others, problems were preferably solved internally and most councillors were ready to support each others' ideas and projects. The conditions were conducive to a relatively rapid creation of local administrative support and, consequently, relatively speedy decision making. Apart from financial commitment, the municipality also agreed to transfer the Rotterdam Municipal Port Management from its traditional location on the right bank of the river to the Kop-van-Zuid.

Moreover, the administrative culture in Rotterdam facilitated the optimum use of the existing formal and informal contacts with the national administrative apparatus. Two factors seem to have been helpful in that respect. Firstly, the scheme for the Kop-van-Zuid represented a fine example of the new policy approach that was advocated in the recently presented national policy document VINO. A central theme of this policy document is the integrated planning of the various urban functions. The document also provided for the possibility of projects propagating the new approach to be labelled as 'key-projects', making them eligible for financial and procedural government support. Secondly, Rotterdam, as second largest city in the Netherlands and as a major economic centre, was in a relatively powerful position. The Kop-van-Zuid project was submitted by Rotterdam for marking as a 'Key-project'. The national government granted that status.

A difficult item for the national government's assessment of the support to be given appeared to be the new bridge across the river Maas. In the eyes of Rotterdam the new bridge was essential to the entire Kop-van-Zuid scheme. Without it the project would lose its attractivity to investors. But not only the bridge itself was deemed essential, the aesthetical quality of the structure was also considered a vital contribution to the high quality of the Kop-van-Zuid project. To convince the government of the necessity of an 'extra' investment in quality proved difficult at a time when cuts were on spending an important element of national policy. Nevertheless, Rotterdam succeeded in its effort and was granted an amount of 279 million guilders to be spent on the bridge. The national government also committed itself to the project by agreeing to transfer several of its services, such as the Court of Law and the Tax Office, to the Kop-van-Zuid.

The public sector's commitment to the project appears to have been important for securing the commitment of the private sector. A group of private investors undertook to develop the housing of the government services. For the development of another part of the Kop-van-Zuid, the Wilhelminapier, a detailed scheme has been drawn up jointly by the Community and development companies from France, England and the Netherlands. For the development of the various housing projects, the commitment of public and private development companies could be secured.

The decision to start realisation was made by the city council in 1991. The project was accepted by the Province of Zuid-Holland early in 1992 and by the central government halfway 1994. By Dutch standards this is a remarkably short period. The first construction activities started in September 1993. The completion of the entire project is scheduled for 2005.

Realisation of the scheme

After the scheme was accepted by the city council in 1991, a project organisation was set up: the Kop-van-Zuid Project Organisation, headed by a project manager. Within this organisation, a Project Group coordinates the activities of various teams representing relevant municipal Services. The teams control activities, commissioners, tenders, etcetera. The Project Organisation is placed in a neutral position, operating on an equal level with the other municipal services. The decisions made by the Project Organisation cannot be overruled by the directors of the respective services. The project manager comes under the direct responsibility of the councillor for Urban Planning. In that constellation, administrative communication and decision lines are kept short. All external communication about the Kop-van-Zuid project is handled by a 'communication-team', which also provides information about housing and office possibilities in the Kop-van-Zuid.

Neighbourhood organisations are also represented in the Project Organisation. Apart from that formal involvement, these organisations are also concerned in an informal way. When important decisions are about to be taken, informal meetings are organised to provide information and give the opportunity to have a say in the events. That makes for better coordination of activities and limits possible nuisance for neighbouring town quarters. An open communication structure has thus been established, which is considered important for winning and maintaining societal support. The limited number of objections that have been lodged thus far are considered an indication of the effectiveness of this method.

At present about 2,000 of the 5,000 projected houses are under construction and the first of these are already occupied. Of all the houses sold, about half are bought by people from the northern part of town. This is considered important because previously there was very limited migration between the two parts of town, because of social and cultural differences between them, and the natural barrier constituted by the river Maas (Mik, 1989). About one quarter of the projected total office floor area of 400,000 m² is under construction. This figure includes offices intended for the public services as well as for the private sector. The financing of these housing and office projects is entirely in the hands of commercial developers. Of the total projected investment of 4,500 million guilders, about 1,500 million is currently in the realisation phase.

Mutual benefits of the project and the neighbourhoods are pursued. To that end a Project Group for Social Return was established, which tries to recruit local residents for the construction projects and also to find work for them when construction is completed. Jobs in catering, security and cleaning are considered serious options. Investments are also made to raise the level of services in the adjoining town quarters. The idea is that project developers and companies planning to settle on the Kop-van-Zuid have an interest in a rising value of their real estate and therefore in the quality of the living environment. Private partners are not obliged to participate in social-return projects. The programme Social Return is run in the framework of the 'Rotterdam Inner Cities Programme' and is partly financed by the European Commission.

An interesting element of the set-up of the Kop-van-Zuid project is that the development of the area is planned in such a way that several attraction poles are realised at an early stage. For instance, a successful hotel cum restaurant ('Hotel New York') draws large numbers of visitors to the area. The impressively designed new bridge, a new theatre and a special quay for the accommodation of cruise ships, all presently under construction, are to fulfil the same function. That way, the entire project holds the attention of the public.

The realisation of the scheme thus seems to be well under way. Since the decision to start it, several circumstances have changed, however. In 1994, after local elections, the local political constellation shifted. The composition of the city council changed significantly. The once sovereign social democratic party was forced to share the power with other groupings. With regard to the Kop-van-Zuid project, new persons were installed in key positions. In recent years, there have also been changes in position in the administrative apparatus. Since the installation of the new city council the necessity of specific elements of the scheme that had already been decided on, has occasionally been put into question. That was the case, for example, of the financing of the modernisation and relocation of one of the existing bridges in the Kop-van-Zuid area. Although such occasions regard project details, they demand an attentive attitude of the project manager to preserve the integral character of the scheme and to prevent negative publicity that might deter potential investors.

Furthermore, market conditions regarding office and business space have been unfavourable since the start of the realisation phase of the Kop-van-Zuid project. The realisation is carried on in the expectation that the market will recover. Recovery, however, proceeds slower than anticipated. Because of the flexible time schedule, the circumstances do not seem to have had serious consequences so far.

Kop van Zuid and organising capacity: analysis

Vision and strategy

In the early 1980s several ideas were circulating about what to do with the Kop-van-Zuid area. These ideas were predominantly grafted on the extensive town-renovation programme that had been in the 1970s. This programme gradually fell out of favour as an answer to the social-economic problems of Rotterdam. That opened the way for new ideas on urban development to gain ground. In Rotterdam, and later on at the national level, a new approach was adopted based on integrality, quality of the living environment and diversification of both the economic and the social basis of the city. In that climate, new ideas for the Kop-van-Zuid could evolve. In the second half of the 1980s a scheme was developed which can be considered a clear exponent of the new policy approach.

The Kop-van-Zuid scheme was thus developed according to a clear vision of urban development. Central themes in the scheme are *quality*, functional, visual and spatial aspects and *accessibility*, good connections with the metro, tram and highway systems, and a new bridge providing a direct connection with the city centre. Other important characteristics of the plan appear to be its integrality; the phased realisation with a flexible mix through time of housing, leisure and office functions; the extensive attention that is paid to the connections with the surrounding neighbourhoods; and the incorporation of several attraction poles at an early stage of realisation. The latter element concerns recreational attraction poles such as a successful hotel and restaurant as well as public facilities such as the Court of Law. All these elements have made the plan innovative, challenging and attractive to all parties involved.

Administrative structure

When the city council understood the need for a new approach to urban development, it appointed the three sub-councils that were to design the spatial-economic, social and administrative renewal. Councillors were thus forced to look beyond the limits of their own portfolios, which contributed to the acceptance of an integral approach. The installation of the sub-councils has probably also stimulated the development of an administrative culture in which collegiality and arguments as regards content were of great importance.

These circumstances appear to have been essential for the development of the Kop-van-Zuid scheme and the winning of support for it on the local level. Because the entire project was so large, support from higher administrative levels was also required. Therefore, the national government had to be involved in the policy networks.

For the realisation of the project, the embedding of the project organisation is in the administrative structure appears to be very important. By placing the Project Organisation on an equal level with the other municipal services, the project management is provided with important competences and short communication lines.

Strategic networks

Because the magnitude of the Kop-van-Zuid project required the involvement and cooperation of a great number of parties, policy networks in various forms have played an important role in the development of the project. In mobilising these networks, a limited group of key-persons seem to have been decisive. This group represented a link between the administrative level of the municipal services and the city council, and its main instrument was an extensive communication campaign. A broad scope, high-quality presentation techniques and a carefully planned approach to target groups were the most important ingredients of this campaign. Key persons involved assumed an open and flexible attitude; plans could be adapted.

To secure local administrative support was essential: a clear, uniform and consistent message was required. The Municipality had to show that it believed in its own ideas presented in the policy document 'Vernieuwing in Rotterdam'. In securing the required support, two factors appear to have been important. First, the citizens of the southern part of the city represented a significant part of the local electorate. Their support was therefore considered not unimportant. Besides, since the extensive renovation programme of the 1970s, neighbourhood organisations had established themselves as an important party in urban development in Rotterdam. Support from these organisations could be secured by agreeing to their demand that the relations between the Kop-van-Zuid and the surrounding town quarters should be paid attention to achieve 'mutual benefit'. The second important factor seems to have been the administrative culture in which collegiality facilitated swift decision making and the external presentation of a 'uniform message'.

Support of the national government was required among other reasons for the financing of the new bridge across the river Maas. This bridge was considered essential for the involvement of the private sector. At an early stage it was clear that private funding of the bridge was not feasible. As Rotterdam itself could not bear all the costs, it had counted on the national government. A difficult point in securing the commitment of the national government was that Rotterdam had, for its aesthetical qualities, selected an expensive design for the bridge. With the careful communication campaign and the good formal and informal contacts with the central administration, Rotterdam succeeded in propagating enthusiasm for the Kop-van-Zuid scheme as a whole. This enthusiasm, combined with the granted status of 'key-project', and the relatively powerful position of Rotterdam due to its population and economic magnitude, led to a positive decision by the national government.

The commitment by local and national government, both financially and in the form of the agreed transfer of several local and national government services, facilitated the involvement of the private sector. With regard to housing, public housing corporations and private development companies were eager to seize the opportunities offered by the Kop-van-Zuid scheme. With regard to offices and business space, private developers became involved at a somewhat slower pace, owing to difficult market circumstances. However, the agreed transfer of government services to the area facilitated the private development of the first major office buildings. This appears to have been an important first step, which probably stimulated the recent development of several other sites in the area. For the development of the Wilhelminapier a separate PPP has been established, involving the Municipality as well as domestic and foreign development companies.

223

The fact that government commitment was secured prior to pursuing private-sector involvement has proved important to putting the project on track. In Amsterdam a scheme similar to the Kop-van-Zuid project has been developed. This was also a waterfront-development scheme projected on the banks of the IJ (IJ-oever project). As with the Kop-van-Zuid, the idea was to have the area developed by a Public Private Partnership. In Amsterdam, however, communication was mainly directed at the private sector. Support from this sector could not be secured because of insufficient and unclear commitment by both the central government and the municipality. It therefore appears that to establish PPPs in the Netherlands, commitment should first be secured from the public sector and then from the private sector, which tends to be conservatist.

In general, the political conditions and good contacts appear to have actively influenced the different networks towards deciding in favour of the Kop-van-Zuid project. That appears to apply specifically to decisions taken on the national administrative level. The most important element of all in mobilising the networks seems to have been that the Kop-van-Zuid scheme is well elaborated in terms of content.

Leadership

Leadership has played a very important role in the development of the Kop-van-Zuid project. A small group of people in the Town Planning Department, the Rotterdam City Development Corporation and on the city council were the initiators of the idea and have exerted themselves to propagate enthusiasm with all administrative and societal actors whose involvement in the project was required. Communication and an open and flexible attitude were their most important instruments.

Political support

Political conditions have been a factor in the development of the project in various respects. For one thing, a significant part of the electorate of the ruling social democratic party lived in the town quarters surrounding the Kop-van-Zuid area. It was therefore a group to be reckoned with. Their critical but constructive attitude has been influential. For another, the plans fitted nicely into the new attitude towards urban development which had been struck at both the local and the national administrative level. A complicating factor was that the Kop-van-Zuid scheme aimed at costly quality at a time when government policy seemed to be dominated by cuts on spending. However, the fact that Rotterdam is regarded as an area important for the national economy has made its position strong enough to influence decisions on the national level.

Political conditions may change after elections. This happened recently in Rotterdam, where the ruling party lost its former dominance. A new composition of the city council led to the occasional putting into question of the necessity of specific details of the Kop-van-Zuid scheme, which had already been decided on. This required confirmation of commitment to the Kop-van-Zuid project by new persons in key-positions. An attentive attitude of the project management is required to cope with changes in political conditions.

Spatial-economic conditions

Spatial economic conditions have been an inducement to develop the Kop-van-Zuid project. With its strong orientation to the harbour and its related activities, the local economy required a broadening of its basis. The Kop-van-Zuid area has a good potential in that respect. Its waterfront location makes it attractive as a place for both companies and residents to settle. Since the start of the Kop-van-Zuid project, economic conditions have improved as far as housing is concerned. In the Rotterdam region the demand for housing has increased. The demand for office and business space, however, has developed less positively, owing among other things to stagnating economic growth in recent years. Although this was already visible when the Kop-van-Zuid project was taken in hand, the recovery of demand for office space is slower than anticipated.

Performance

The realisation of the project is currently in its fourth year, which is roughly one third of the projected time horizon. In this period about one third of the total projected investments have been carried out. Major infrastructural projects like the new bridge across the river Maas, the new subway station, new tram tracks and a road connection with the ring highway are all under construction. So, the project seems well under way.

The greatest achievement was made, however, in the period preceding the first construction activities. The time period between the first development of the Kop-van-Zuid scheme and the actual start of construction was about seven years. In this period the initially small group of people succeeded in making the ideas they had envisaged real. Because the scheme which

225

emerged after elaboration of the initial ideas was of huge dimensions, many parties with different interests had to be persuaded, often against considerable scepticism. The sceptics could only be swayed after others had shown their clear commitment. Even though circumstances were generally favourable, that the required support could be secured in what is by Dutch standards an exceptionally short period is a remarkable achievement, which indicates a significant organisational ability of Rotterdam.

Conclusion

The dramatic effects of the energy crises during the mid- and late 1970s put an end to the sustainability of the strongly social-oriented policy which had been pursued in Rotterdam since the early 1970s. Rotterdam, like other traditional European harbour and industrial cities, threatened to fall into a serious socio-economic crisis unless the negative trends were energetically opposed. In the course of the 1980s the municipality became aware of the severity of the situation. Action was taken to create favourable circumstances for the development of new ideas. The guiding principle appeared to be an integral approach to the problems. Urban policy was therefore to be directed at the same time at economic, social and administrative renewal. Three sub-councils were formed around these three themes to generate ideas and to mobilise the various municipal services. Furthermore, a commission of external experts was commissioned to advise on tackling persistent unemployment in the city.

The implication is that Rotterdam had thus created a climate in which new ideas could develop and in which administrators were forced to look beyond their traditional policy domains, thereby stimulating an integral view of the issues in hand. Remarkably, while this climate was created, the newly appointed director of the municipal service responsible for town development revealed herself as an energetic generator of new ideas based on an integral approach. In the new administrative climate she could be given a wide berth to develop and elaborate her ideas, one of which concerned the deserted harbour grounds know as the 'Kop-van-Zuid'. In cooperation with a small group of people in her own department and the city council, she succeeded in propagating enthusiasm for the project so that all local actors viewed it as a promising possibility for revitalisation. In that situation commitment of other actors, such as the national government and commercial and public development companies, could be secured. In this process Rotterdam was the director, actively orchestrating the circumstances and the required networks.

The results, the relatively short development and decision period and the realisation largely according to schedule, can be regarded as an impressive proof of the capacity of Rotterdam to organise itself.

If the Kop-van-Zuid project was mostly hatched and launched 'in-house', the ROM-Rijnmond project originated outside Rotterdam. In the late 1980s the national government adopted a new approach to spatial planning, based on the view that economic growth, accessibility and environmental quality should go hand in hand in order to achieve sustainable development. The Rotterdam region was appointed one of the areas where the new policy was to take shape. In this area a tension is evident between mainport development and the quality of the living environment.

During the Kop-van-Zuid process Rotterdam realised that its previous urban policy had laid too strong an emphasis on limiting polluting activities in its region. The environment was of course recognised as an increasingly important location factor, but it should not frustrate harbour and industrial activities which still are a dominant factor in the local economy. A balance between economic development and the environment was therefore considered necessary. Since this was the main objective of the ROM-Rijnmond initiative of the national government, the project can be regarded as an important contribution to an improved location environment in the Rijnmond region and therefore as complementary to the Kop-van-Zuid project. Rotterdam, however, was used to minding its own matters, as is also illustrated by the Kop-van-Zuid process. The first reaction of the city to the initiative of the Ministry of VROM to develop the ROM-Rijnmond project was therefore hesitant. Uncertainty about the project objectives and the fact that Rotterdam had not yet developed a strategic plan for the harbour were other factors which contributed to a hesitant reaction.

With the strategic port plan eventually completed, Rotterdam participated in the process in order to limit the involvement of the national government in regional matters. Besides, the project objectives were gradually becoming clearer and in essence was considered important. By active participation Rotterdam succeeded to a large extent in taking over the initiative. For instance, the strategic port plan was accepted as an important element of the ROM-Rijnmond project. Nevertheless, Rotterdam had to accept the fact that other parties, such as the Province of Zuid-Holland, assumed important parts for themselves.

Because the issues concerned the entire Rijnmond area, the involvement of the other Rijnmond communities was required. The attitude of Rotterdam, which was used to handling port matters itself, posed problems of cooperation with the other communities. Gradually, however, Rotterdam realised that a more cooperative attitude was required, also with a view to other problems to be solved outside the scope of ROM-Rijnmond. The project seems to have helped towards the establishment of the OOR consultative body. With the major obstacles removed, the region succeeded, in cooperation with the national government and the Province, in putting ROM-Rijnmond on track in a relatively short period. This reveals considerable organising capacity. The ROM-Rijnmond project has strengthened this capacity in a regional context, more or less institutionalised in the form of the OOR consultative body.

The development of both the ROM-Rijnmond and the Kop-van-Zuid projects seems due to a unique combination of only a very few people. On the one hand this is an intriguing observation, on the other hand there seems to be no blueprint for the establishment of such a unique combination. That many projects are less successful than the two discussed here, might well have to do with the fact that unique combinations of key persons are far from common. Another fact to consider is that key people may change positions, thereby stripping a project of its 'bearers'. That is what seems to have happened to the ROM-Rijnmond project. This long-term project, which is now in its realisation phase, has trouble maintaining its momentum. Apart from key people having gone to another position, there are other problems. One is that thus far, the project has not produced any clear, visible results. Another problem is that the project management has not been given adequate competences. Maintaining the momentum might also be hampered by the fact that the citizens of the region are not actively involved. Their involvement could have provided a broader support for such matters as the new land-reclamation scheme and the attempt to decrease the use of private cars in the region. It might also have made it easier to secure financial commitment from the business community, for instance for the financing of environmental projects. Involvement of the public might have made businesses more worried about their environmental image.

Although Rotterdam and the region have shown the ability to organise, the challenge is to maintain the momentum once developments have been put in motion.

Abbreviations used

ROM   Spatial Planning and Environment
OOR   Rijnmond Municipalities Consultative Body
RMPM   Rotterdam Municipality Port Management
VINO   Fourth Policy Report on Physical Planning in the Netherlands
VINEX   Fourth Policy Report on Physical Planning Extra
SVV   Policy Report on Transport
VROM   Ministry of Spatial Planning and the Environment
NMP   National Plan for Environmental Policy
V&W   Ministry of Transport
TPD   Rotterdam Town Planning Department
RCDC   Rotterdam City Development Corporation

Notes

[1] Co-author: drs. P.W. Poppink
[2] ROM: Ruimtelijke Ordening en Milieu (Spatial Planning and Environment)
[3] On the national level, the 'growth-core policy', aiming at guided deconcentration of town leavers to a limited number of suburbs (through the allocation of housing contingents), was replaced by a 'compact-town policy', by which extensive housing locations were allocated to the major cities.
[4] In 1992, Amsterdam accounted for 5.7 million square metres and The Hague for 4.5 million square metres of office floor area (VGM, 1992).
[5] This part is based on L. van den Berg, A.H. van Klink and J. van der Meer (1993), *Governing Metropolitan Regions*, Aldershot: Avebury
[6] ROM: Spatial Planning and Environment
[7] In 1992 Rotterdam had a population of about 600,000 while the second largest cummunity, Vlaardingen, had a population of about 73,000. All other communities have smaller populations.
[8] Nationaal Milieubeleidsplan, 1989
[9] Voortgangsrapportage 1994 ROM-Rijnmond, Hoofdrapport, 1994

9 Turin[1]

Introduction

The city of Turin is situated in northern Italy and belongs to the 'First Italy', which is the traditional industrial heartland of the country. Turin is well known as capital of the FIAT company. Since the late 1970s, the automotive industry all over the world has been highly dynamic, facing new methods of production, new markets and new competitors. The region of Turin has to cope with the spatial-economic and socio-economic implications of these dynamics, such as the closure of factories, the vacancy of outdated industrial sites and the unemployment of industrial workers.

The subject of this chapter is the way in which the city and the metropolitan region of Turin have organised themselves to cope with the restructuring process in its economy. The chapter sketches a general profile of Turin and describes the main characteristics of the spatial-economic development of Turin. The administrative structure is discussed next. Thereafter, attention is focused on two specific projects: the restructuring of the Lingotto complex, a former production site of FIAT, and the development of the Environmental Park. The chapter finishes with some general conclusions.

Profile

Geography

Turin is located in the Po-valley, to the left of the river. The French border is at a distance of 80 kilometres, while Switzerland is some 100 kilometres away. Turin is the capital of the Piemonte region. Piemonte has a highly industrialised economy, with car manufacturing and mechanical industries in Turin, information technology in Ivrea and biotechnology in Verbano. The city of Turin covers an area of 130.7 square kilometres. With 955,827 inhabitants at present, the density of population is 7,342 persons per square kilometre. Its metropolitan region comprises 53 municipalities and has some 1.8 million inhabitants. The phenomenon of suburbanisation is relatively recent in the case of Turin. In the period between 1981 and 1991, 13.8% of the population was lost. As result of the suburbanisation, a metropolitan region has arisen. Because much employment is concentrated in the city of Turin, intensive commuting traffic has developed: every day, some 203,000 persons move to the city centre from the suburbs.

History

Turin was founded in 30 B.C. under Augustus. In the year 1560, the Duke of Savoy retrieved Piemonte from the French and decided to move his capital from Chambéry to Turin. This decision was based on the strategic location of Turin in the foothills of the Alps, as an entry-point to Italy. To supply the Savoy army with weapons, an arms industry arose in the city. In 1861, Italy was unified and Turin was relieved of its role as state capital. The administration was moved from Turin first to Florence and then to Rome. In the industrial climate already existing, activities related to the manufacturing of textile, food and automobiles developed in the second half of the 19th century.

Turin: capital of the automotive industry

In 1899, Giovanni Agnelli, born in Turin, established a car manufacturing company in the city. It was to grow into the multinational FIAT (Fabbrica Italiana Automobili Torino). In the first decades of this century, besides FIAT, some thirty other car producers were located in Turin. In 1905, FIAT sold 250 cars; within ten years, sales had grown to 7,000 cars. Thanks to the World Expo in Turin in 1911, the Italian car got international fame. To cope with the ever increasing demand for cars, Fiat built two large plants in the Turin area: Lingotto (1922) and Mirafiori (1936).

The automotive industry employed some 9,000 persons in Turin in the 1920s (Gabert, 1964, p.124). In 1960, FIAT had over 78,000 employees in the Turin region (some 30 per cent of total employment in the province) (Gabert, 1964, p.169). In the late 1970, FIAT employed as many as 150,000 persons in the Turin region, of which 60,000 worked in the Mirafiori plant alone. The growth of industrial activities in Turin resulted in a strong demand for labour. As a consequence, immigration from southern Italy came up. The population of the city grew from some 300,000 inhabitants in 1921 to 700,000 in 1940 and 1,200,000 in 1974.

From the development of FIAT all kinds of related activity emerged in the Turin region, like the production of components and activities in research & development. One example of the latteris the design of cars. With Italdesign, Pininfarina and Bertone, Turin possesses a set of services in car design that is unique in the world. The emergence of related activities resulted in the rise of an industrial complex based on car manufacturing in Turin. From the 1960s onwards, the FIAT company diversified into new directions, such as producing air planes and publishing newspapers (for example *La Stampa*). Many of these new activities had their basis also in Turin.

FIAT not only dominated the metropolitan economy of Turin, it also was an important factor in the city's social life, as the company financed all kind of facilities. For instance, FIAT organised bus services in the region to provide efficient transport for its workers. The company also invested in the education system to have well educated and trained workers at its disposal. The Turin-based management school of ISVOR-FIAT is an example.

The restructuring in the car industry

The motor vehicle industry has been one of the key manufacturing industries of the 20th century. However, in the late 1970s the growth of the car industry stagnated worldwide, owing to the oil crises, the economic recession and the societal attention to energy savings (Dicken, 1986, p.279). Besides, new car producers came up in Newly Industrialising Countries (NICs) in Asia.

To fulfil new customer demand and to cope with new competitors, the established car producers had to reorganise their production systems. That held also for FIAT and other Italian car manufacturers. They streamlined their relations with subcontractors, automated their production systems and reduced their labour force. Between 1979 and 1984, 130,000 jobs were lost in the automotive industry in Italy (Dicken, 1986, p.294). FIAT reduced its labour force by 35 per cent. As a consequence of the geographical concentration of the Italian car industry in the Turin region, the employment reduction was felt heavily here. Since 1971, some 65,000 jobs have been lost. For instance, while the Mirafiori factory employed some 60,000 workers in the 1950s, it offers work for only 20,000 persons nowadays. Besides the loss of employment, industrial sites in the city were abandoned as they became redundant and unsuitable for modern production techniques.

The loss of production activities in Turin was caused not only by the reorganisation of existing plants, but also by the relocation of activities to other places with more competitive location circumstances. In the case of FIAT, the national government pushed the company to open production facilities in southern regions in Italy, to stimulate their economic development.

Despite fundamental changes in the market and the production system, the Turin region is still the industrial heart of Italy. With just over five per cent of the national population, the region supplies almost 10 per cent of the industrial employees. FIAT has some 80,000 employees in Piemonte. FIAT and Turin still have strong mutual links. However, the relationship has shifted from manufacturing activities to service activities. At present, Turin functions as a major intelligence centre for car design, production and marketing in the world. For instance, the production sites in Southern Italy make use of specialists from Turin. Its know-how has attracted foreign producers of cars and automotive components.

Economic diversification

The FIAT company and its industrial complex have been recognised as an asset for the Turin economy. However, as many activities in the FIAT Group are footloose, traditional manufacturing is vulnerable to changes in the global economy and their added value is diminishing in terms of employment, there is a need for economic diversification in Turin. To strengthen the economic base of the city is also required in order to solve the problems that have originated from the transition towards a post-industrial economy. Main problems are the relative high unemployment (14 per cent) and the large reservoir of vacant land in the city (about one tenth of the city's area). Given the problems related to the economic transition and the negative effects of the economic recession of 1992-1994, Turin was defined in 1993 as objective II area in the framework of the European Structural Funds.

The strategy to diversify the economy is mainly aimed at strengthening the service sector. Services offer work for 56 per cent of the professional population of Turin. That is significantly less than in other cities in Italy and Europe. The service sector of Turin consists out of various activities. The city houses the head office of some large Italian banks. Turin is also the headquarters of three of the country's ten major insurance companies and some publishing firms. Finally, car design can be categorised as a major service sector in Turin. With respect to the banking sector, it is important to notice that the public banks in Italy nowadays are governed by foundations. In the foundations of Turin based banks, the city of Turin and the Chamber of Commerce are represented. The economic structure in terms of employment in the various sectors is presented in the table below.

Table 1
Employment in Turin (city and metropolitan region) and Piemonte (1991)

	City of Turin	Metropolitan region	Region of Piemonte
Total number of jobs	394,82	736,26	1,808,27
Share of sectors:			
Agriculture & energy	1	4	7
Manufacturing	38	37	35
Construction	5	6	7
Trade	19	17	17
Transport	5	5	5
Education	5	6	5
Health care	5	4	5
Public sector	6	6	6
Other services	16	15	13

Source: IRES

The strategy of diversification has not produced many concrete results yet. A sound alternative for traditional manufacturing activities has not been found. Diversification of the economy appears to be difficult, for one thing, because Turin does not have a tradition as a service centre and location of small and medium-sized companies. The mentality of its workforce is oriented towards technology rather than commerce. An important barrier to the attraction of new activities in services and high-grade industrial activities is their demand for a modern location climate. Turin has much space available, but the land is polluted as a result of industrial use in the past. High investments are required to clean it and restructure it for new uses. The local government lacks financial means for these investments. The municipal policy aims at involving the owners of the land in the restructuring of land.

To stimulate international companies to locate in Turin, a new airport was opened in December 1993. It has a capacity of over three million passengers a year. The airport will get a railway connection with the city. In a few years, Turin will be linked to the European high-speed railway system (Lyon, Milan and Rome).

Town planning

Town planning in Turin has a long history. In 1959 the first town plan was approved. It was based on fascist law and had a hierarchical and purely economic orientation. Socialists criticised the lack of attention for public transport, the historic inner city and new living quarters. To protect citizens against negative effects of strong economic growth on their quality of life, a new town planning law was passed in 1968. It provided for a city to have 18 square metres of public space per citizen (Turin had only five square metres). To meet the new law, Turin developed a new town plan, whose aim was to relocate industries to surrounding places to create more public space. The left-wing opposition opposed the plan, as they feared land speculation and loss of employment in the city. In 1975, communists came into power in the municipal council. They decided to develop a new urban planning scheme. A central element of the new plan was the improvement of public transport as a means to balance land values in different parts of the city. However, the required investments in public transport could not be found and the plan failed.

In 1985, again (!) a start was made with a new town planning scheme. That has resulted in the present plan, which was finally approved in May 1995. Just to have reached this stage in the planning process is considered a success in Turin. This success is due to three factors. First, the local politics saw the importance of a town planning scheme as a framework to coordinate various projects in the city and as an example of the renewed administrative capability of the municipality. Second, the plan was developed with a bottom-up perspective and took the present structure as starting-point.

Finally, the planning was carried out by professionals with an independent position.

The implementation of the plan (the *Piano Regolatore Generale di Torino*) will involve the investment of 28,000 billion lires. The plan envisages the reconversion of some 8.5 million square metres of land in the city. The land has been segmented along three axes in order to integrate as many parts of the city as possible in the projects. The following axes are considered:

- the east axis along the river Po;
- the central axis through the city centre and the railway system;
- the west axis along the planned ring road.

The central axis - the so-called *Spina Centrale* - covers an area with a length of 6 kilometres. It consists of space that has fallen vacant after the closure of industrial activities and as a result of the tunnelling of fifteen kilometres of railway line, which is in progress. In the Spina Centrale, various projects will be undertaken. They will be coordinated in order to develop a logical chain of activities with maximum positive effect on the city. Important elements of the Spina Centrale are the development of new parks, the construction of office space, the building of dwellings and retail space, and the realisation of a new campus for the Polytechnic. In the central axis, half the space will get a public destination.

To realise the projects, the collaboration of the land owners in the development axis is essential. To get their cooperation, the municipality operates an innovative system of exchange of land and property rights. The municipality transfers building rights to the owners of land in exchange for the ownership of land with a public destination. Private owners are allowed to build up seventy per cent of their land in the development area. They are also allowed to sell their building rights. Owners of land have to develop plans to rebuild their area together, in accordance with the directives of the planning scheme. Because the greater part of the land is in the hands of just a few industrial companies, the transfer of land progresses relatively well. The vision and persuasive power of the local government have also contributed to the progress made already.

The planning for the central axis incorporates the Lingotto project (discussed further on). Formerly, the reconversion of the Lingotto factory was not an element in any municipal planning. As elements of the central axis (especially Spina III) as well as Lingotto aim at the development of space for offices and research activities, there is a risk of competition between the two. That holds in particular for the relocation of laboratories and other facilities of the Turin Polytechnic: both the Spina Centrale and the

Lingotto project have opted for their location. To prevent such competition, coordination between the projects is required. To coordinate and phase them in time requires a strong local government. However, the municipal instrument to phase projects was removed by the Berlosconi government in 1994 to give more freedom to the market. At present, the municipality can phase projects only without legal instruments, for example through negotiations with the project developers and through phasing municipal investments.

Administrative structure

General

Italy has four levels of administration: state, regions, provinces and municipalities. This administrative structure gives the Italian state a decentralised unitised nature. However, in practice, the Italian government is very centralised: 'Rome' has a say in many decisions. Directly through representatives of the state, or indirectly through enterprises in which the state holds a share. These state shareholdings, either as a legacy from Fascism or acquired in the 1960s, involve the state right across economic life.

In Italy, there are twenty regions. The responsibilities of the regions are in administrative supervision of local government, public order, public services (such as health care, regional transport and inland navigation), economic development (tourism, road maintenance, agriculture) and environment (urban planning, protection of flora and fauna). The regions manage one tenth of all public expenditure in Italy (Mény, 1990, p.252). In the future, a state reform aimed at decentralising power to the regions may be carried through.

Alongside the regions, provinces and municipalities function. The one hundred Italian provinces have few competencies of their own. They are comparable to the French departments. The provinces share competences in environmental protection, social services and transport with the regions and municipalities. In Italy, there are 8,102 municipalities. Traditionally, they have a mere executive role. There are no administrative structures for metropolitan regions, although a law on metropolitan government has been approved (Ferlaino and Piperno, 1994). Given the large number of municipalities, the weak provinces and the absence of metropolitan authorities, local government in Italy is fragmented and lacks power to deal adequately with complex problems.

In Italy, public administration has traditionally been relatively weak. The political instability, expressed in many changes of coalitions and responsible persons, has been a major cause. Given the weak position of the government in Italy, the primate of decision making has been in the private sector. Owing to the unbalanced division of power between public and private sector, the relationship between the government and the business sector is not well developed.

Under influence of fundamental changes in economy and society, it has become clear that the private sector cannot manage the renewal of the Italian economy alone any more. The questions become more diverse and complex. To guide the development of the economy in a strategic and sustainable way and to unite diverse interests, the need for a strong and stabile government at all administrative levels is increasing.

One way to strengthen the power of local government has been the introduction of a new act on the appointment of mayors, which came into force in 1993. Previously, mayors were elected by municipal boards. Those elected as mayor were the leaders of the majority in the councils. Consequently, the function of mayor was a political one. The new law orders that mayors are to be elected directly by the population, simultaneously with the election of the municipal board. It also provides for persons who are not affiliated with a political party to seek election. The mayor cannot be sent home by the council, otherwise than by the council's resignation. The new law seems to have given a more independent status to the mayor and have brought more administrative power to local government.

Administrative circumstances in Turin

Turin was one of the first large cities in Italy with a mayor directly elected by the population. The mayor, Valentino Castellani, who had been a professor at the Polytechnic of Turin, is backed by three fifths of the municipal council. He has a strategic position in local policy making. Since he has been elected by the population, the mayor has to maintain close relationships with the citizens. He is highly visible in Turin and plays an important role in communicating municipal policies to the population.

Since 1993, in Italy aldermen can only be appointed from outside the municipal council. In May 1995, a national law provided the large cities to extend the number of aldermen from eight to twelve. The recruitment of non-political experts as aldermen is considered another way to professionalise the city's administration and to strengthen its administrative power. Managers of municipal services can be recruited from outside the local corps of civil servants too. That this last measure has met with resistance from the civil servants goes without saying.

Turin has been the first city in Italy with an alderman responsible for economic development. He was appointed in May 1995. The absence of an alderman and a Department for Economic Affairs illustrates the traditional orientation of municipalities in Italy to the passive execution of rules and regulations. As the city of Turin started its involvement in economic development only recently, the municipality has no staff of experts available. Therefore, it makes often use of private consultants. The municipality also lacks policy tools of proven effectiveness.

Besides a Department for Economic Affairs, the city of Turin recently created a Department for Environment and Sustainable Development. This department is responsible for, among other things, the project Torino Citta d'Acqua, the architectural quality of the city, energy conservation programs and pollution reduction programmes. The department also leads the Environmental Park project.

Despite the development of a functional urban region around Turin in the past decades as result of suburbanisation, the region of Turin lacks a metropolitan government. The present relations between the municipalities in the region are characterised by competition. To govern the metropolitan region and to prevent intergovernmental conflicts, the Turin region needs a form of metropolitan authority. As the law on metropolitan government cannot be used yet, the establishment of technical committees to coordinate individual (infrastructural) projects in the region has been proposed. Notwithstanding the competition between Turin and its suburbs, the contacts between the city and the region of Piemonte are well developed.

Like other Italian towns, Turin has been hit seriously by the financial reform of the state. The share of state subsidies in the municipal income has declined from eighty to fifty per cent. Local taxation, such as tax on real estate, has become more important as source of income. However, the decrease of transfers from the central government cannot be balanced by an increase in local tax income. Turin's tax base is relatively stable.

owing to the economic downturn of the city in the last few years, buildings in the city have decreased in value and only a few new buildings have been constructed. Therefore, the base for taxation has caved in. Given the reduction of state subsidies and the contraction of the tax base, the total income of the municipality has declined.

The dominance of FIAT in Turin stretches to the city's government. The municipality maintains close relations with the company. Some discussion partners have indicated that the relation between the city and FIAT needs to be examined critically. That the city is able to follow its own course, appeared recently when FIAT was passed over in the supplier selection of wagons for the new subway system of the town.

Local politicians are expected to regain some of their credibility in the future through the success of the present 'business-government'. That will not change the political arena, as there is consensus on the future development of the city among the political parties. The opinion prevails that the main strategies of the municipalities will continue after the elections of 1997, whatever the political colour of the majority in the municipal council.

A hundred projects after five years

In 1995, IRES Piemonte (Instituto Ricerche Economico-Sociali) concluded a qualitative evaluation of 100 projects related to urban development and infrastructure in the region of Piemonte. Projects of both public and private actors were incorporated in the evaluation. According to the researchers, the progress of many projects investigated had not been smooth in the last five years. In some cases, strategic frameworks are lacking and implementation procedures unclear. What with long decision times, competition among actors involved (also competition among different public entities), lack of funding, and premature changes in project schemes, the implementation of many projects proceeds inefficiently. For lack of administrative power in public organisations, the projects with the highest success rate in the former days were those which did not require cooperation between the private and public sectors.

From the study, four types of ingredients are required for a smooth project development:

– legal framework. The legal framework in Italy requires streamlining and a clearer definition of responsibilities and competences. Present decision making is characterised by non-coordinated actions of autonomous actors.
– know-how. The Italian administration lacks knowledge. Government agencies normally turn to external sources, such as consultants. This might entail a loss of initiative on the part of the public sector.

- finance. As a result of the financial crisis in the Italian public system, many projects lack resources. Private funds should be tapped. One precondition to deal more efficiently with available funds is timing between financial and legal procedures.
- political support. At present, support from politicians for individual projects is difficult to secure. Minority groups can have great influence and can easily change a project's schedule. That makes private participation difficult to realise.

One recommendation of the IRES research is to improve each of the four ingredients mentioned above. Besides, finance, know-how, legal structure and political support have to be combined in a better and more explicit way in project development processes. Another recommendation was to stimulate cooperation between the public actors in the projects. Trust among the actors provides the basis for the success of the project. For public-public partnerships, two ways are open: direct cooperation by the actors involved or indirect collaboration through a mediator.

The reconversion of Lingotto

Lingotto is the name of a former plant of FIAT, located in the southern outskirts of the city. The plant was built between 1916 and 1922. The Lingotto site covers an area of 280,000 square metres. The main building of Lingotto is an impressive example of the industrial architecture of the beginning of this century. It has two longitudinal bodies, five stories high, 24 metres wide and over 500 metres long. The different stages of the car production were located in a logical order in both bodies. On the building's roof, a track for testing cars is situated. Next to the industrial site, a railway complex is situated. Just before World War II, the plant employed some 8,000 workers and produced some 53,000 cars per year.

In 1982, the manufacturing of automobiles in Lingotto was ended in the framework of the reorganisation of FIAT's car production. The announcement of the closure of Lingotto resulted in a strike among employees and much commotion in the Turin society, as the factory was the very picture of the presence of FIAT in the city and the importance of car production for Turin. Closing Lingotto gave citizens the impression that FIAT washed its hands of the city.

Given the opposition in society against its decision to close Lingotto, the socio-economic problems that resulted from the reorganisation of car production in the city, and the close relation of the Agnelli family with Turin, the FIAT company took the initiative to give Lingotto new functions. The fact that the State Department of Culture decided that the Lingotto site should be kept as a heritage of architecture, was an impediment to the renovation. FIAT invited twenty architects to present their ideas about the future of the complex. The company consulted the municipality to discuss the new functions of the complex. Over 140,000 persons visited the display of the architects' visions in Turin. To show the potentials of the new use, concerts, exhibitions and conferences were held in an experimental way in the building. In 1990, FIAT chose the design of Renzo Piano to transform the factory into a polyfunctional service centre. The city council approved the plan for revitalisation of Lingotto. However, only with the new urban plan became the project incorporated in the spatial-economic strategy of the town.

To undertake the revitalisation and to manage the transformed complex, a public-private partnership has been established: Lingotto srl. Main shareholders in this partnership are FIAT (54 per cent), the municipality of Turin (6 per cent), the S. Paolo bank (10 per cent), the insurance company Toro Assicurazioni (10 per cent) and the railway company (10 per cent). The representation of the railway company is based on its ownership of the land of the nearby railway complex. The city of Turin has invested 3 billion lires in the Lingotto project. To stimulate congresses and tradefairs in Lingotto, Expo 2000 has been established. This is a public-private partnership, in which FIAT, the Society of Industrial Enterprises, the region of Piemonte and the Chamber of Commerce have shares.

Since 1990, the basic infrastructure of the Lingotto complex has been renewed. An exhibition centre of 50,000 square metres has been realised as well as a conference centre of 23,000 square metres. The complex boasts a panoramic VIP-lounge, a four star hotel with 240 rooms, a heliport and parking facilities for 5,000 cars. In the building, some 40,000 square metres for office space have been developed. The first floor of the complex consists of eighty shops with a total area of 70,000 square metres and situated along an internal arcade. The shops will be opened in Spring 1996. With its new functions, the Lingotto complex is planned to work as an engine of the tertiary sector. Up to now, nearly 1,000 billion lires have been invested (1995 prices).

The big commercial success for Lingotto has so far failed. The economic recession of the last years is mainly to blame for this. Only a small portion of the office space is rented at the moment. A number of tradefairs have been held and several large conferences organised in Lingotto, but these activities cannot make good the investments. The ambition to develop a technological park for research activities of Turin's Polytechnic and other research institutes could not yet be realised yet on account of financial problems of the government and the supply of alternative locations for these activities in the Turin area.

Besides the general economic situation, the location of the Lingotto complex seems to be a reason for the lagging commercial success. The former factory is located alongside a residential quarter in relatively unattractive surroundings. The quarter was built in the 1950s to supply dwellings for workers of the Lingotto plant. Lingotto lies at four kilometres from the inner city and on the opposite of the town from the airport. As a consequence, Lingotto is relatively badly accessible for (international) visitors[2]. It is planned to connect the Lingotto complex with the nearby railway station via a light railway. However, this connection will be ready only after the year 2000. The unfavourable location of Lingotto can be considered a handicap from the start.

The enormous investments required to transform the complex and the disappointing commercial results induced Lingotto srl to undertake a financial restructuring in 1995. The tradefair and the conference centre have been sold to FIAT for 360 billion lires. For another 300 billion lires the space used for the hotel, offices and shops have been sold to a newly created company, in which some shareholders of Lingotto srl are represented. The money received from the sales has been used by the project organisation to get new loans. To strengthen the commercial basis of the project, FIAT plans to relocate part of its offices to Lingotto.

Among the population of Turin, the reconversion of the Lingotto factory is a delicate subject. That many citizens take a critical attitude towards the project has several grounds. Some of the opposition stems from the closure of the factory in 1982, which was a smack in the face of the population. The criticism is also related to the fact that the project is not embedded in its surroundings. In the quarter live many retired FIAT employees. They have a 'natural' critical attitude towards the project and they do not see any (economic) advantages to it. The last source of opposition is the absence of commercial success from the project for some time.

The above analysis indicates that the Lingotto project has come to a new stage in its development process. The time seems to have come for a better spatial and social integration of the project in the city. To secure the utilisation of its potential, the project should be coordinated with other projects in the town and the accessibility of the location should be improved. In addition, the population of the surrounding quarter should be involved in developing additional activities around the complex with positive spin-off on its surroundings.

Organising capacity and the reconversion of Lingotto: analysis

The challenge and the need for organising capacity

To use outdated industrial sites for sustainable economic growth is one of the general challenges of the city of Turin: about one tenth of the city's acreage is available for new activities and there is a great need to broaden the city's economic base. For the FIAT company the challenges have been to find a new purpose for its outdated factory and to keep the support of the population. The public and private challenges have converged in the development of the Lingotto project in the late 1980s. The Lingotto polyfunctional centre is planned to work as an engine for the development of the tertiary sector in Turin.

Given the proposed function, the reconversion of Lingotto needs to be regarded as a strategic project for the city. The project is also complex, given its peripherical location in the city, its impact on the surrounding district, its position in the international market of conferences and tradefairs, and the potential conflicts with other projects in Turin. As the population is not convinced yet of the its appropriateness and importance, the implementation of the project is also rather delicate. The strategic, complex and delicate nature of the Lingotto project makes a high level of organising capacity indispensable for its successful implementation in the city's economic, social and spatial structure. In the phases of problem recognition and project design, the private sector took the lead in the organising efforts. Now that it has become clear that the project needs to be embedded better in the city, more is expected from the public sector as an organising entity.

Spatial-economic conditions

Fundamental economic and technological changes induced industrial companies to reorganise their production and to close factories in the Turin region. In the city itself, many buildings became empty and large plots of land became vacant. Besides the land that has fallen vacant, the transition to a post-industrial era has resulted in a high rate of unemployment in the Turin region. The economic recession of the last few years has worsened the employment situation. In 1995, the unemployment rate was over 14 per cent.

245

The vacancy of land and the unemployment are both a threat as well as an opportunity for the city. They might affect the quality of life negatively and put off new investors. However, the vacant land and the unemployed workers can also be considered unexploited potentials for the city. They can be used to develop and house new activities. In that line of thought, the Lingotto project was developed in the late 1980s.

Political support

During the phases of design and realisation of the Lingotto project, the Turin city government did not distinguish itself from the administrative situation in Italy in general: chaos, instability, unreliability, nepotism and short-term orientation were keywords for the town's government in the former days. Because of its weak position and the strong (financial) involvement of FIAT, the municipality could play only a minor role in the Lingotto project. It just fulfilled the necessary legal procedures and took a share in the project organisation, but the municipality failed to embed the project in the city.

The physical reconversion of Lingotto has now been realised for a large part. The project seems to have entered a new phase: social support needs to be enforced and the project needs to be better integrated in the town's spatial-economic structure. The private sector cannot undertake this alone. The municipality seems to have to play a key role and can do so, because political conditions have altered recently. The direct election of the mayor by the population and the appointment of non-political aldermen have changed the administrative situation. The city of Turin has professionalised its management. Consequently, it has strengthened its administrative power in such a way that it will be able to guide the further development of the Lingotto project.

Vision and strategy

The FIAT company has been the main stakeholder in the project. It initiated the project, invited architects to develop plans for new functions, and chose the concept of Renzo Piano. Therefore, the plan on which the reconversion of Lingotto is based can be considered mostly a private vision. The community's only involvement in the planning was that citizens were invited to visit the display of the architects' visions and the concerts that were held in the building. From the start, the municipality has supported the vision of the project initiator, because the municipality expected that project to make an unique contribution to the city's location climate for service activities.

The goal of the Lingotto project is to preserve the old factory and to add facilities, like an exhibition hall, conference rooms and a hotel, to the service infrastructure of Turin. The ultimate aim is to make the former factory function as an engine for the tertiary sector of the town. The strategy designed is to reconvert the factory in a few years and with the help of private and public partners into a modern service centre. According to criticasters, the project has not sprung from a strategic plan, but is merely due to the generosity of FIAT. That cannot be denied, given the enormous amount of money invested by this company.

The strategic aim of the project is clear and will have a profound effect on the position of Turin as an international service centre. However, the project is handicapped by a lack of integrality in its planning. The Lingotto project has not been developed with an eye to the existing spatial-economic structure in the city and the direct surroundings of the Lingotto site. Neither has the project be coordinated with the other projects in the town and the metropolitan region. Thus Lingotto runs the risk of developing into a stand-alone 'island of glamour services' in the town, which might be detrimental to its commercial potential. To prevent such a development, the municipality has taken the initiative to incorporate the project in the new town planning scheme.

The role of formal administrative entities

Its relative weak position in political, organisational and financial terms and its inward orientation have prevented the local government from participating strongly in the project in the past few years. The government has had a rather modest role in the project and can be characterised as facilitator. The municipality has taken a share in the project organisation Lingotto srl and has looked after the fulfilment of legal procedures. The need better to integrate the project in the city seems to entail in the near future a shift in the municipality's role from facilitating the realisation of the project towards guiding the integration of the Lingotto project in the city.

Leadership

Many networks are centred around one actor, who has 'economic control' (Ohmae, 1989). It goes without saying that in the case of the Lingotto project FIAT has been the leading actor. It was the owner of the Lingotto site and had the financial means to undertake the reconversion. Its financial strength and strong position in the city gave the company the power to carry out the renovation efficiently. Now that the project has nearly left the phase of design and realisation, another type of leadership seems required to integrate the project in the city.

Strategic networks

As said before, Italy has for many decades been governed by rather informal networks of private industries. That has also been the case of the city of Turin. The Lingotto reconversion project has been supported by a strong policy network led by the private sector. Otherwise, many of the actors in the network have a public nature, as they are state-owned. That holds for example for the banks and the national railway company. The policy network has been formalised in the project organisation Lingotto srl, which has been responsible for the realisation of the project and the exploitation of the reconverted building. Its responsibility does not exceed the territory of the Lingotto site. The network recently changed its constitution after the financial restructuring that was carried through.

Although the municipality is a shareholder of Lingotto srl and thus directly involved in the project, for the interface between the project and the local government a special committee has been established. This permanent committee studies legal procedures and discusses other matters. Both the municipality and the project organisation Lingotto srl have a seat on this committee. Lingotto srl considers the relationship with the municipality positively: whenever necessary, the municipal organisation has properly collaborated.

Performance

The incentive to start the Lingotto project was the social resistance against the closure of the factory and the decision of the State Department of Culture to protect the site as a cultural heritage. The reconversion of Lingotto is a very important project in the revitalisation of Turin. The results of the physical reconversion are already impressive and worth seeing. It is expected that the project can have a substantial spin-off effect on the metropolitan economy. However, up to now, the success of the project for its investors and for the Turin economy has not yet become apparent. That is no surprise, given the long pay-off time of large renovation projects in general and the present unfavourable economic climate in Turin. The absence of commercial return from the project has reinforced the negative feelings among the population towards the project.

For Lingotto to become an engine of the economy in the near future, the project should be integrated in the city's spatial-economic structure. The actors involved in the project have not given enough attention to that aspect. As a consequence, the project is hampered by inadequate accessibility, unattractive surroundings and potential conflicts with other projects in the city. The lack of integration can be explained by the fact that to reach integrality was not the direct responsibility of the private partners and that the municipality lacked power and know-how to enforce it.

The integration of the project has been neglected not only in spatial-economic terms, but also in social terms. The population is hardly involved in the development of the project. Given the delicate history of the project (the first factory of FIAT, the very picture of the presence of FIAT in the city), the lack of public involvement in the project should be considered a serious shortcoming in the project development. This failure can again be explained by the dominance of the private sector in the project. On the other hand, as other case studies have shown, neither is the involvement of the public sector a guarantee for the social acceptance of projects.

Now the time seems to have come to put the project in a broader perspective. The incorporation of the project in the town plan has been a first step. The establishment of a new management team in the municipality can be considered to supply the momentum to change the project's position. With a stronger and more professional government, private and public power can be rebalanced to lead the further development of the project. With a more public orientation, the project's position in the city can be considered better. That should bring a sustainable contribution of the Lingotto project to the economy of Turin within reach.

The development of the Environmental Park

In 1993, Turin was assigned the status of objective-II area in the framework of the European Structural Funds. Four of the ten districts of the town met the objective II criteria. In order to benefit from this status, Turin started to develop projects. The municipality organised meetings with the business society and non-commercial organisations to define projects. Three of the proposed projects were elaborated by special committees: the relocation of laboratories of the Polytechnic to Lingotto, the development of a multimedia training park, and the development of an Environmental Park. This last project appeared to be the most serious and realistic. The project was presented to the European Union for funding. In December 1995, the project got a subsidy of 50 billion lires from 'Brussels'.

The Environmental Park was intended as a catalyst in the strategy of diversifying the economy and improving the city's sustainability. The underlying question was "what will be the environmental regulations of the European Union in the future and how can we meet them?". Comparative advantages of Turin that support the Environmental Park are the establishment of the National Research Council and the good reputation of the Polytechnic in Turin. The project wants to be more than a real-estate operation. Beyond the realisation of a business park for research & development in the sphere of new techniques for environmental protection and the attraction of (foreign) enterprise to this park, the project aims at promoting new know-how in environmental protection. Possibly, the project will also get a function as a centre of education in environmental protection and sustainability ('ecological tourism'). Many potential functions of the Environmental Park were generated at two workshops in december 1994.

The project has been initiated by the Department for Environment and Sustainable Development of the city of Turin, and set up by the Promoting Partners Committee. Important members of this network organisation are the city of Turin, the regional development agency of Piemonte, the Polytechnic of Turin, the National Research Council, FinPiemonte S.p.A. and the Chamber of Commerce. The municipal utility companies are partners in the project too. Remarkably, the FIAT company is not involved in the project. The discussion partners ascribe the absence of FIAT to the fact that the Environmental Park is not a pure real estate project. They also indicated the potential competition between this project and the housing of research activities in Lingotto.

The Environmental Park will be developed in Spina III (the third part of the central redevelopment corridor). The former steel factory in this area closed ten years ago. The land is severely polluted. The site is surrounded by residential quarters. The success of the project seems to depend in part on the revitalisation of these quarters and their integration in the project. Probably, the revitalisation of the living quarters will be submitted as a project for the URBAN-program of the European Union. The project organisation has already started a communication campaign to get the project accepted by the population.

The project has now come to the stage of finding additional financial means and selecting the architect who will design the Environmental Park. In September 1996, the architectural plan will be selected. Hopefully, the construction of the park can start in the Spring of 1997. In the meantime, enterprises with a potential interest in the project will be identified in Italy, Europe, the United States and Japan. For the overseas marketing, agents will be used.

Organising capacity and the Environmental Park: analysis

The challenge and the need for organising capacity

In the case of the Environmental Park the need to find new activities to diversify and strengthen the economy and to re-use outdated industrial sites has been a primary challenge. Another challenge has been to improve the lagging position of Italy in developing new environmental technologies and meeting (European) environmental standards. Given the presence of high-grade research institutes in Turin - the Polytechnic and the National Research Council - the city was expected to be able to take up this challenge and to develop a competitive location climate for high-tech activities in research and development in the sphere of environmental protection and sustainability.

The momentum to take up the challenge of developing the city into a centre of environmental technology came when Turin got the Objective II status in 1993. In order to capitalise this status and to get European subsidies, the city had to draw up project proposals. The development of the Environmental Park appeared to stand the best chance. To design the contours of the project required organising capacity to bring organisations and persons together and to decide about the strategic course of the project.

Spatial-economic conditions

Several spatial-economic conditions have supported the development of the Environmental Park project. In the technologically orientated professional population, the National Research Council and the good reputation of the Turin Polytechnic, the city possesses some comparative advantages in the field of research and development. In addition, the city is situated in the Alpine region, which has shown strong innovative dynamics in the recent past. A spatial-economic condition that has been a motive to utilise the comparative advantages in technology has been the stage of restructuring of the Turin economy. To pass successfully from an economy based on traditional manufacturing towards an economy with modern production and services, new engines for the economy have to be developed. The Environmental Park is considered such an engine. A final relevant spatial-economic condition has been the vacancy of land in the city. The Environmental Park has been allotted a role in the reconversion of industrial sites.

Political support

Nowadays, environmental protection and sustainability are keywords in politics in many countries and cities. Jokes have it that to get funds from the European Union, these words should be mentioned in the project proposal. In the case of the Environmental Park, environmental protection and sustainability seem to be elaborated effectively. In the development of the project, the recent professionalisation of the government has proved invaluable. In the old situation, the project would not have been raised and it would certainly not have developed in the present direction. The new municipal councillors have promulgated ambitious visions. Their credibility and outward orientation have improved the municipal contacts with the business community and other organisations.

Vision and strategy

The initial vision of the Environmental Park came from the municipality, more in particular from the Department of Environment & Sustainable Development. The present vision has been developed step-wise with the help of many actors. International workshops have been organised to develop the vision and to get support for it. As the project is still at the phase of design, its future direction has not yet been fully determined. The goals of the project are at the least to promote new know-how in environmental protection and sustainability, through the realisation of a business park for research & development and the attraction of (foreign) enterprise to the park. Possibly, the project will also get a function as a centre of education in environmental protection and sustainability. The present strategy concentrates on developing the business park and promoting Turin as a location for environment-related activities in research & development.

The role of formal administrative entities

In 1993, the municipality has established the Department for Environment and Sustainable Development to express its interests in an environmentally healthy city. The responsible governor has been recruited from outside the municipal board. The new organisation was able to start with a clean slate and to develop new ideas and visions. For instance, plans have been developed to reorganise and privatise the public utility companies of the city. In the case of the Environmental Park, the department has a central role. There are good contacts between the department and other organisations. According to the discussion partners, the cooperation between the municipality and the region of Piemonte, which has its own responsibilities in environmental protection, is good.

Leadership

In the initiation of the Environmental Park project, the public sector has taken the lead. The municipality, in this case the Department for Environment and Sustainable Development, has played an active role in calling attention to environmental protection in the city and promoting the concept of the Environmental Park. In its efforts, the municipality has been assisted by FinPiemonte. This regional agency is responsible for financing new projects in Piemonte and has some experience in developing business parks for technological activities. FinPiemonte will be given an important role in the marketing policy for the Environmental Park.

Strategic networks

The project of the Environmental Park has been developed by a public-private partnership: the Promoting Partners Committee. Important members are the Department of Environment & Sustainable Development, the regional development agency of Piemonte, the Polytechnic of Turin and FinPiemonte S.p.A. In the committee, each of the parties is represented by one delegate. The committee has a rather informal nature, it lacks a formalised organisational structure. Given its stage of development, the informal character of the present network is an advantage. However, when the project enters the phase of implementation, a more formalised organisational structure, in which both public and private interests are represented, seems desirable to guarantee continuity and a clear division of responsibilities.

Performance

Measured in terms of subsidy received from the European Union, the performance of the Environmental Park project should be judged positively: in December 1995, the project was allotted a European subsidy of 50 billion lires. However, in non-monetary terms, too, the project development is progressing positively. The initiators of the project have been able to unite various actors in the project's committee and to generate a strong and innovative vision based on results of several workshops. The Environmental Park project is an example of the new role of the local government as a professional actor in processes of socio-economic and spatial-economic development.

When the planning comes true, the realisation of the Environmental Park will start in Spring 1997. It is expected that the project will make a valuable contribution to the sustainable diversification of the Turin economy. The project has potentials for attracting new economic activities and for turning the abstract concept of sustainability into an object of tourist interest. However, the potential threat of competition from other cities in this sphere should be kept in mind constantly, as 'environment' and 'sustainability' are used as slogans everywhere.

As in the case of Lingotto, to integrate surrounding residential quarters in the project is a precondition for the economic success and social acceptance of the Environmental Park. Neighbouring areas should be upgraded and unemployed citizens in nearby quarters should be offered new chances. The importance of spatial and social integration of the project in its surroundings seems to be well understood in the project organisation. Actions to integrate the project in its surroundings can be expected in the near future.

Conclusions

The case study of Turin shows the need for organising capacity. After many decades of economic growth, the city and region of Turin were hit in the 1970s and 1980s by fundamental reforms in the automotive industry. These reforms have had economic, spatial, social and psychological implications for Turin. To take up the challenge of diversifying the economy and re-using former industrial sites, the city needs to be well organised. In developing organising capacity, Turin is exceptionally circumstanced. Firstly, despite the contraction of the car industry, the dominance of FIAT is still perceptible in the city. Secondly, owing to recent administrative reforms, the traditional instability of the public sector seems to have been reduced in the city's management.

This chapter illustrates the various forms that organising capacity can take. In the case of Lingotto, the FIAT company has been the project's engine. In the case of the Environmental Park, the municipal Department of

Environment and Sustainable Development has been an important actor. The difference can be explained from the different nature of both projects. However, it also proceeds from a difference in momentum, due to the dynamics of the Italian administrative system. The Lingotto project dates from a time, when the private sector was the leader for lack of a strong public sector. The project of the Environmental Park belongs to a new era, in which the public sector is gaining stability and professionalism.

The relatively weak position of the local government and the lack of a comprehensive planning scheme have prevented the Lingotto project's placing from its start in a city-wide perspective. The isolated development of the project has resulted in an overlap of ambition with other projects, in particular with respect to the development of office space and the relocation of facilities of the Polytechnic. The incorporation of the Lingotto Project in the new urban planning scheme makes a more balanced development possible. However, the municipality lacks legal instruments to phase projects in time, which hinders the coordination of projects. Therefore, to avert competition between Lingotto and Spina III can be considered a first test case for the new leadership of the local government.

The reconversion of the Lingotto factory shows the importance of creating social support as early as possible in the project's development process. Because the population has not been involved from the start - for instance by communicating the project's goal and relating the neighbouring quarter to the project - the project still seems to suffer criticism among citizens. That might by a handicap for the further realisation of the project and its integration in the city's economy. In the case of the Environmental Park, communication has been considered necessary from the start.

The capacity of the local government in Turin to act efficiently and strategically has grown in recent years. That makes a shift in organising capacity from private to public primacy possible. Such a shift is required to guide the development of projects in the city and metropolitan region more integrally and strategically. The strengthening of the local government in the case of Turin argues the convergence between the administrative systems of North-west and South Europe: in North-west Europe the role of the private sector is being activated, whereas in the southern states the public sector is slowly gaining power.

In the process of professionalising the local government, care should be taken that it should not hinder to the participation of the private sector. The challenge is to find such a balanced division of leadership and responsibilities that specific strengths of public and private partners show to full advantage for the city as a whole. Another challenge for the further development of organising capacity in Turin is the integration of urban renewal projects in their social and spatial context. This integration of projects in the city is necessary to make the fullest use of their potential for sustainable economic development in the future.

Notes

---

[1] Co-author: Dr. H.A. van Klink

[2] For that reason, municipal town planners opted for an exhibition centre on the north-western side of the city in the direct vicinity of the airport and the highway.

10   Synthesis

Introduction

Despite the wide variety of projects, there are three clear similarities. First, all projects set out to reinforce the city's or metropolitan area's competitive position. Sometimes it is the most important goal, but at the least it is one of the serious arguments underlying every project. That finding seems to confirm the impression that European cities are more and more feeling the hot breath of competition. Second, nearly all projects appear to relate to more than one policy area and to as many interfaces between them. That fact indicates that among revitalising projects integrality is the rule rather than the exception. Thus integrality is a crucial factor with respect to organising the projects. That applies to the preliminaries, implementation and management of such projects. Third, while, as we have stated above, projects have been consciously selected from the areas of economics, transport or the environment, most projects combine those aspects. A sign that accessibility and the quality of the living environment increasingly are regarded as a necessary condition for economic revitalisation. The projects differ in spatial scale, size, funding, lead actors, time horizon and policy areas, but the differences do not affect the three main characteristics mentioned above. These three characteristics determine to a large extent the need for organising capacity.

This chapter recapitulates the principal findings of the case studies. The purpose of the investigation was to get an insight into the organising capacity of eight Eurocities and their regions. What are the critical factors of failure and success? The investigation started from the theoretical framework drawn up in the first chapter. Each city has submitted two projects to serve as input for the analysis; only in Lisbon has the analysis been limited to one large project. We want to emphasise that to give a mature judgement of the organising capacity available within the entire urban region on the strength of just two projects is not realistic, the less so as we have consciously chosen to include both successful and less successful projects in the investigation, the more clearly to expose how the different theoretical elements are weighed. What lessons can be drawn from the experiences gained in the eight cities concerned with the fifteen projects we have analysed? To answer that question, we confront the theory with the facts. How important are the different elements, and is the theory supported by the facts? Finally, the chapter concludes with some final remarks on how to *deal* with the elements of organising capacity.

Main findings of the analysis

In the first chapter a theoretical framework was drawn up, identifying the main factors that are important for organising capacity and also describing the relations between the various elements. In this chapter the theory is confronted with the facts from the case studies. *What can be learned from the experiences in the eight cities?*

Is leadership a necessary condition for organising capacity?

Projects which lack clear leadership do not produce the desired results. For instance, an important question in both the Munich projects is: who will take up the challenges, who will assume leadership? The first project concerns the challenges that face Munich's public transport region. The institution that has co-ordinated regional public transport (MVV) can no longer continue in its present form because the Federal Government decided that the responsibility for intra-regional transport had to be ceded to the state of Bavaria and at the same time that conditions for competition in public transport must be created. Moreover, Munich's regional public-rail system (S-Bahn) is in need of infrastructural adjustment. The new circumstances demand an initiative from the state of Bavaria. None of the other actors (city, eight counties, the former national railway company) can take the lead at the moment. Whether the state will take up the role of leader and how things will work out eventually remains to be seen. Bavaria is not 'free' to play the leadership role to the full because it has been made responsible for regional public transport in the whole area of Bavaria. It has to balance the interests of the urban region of Munich and of the more rural parts of Bavaria where public transport is extremely costly.

The second project is concerned with a reverse side of the economic success of the Munich region: the tendency to chase necessary but unattractive distribution and transport activities out of the region. Proposals have been made to start up an agency for the co-ordination of regional economic development. Especially the city of Munich is an advocate of such an agency. However it would have very little scope to fulfil a pioneering role. In the eyes of the smaller municipalities and counties in the region, the city is 'too big' a factor in the region. In neither project is the condition of leadership fulfilled. Consequently, their results have not been satisfactory.

Another illustration is one of the projects in the Rotterdam region: ROM-Rijnmond. That project aims at simultaneously strengthening the mainport function of Rotterdam and improving the quality of the living environment. In 1989 the responsible Ministry had initiated a discussion with the city of Rotterdam and the Province, and later on with the 14 municipalities in the region. Clearly, however, on the regional level all those involved shared the ambition to reduce the role of the central government. At the start, there was a debate about whether leadership is a task of the Ministry or of the region itself. That debate is repeated now that the project enters the realisation phase. At the moment, a small group of people keep the process going but it is in the interest of all actors involved to finish the leadership debate soon.

In general, leadership has much to do with formal and material competence. In some cases the role of leadership is taken in hand by the institution that has the formal power to do so. The Lingotto project in Turin is orchestrated by the FIAT company because they own the factory. The EXPO project in Lisbon is led by the central government because they have the means and legislative power to complete the project at the required pace. Antwerp's ICA has been made responsible for informatics in the city and 'Intelligent City' is their project.

Sometimes the final leadership is not given to the potential leader. To a certain degree, competence can be created. In Italy, the national government has enacted a law for the creation of a metropolitan government for Italy's larger urban regions. The initiation of that adjustment was entrusted to the regional authorities but they are not fully equipped for that task. In the case of the Greater Bologna area, the city and province of Bologna took over the leadership role from the Emilia-Romagna region, the appointed leader. That bottom-up approach has produced better results in Bologna than elsewhere in Italy. In 1994, 50 out of 60 municipalities signed an agreement (Città Metropolitana) expressing their commitment to the new metropolitan government. The combination of the city and province had created the competence to accomplish that. It produced two persuasive arguments for the municipalities to join in: first that in the new situation the province will be dissolved and replaced by the metropolitan authority, and second that the city of Bologna will be split up. The results have been good so far, but it is not just leadership that matters and therefore the final success is still questionable.

Leadership is not inherent in persons alone. The successful revitalisation projects involved in the inquiry appear to have been orchestrated by a municipality, agency, person, group of persons, business company or government agency. So, leadership can also be based on the strength of an organisation. In Turin, FIAT took the lead in transforming one of its old discarded factories, Lingotto, into a modern service centre. It is not so much the Board, but the strength, status, influence and contacts of the company that underlie strong leadership.

It is clear that leadership is required, but the specific circumstances of a city or project sometimes call for specific leaders. In the case of EXPO in Lisbon, different layers of government co-operate in the company Parque EXPO'98 under strong leadership from the central government. As we know from other research[1], the central government still plays a very important role in matters of urban development and problems. Because of that tradition the strong leadership of the national government works well in the Lisbon case. But that does not necessarily mean that this model would also work elsewhere in Europe.

Leadership comes in different disguises. Leadership is important at all stages of the projects. However, different projects and different stages of a project sometimes call for different forms of leadership, and therefore sometimes for different leaders. Indeed, a succession of leaders may be involved in a project. The Stimulus programme in the Eindhoven region is a good example. The Stimulus programme aims to reinforce and anchor small and medium-size business to the region by means of economic clustering. The mayor of the city of Eindhoven took the lead in creating the necessary (financial and organisational) conditions for the programme to take off, but in the end it is the companies that have to give substance to the programme. A large international producer of copiers in the adjoining Limburg area -Océ van der Grinten- recognised the possibilities of the programme and initiated a high-quality supplier network in the Eindhoven region. That shows that the search for the most suitable locomotive need not stop at the regional border.

How important are vision & strategy?

The research supports the argument that a project should fit within a wider vision of urban development. That the Kop-van-Zuid project fits so nicely into the new approach towards the development of the city of Rotterdam has been beneficiary for the project; it reduces the risk of the Kop van Zuid developing in isolation of the city and in turn and thus improves the chances of commercial exploitation of (elements) of the project. The importance of that fact can also be found in the case of Lisbon, where plans have been developed to integrate the EXPO URBE project in the city. The Westcorridor Key project in Eindhoven has sprung from a general vision that had been developed for the urban region. But there, other factors have played a decisive role as well.

If a project does not fit in a more general vision of the development of the city or region, serious problems may arise. The Lingotto project in Turin is concerned with finding a new purpose for an outdated factory of the FIAT company. The strategy behind the project is to reconvert the factory with the help of private and public partners into a modern service centre. The strategic aim of the project is clear. However, the project has not been developed according to the existing spatial-economic structure of the city and the surrounding area. The municipality supports the project, but all the decisions have been taken by the FIAT company alone. That can be an important handicap. Lingotto runs the risk of developing in isolation of the town, which might reduce its commercial potential. In addition the location is not ideal for such a modern service centre. The airport is on the other end of the town and the accessibility of the location itself wants improvement. Besides, that situation increases the possibility of intra-urban competition with other projects in the city that are more accessible.

In none of the metropolitan areas has a vision for the development for the entire metropolitan area been worked out into a strategy. That can be a serious handicap as far as organising capacity is concerned. The two Munich projects that have been objects of study had directly to do with problems on the scale of the metropolitan region. Clearly this has had repercussions on the organising capacity of the Munich region. In some metropolitan areas a vision of the development of the metropolitan area has been developed but for lack of political support, delay of administrative reform, and other reasons, the vision has not been elaborated into a strategy.

What is the role of the strategic networks and the more formal (administrative) institutions?

Collaboration in strategic networks makes for easy starting-up of challenging and innovative projects. Hardly any come under the competency of one single actor, for instance one municipality. Apparently, if all relevant actors are involved, a strategic network can be an instrument to generate new ideas, organise support for them and orchestrate their implementation. In the Bilbao region representatives of the formal public authorities as well as the business community and other institutions co-operate in Metropoli-30, whose principal task is to revitalise the Bilbao region. There is still a long road ahead, but the partnership has been effective up till now. A traditionally positive attitude towards co-operation in the region concerned has been a great help. Such constructive and structural public-private co-operation on that scale is remarkable. Strategic networks have also played a major role in drawing up the Stimulus programme in the Eindhoven region. Practically all public actors who had anything to do with the challenge ahead were involved, as well as representatives of the private sector. The formal and informal contacts in the network could be effectively used to organise the programme through the competency of the various actors involved.

If the strategic networks are not used to the full, efforts to start up innovative projects along strictly formal channels founder on inflexibility. An illustrative example is the Westcorridor project in Eindhoven, a large urban-renewal project in the western part of the city. Initially the project found insufficient support among other important actors in the city, so that the project was carried mainly by the Department of Town Development. That situation continued for too long. The case study shows a project on that scale, with numerous implications for the city and other actors, cannot take off within the 'formalised' structure alone. Apart from the municipal organisation, all the available capacity and competency in the town has to be enlisted to keep the project on the move and complete it successfully. So, the research supports the idea that strategic networks can ensure the necessary flexibility and increase the organising capacity.

Projects that aim at sustainability are often projects involving both public and private parties. The research has paid attention to the composition of the networks, whether of a public-public, public-private or private-private nature.

In some cases public-public networks and in others private-private networks are appropriate. In most cases though, the interest and competency of public and private actors is at stake. In Italy the emphasis tends to be on private-private networks; traditionally the local public authorities are less involved in renewal projects. The case of the Lingotto project in Turin supports that argument: as said earlier it is mainly an initiative of the FIAT company assisted by other private parties. As a consequence, the project runs the risk of development in isolation from the town. In addition, the measures required to improve the infrastructure to safeguard accessibility of the building have not been taken. Perhaps better contacts between the public and private sectors could have prevented some of the difficulties.

The network approach has certain limitations with respect to continuity, and that is where the more formal institutions come in. Given the right actors, strategic networks are a good breeding ground of new ideas and initiatives, and provide the flexibility required to start up innovative projects. In the short and the medium run that can lead to a good performance. That is not to say, though, that strategic networks do not have their limitations. The research reveals at the same time the need to span the gap between the networks and the formal structures. To ensure *continuity*, a link with the formal, authorised bodies has to be accomplished. From the investigation, the successful projects appear to be those that have managed to create that link. The case of the metropolitan railway network in Bologna illustrates that at a certain point, the flexibility of the strategic networks should be supplemented with the reliability of the more formal institutions. The idea to improve the existing rail network and to approach the matter of public transport on a metropolitan scale is a result of the Città Metropolitana conference. The relevant actors have been involved and the project is under way. However, the implementation would be greatly helped if a single public transport authority for the metropolitan area were established. For the time being there is no legal framework for such an authority (see the comments on the other project in Bologna).

In the case of EXPO'98 in Lisbon five ministries, two municipalities and some regional bodies are parties in the process. Despite the central leadership of the national government, mutual adjustment is called for. To that end Parque EXPO'98 has been founded as the means to create a formal, well-defined basis for consultation with enough power to bring the project to a positive end. The predominantly public-public network can be said to have been given a formal basis to manage the project properly. The company can wield extensive power within the selected 330 hectares: 'it is a city in its

263

own right'. Up till now the construction has worked remarkably well: the organisation has proved itself capable of putting the project on the rails in very little time. In sum, the research strongly supports the idea that the strategic networks and the formal structures are complementary.

There is a tendency for the approaches in the North and the South of Europe to converge. Earlier on, in cities like Turin and Bilbao, it was the private sector that initiated urban renewal, and a network approach prevailed. In the Dutch cities it was predominantly the public sector that did the work, with emphasis on the formal procedures. From the research the picture seems to be changing. The Environmental Park project in Turin has been initiated by the public sector, and so has Metropoli-30. In the Stimulus programme in Eindhoven the public sector still had the lead, but the involvement of the private sector through strategic networks indicates a change in the approach. Nor have the two Rotterdam projects spring from the strictly formal channels of municipal planning. Possibly there a trend towards a more balanced approach in Europe with respect to the role of the public and private actors as well as the formal and network approaches.

Is it true that spatial-economic problems have a positive effect on organising capacity?

Spatial-economic problems have worked as incentives to co-operation. That applies to nearly all the cases, though in different forms and to various degrees. The case of Bilbao shows that the heavy problems caused by the decline of the region's main traditional industries induced public and private actors to co-operate in Metropoli-30. The Stimulus programme in the Eindhoven region owes its existence to serious problems of two leading firms in the region; the slimming-down operation of Philips followed by the unexpected collapse of DAF company, brought all the relevant actors together and resulted in the Stimulus programme, which aims to reinforce and anchor small and medium-size firms in the region.

The conclusion in the previous paragraph is further supported by the evidence from the Munich case. In general, the spatial-economic conditions in the Munich region are still favourable, but the scores on organising capacity of the projects have been lower than in the other cases, and a major problem is the lack of co-operativeness on the part of the majority of municipalities and counties. The city of Munich strongly advocates a new economic-development agency for the region, for better co-ordination of the region's development. Recent developments call for such an agency. The tendency to drive necessary but unattractive distribution and transport activities out of the region -the reverse side of the economic success- may jeopardise the competitive position of the region in the long term. That potential threat is masked by the overall favourable situation.

To what extent does political support impede or stimulate urban renewal?

Without clear political support, innovative renewal projects have difficulties taking off and sometimes fail to produce satisfactory results. That applies to the support in the local political circles as well as from the national government. The experience of all the projects confirms that conclusion. For instance, the lack of progress after the drawing-up of a Strategic Plan for the Region of Antwerp is -among other reasons- due to the absence of actual support of local authorities. Although the city council accepted the plan in 1993, it has not made it an explicit part of urban policy. In the case of 'Intelligent City', the other Antwerp project, the political support came about because the renewal -a modern inter-municipal telecommunication network- was attended by substantial financial advantages for the city.

The initial development of Eindhoven's Westcorridor project was boosted by the recognition of its importance. In the national policy document on spatial planning of 1991 the project had been given the status of potential 'key project'; a covenant between the State and Eindhoven region was to confirm that status. But from that point onwards the positive impulse soon faded away. The negotiations between the Ministries and the region took far too long. The national recognition had given rise to expectations about financial support that the responsible Ministries could not or would not fulfil. As late as the summer of 1995 the covenant between the State and region was finally signed, ensuring only partial financial support from the government.

Good communication of the project is of crucial importance to obtain political support. Naturally, lack of adequate information on the problem and its solution (the performance expected from the implementation of a specific project) to the parties involved (for instance, other departments within an organisation or other public authorities and/or agencies involved) is not conducive to the creation of organising capacity. Organising capacity by our definition implies the involvement of all relevant actors, and good communication is an essential condition to achieve that involvement. However, good communication does not automatically lead to cooperativeness. Other elements will be decisive in that respect. To make the project as widely known as possible is indispensable to create organising capacity, but the case studies have not given clear evidence of any project falling through for lack of political support due to bad or failing communication.

Is societal support regarded as important?

Societal support is considered to be of eminent importance. In the Kop-van-Zuid project efforts have been made to organise societal support. In an attempt to gain support from the population in the surrounding neighbourhoods, the 'Social-Return' plan was established as a part of the Kop-van-Zuid project. These neighbourhoods suffer much from unemployment and social exclusion. Social Return tries to recruit local residents for the construction projects and also to find work for them afterwards in, for example, catering, security and cleaning. Up till now Social Return has found it hard to get the local population involved. It is too early too judge whether Social Return is a success or failure. Societal support is also an important factor in Eindhoven's Westcorridor project. In 1994 the strategy of the West Corridor was changed to take better account of the needs of the population in the selected area. It is a long-term project, but short-term concrete results are needed to increase and maintain popular support.

Another lesson can be drawn from the Città Metropolitana project in Bologna. At the end of the process towards the new metropolitan authority, the population will get a chance to give their opinion on the Città Metropolitana developments. Failure to organise societal support for the new government will put the feasibility of the entire project in jeopardy. This was shown by the recent development in Rotterdam, where the population by referendum rejected the idea of the split-up of Rotterdam into eleven parts to make way for a metropolitan government. To complete the administrative reform in Bologna a lot of effort and resources has to be put in to secure support of the population.

The population as well as the business community are often the markets that the projects aim at. Parque EXPO'98 recently launched its campaign to bring the EXPO to the attention of the Portuguese population. At the same time Portuguese and foreign investors are invited to take part in the project, and the benefits of a future location at the EXPO URBE site are brought to the attention of the business community. Their commercial success is directly related to societal support. Therefore, and to have the necessary knowledge available at home, the company has consciously recruited part of the staff from the private sector.

Societal support can be organised, at least to a certain degree. The examples show that efforts have been made to organise societal support. Whether the efforts will be successful remains to be seen. Much depends on the specific circumstances of the project. In Turin the Lingotto project is concerned with the transformation of a former FIAT factory that had to be closed down in the early 1980s, an event that resulted in mass discharge of employees. The building is situated in a neighbourhood that is dominated by (former) FIAT employees. Despite the effort and investment of FIAT in the re-use of the building, the population in the surroundings still associate the building with their former workplace. Under these circumstances, support of the local population is very difficult to organise.

A good communication strategy is a principal condition for creating societal support. If the population and market parties involved are not convinced that a project will contribute to their needs and wants, the support will be minimum. Although the Lingotto project in Turin proves that explicit support by the population is not always needed to reach specific project objectives, it does tend to speed up project development, as the Kop-van-Zuid project shows. Besides, the Kop-van-Zuid project has been very well communicated by the media to the Rotterdam population, which is also reflected in the successful sales of many of the new houses even before they had been built. If a sound base in society is missing, the project runs the risk that the objectives will not be met in the end. That holds in particular for obtaining the interest of (commercial) market parties, such as private investors and end-users of offices. Especially the projects aiming at economic revitalisation (such as Kop van Zuid in Rotterdam, Lingotto and Environmental Park in Turin, Metropoli-30 and Ria-2000 in Bilbao, EXPO URBE in Lisbon and West Corridor in Eindhoven) rely on the market to invest in the new business opportunities (office space, commercial housing, shopping) which the projects will create. In these projects, marketing is highly important. Communication is an integrate part of marketing, and its neglect will certainly have a negative effect on the performance of the project. We repeat what has been pointed out earlier: while good communication is a precondition for success, the ultimate success will not be determined by communication alone. Other factors will be decisive in that respect. A sound communication strategy, based on giving the right information to the right groups in society at the right moment, is an important means to convince the public and the market of the necessity of a project. With respect to the influence of communication on the behaviour of (commercial) market parties we have not obtained a clear picture. Some projects show have already attracted investors (for instance, Metropoli-30, Lingotto) but for the majority of projects market parties still have to decide about investment (Kop van Zuid, Ria-2000, Environmental Park, EXPO URBE, Westcorridor).

Can we conclude from the case studies that organising capacity is determined by the combination of elements of the theory?

The research supports the notion that the combination of leadership, vision and strategy, strategic networks and formal institutions, spatial-economic problems, societal support and political support, has a clear impact on the performance of the projects. All the elements of the theory make up a coherent system, and are linked by a variety of relations. A serious problem concerning one element will have an impact on the whole system. That implies that almost by definition it is the combination that determines the organising capacity. Examples of two crucial relations illustrate that.

Without leadership to direct them, strategic networks cannot be activated and put in as instruments. The research offers extensive evidence of the relation between the elements. Every case study can be used to support that argument. As said earlier, unfavourable spatial-economic conditions tend to make local parties willing to address the problems together. That increases the possibility of strategic co-operation in strategic networks. That important lesson is aptly illustrated by the strong signal which the problems with Philips and DAF in the Eindhoven region gave to all relevant actors. The problems induced them to take a more positively attitude to co-operation. But the need remains for a distinct puller to give direction to the emerging policy network. At the start the city of Eindhoven and the mayor in particular, undertook to bring about the conditions needed to solve the problem and to activate the policy network.

Political and societal support are vital to the design of a clear and broadly supported vision. In that way the vision and strategy (and the goals) can bind the various actors and contribute to the balance between the networks and the formal institutions. An interesting example is the Strategic Plan for the Region of Antwerp. The economic development in the Antwerp region was lagging behind that of Flanders as a whole, and the Chamber of Commerce wanted to put an end to that situation. The decision was made to draw up a strategic plan to deal with the region's problems coherently and integrally. Two energetic key figures, the mayor of Antwerp and the president of the Chamber of Commerce, set the process in move in conjunction with the representative of the Bank of Belgium, and a plan has been ready for implementation since the end of 1992. Unfortunately, However, the necessary support for the vision embodied in the plan, especially political support, is highly questionable. That has to do with the troublesome political climate in Antwerp at the moment. The lack of support blocks further progress, despite the efforts of the pullers of the project. As a matter of fact, the two key figures have retired from their offices and whether the new persons in office will take over their role is uncertain.

The Rotterdam Kop-van-Zuid project illustrates how crucial is wide support of the vision by the relevant societal and political actors in the city or region. In that project, much has been invested in the development of a clear vision and in communicating that vision within the city and to the national government. That has facilitated the orchestration of the actors for effective implementation. It has enabled the initiators to build and organise a network as an instrument to keep the process going. From that position they managed to introduce the project into the formal structures.

What can be said about organising capacity and dynamics?

As pointed out earlier, time is an important aspect of organising capacity. To analyse the dynamics of comprehensive urban-renewal projects a distinction between different stages of project development can be helpful. A few remarks may be clarifying.

It is essential to organise political and social support at the earliest possible stage. For a project to contribute to sustainable development, a fundamental condition is to agree on what the problem or challenge actually is, and on the necessity to take it up. In many cases 'bad' spatial-economic conditions have helped to overcome differences in opinion. In Bilbao there appeared to be sufficient political and social support for Metropoli-30. Nobody could deny the economic distress of the region. As a result, support could be easily organised. The same applies to the Eindhoven project, Stimulus; the great stir provoked in the media by the collapse of DAF entailed general awareness. At the same time a leader is required to organise the support wanted.

As the stage of implementation draws near the commitment of the actors in networks has to be given a more formal basis. The construction of the metropolitan railway network in Bologna will benefit from Città Metropolitana, as stated earlier on. Several public parties are involved in the project, and much consultation and co-ordination is needed to get them all aligned. There is sufficient cooperativeness and the right networks seem to have been activated. There is, however, a distinct need for a more formal organisation to smooth the execution. So far, such an organisation is lacking. The project in Lisbon is already in full implementation. For indeed, the EXPO is scheduled for 1998, and by that time the exhibition part has to be complete. But a beginning has also been made with EXPO URBE. All government parties involved back the idea to put in the EXPO as an instrument for the revitalisation of a backward area on the outskirts of Lisbon. The long-term success depends on the degree to which the market parties can be interested in the projects of EXPO'98 and EXPO URBE. There is at any rate a clear point of address with the necessary expertise: *Parque EXPO'98*. All the government parties involved, national as well as local, are united in this 'company'. Parque EXPO'98 is adequately equipped with means and competencies. Without this -provisional- formal agency, an operation like EXPO'98 cannot be carried through in the time envisaged. Even now, whether everything will be ready on time remains to be seen. That depends not so much on the organisation as on the gigantic dimensions of the project and the lateness of the preparations.

It is important to keep up the momentum: organise for change. All projects investigated stretch over a number of years. Given the duration, the number of actors, the number of variables and the complexity of renewal projects, one or more elements of organising capacity will inevitably change. The challenge is to prepare for change in order to keep the project on track. It is one thing to get the conditions right, it is another to keep them right. Sudden changes will occur, and organising capacity also implies the ability to anticipate and be flexible enough to cope with them. Strategic networks provide the framework to realise that in some degree. One of the instruments to keep up the momentum is early and regular communication of the results so far achieved. The Stimulus programme in Eindhoven was triggered by the commotion around the DAF-bankruptcy in 1993. The problem -the loss of dominant economic locomotives- was clear and the willingness to do something about it appeared great. The strategy -to reinforce and anchor small and medium-size business in the region- was generally supported. But then it took more than a year for European recognition and support to materialise, and even longer for the effective starting signal to be given. To keep up the spirit and willingness of 1993 -the momentum- for so long

270

without concrete results, has proved exceptionally hard. For that reason, a point has been made right from the start of communicating forthwith the first results of the programme.

Another instrument is flexibility. The experience from the Kop-van-Zuid project is that the vision must be flexible enough to cope with changing market conditions. At the start, the project gave much weight to the development of offices. However, when the market for office space fell into a recession, those responsible managed to switch to high-quality housing for which the demand had grown. Because of that flexibility the Kop-van-Zuid project is still on track.

Final remarks

The theory has been confronted with the facts. The conclusion can be that the research supports the theory of organising capacity as developed in the first chapter. Leadership, vision and strategy, strategic networks, spatial-economic problems, political support, societal support can all be regarded as critical factors of failure and success in terms of organising capacity. At the same time, the research reveals that there is no blueprint for organising capacity; organising capacity comes in different disguises. However, some suggestions concerning the elements can be made. Organising capacity is defined as the ability to enlist (leadership) all actors involved (strategic networks) and with their help (political and societal support) to generate new idea and develop and implement a policy (vision and strategy) designed to respond to fundamental developments (incentive form spatial-economic problems) and create conditions (coherence of the elements, momentum) for sustainable development (in the metropolitan area). The suggestions, in combination with the definition and the elements of organising capacity to which they refer, are systematically presented in the overview below.

Finally, organising capacity implies a new style of urban management. Organising capacity is really the key to the successful attack of problems and attainment of objectives. In view of the increasing integrality of more and more problems of urban policy, the road to success is almost always by the joint endeavours of various public and often also private parties. The challenge to the local and regional authorities is to mobilise the competency, knowledge and energy present in the metropolitan area. That calls for another type of urban manager than those prevailing until a short time ago. An enterprising attitude putting the activation of networks and communicative abilities first, commands the future.

| **Organising capacity is:** | | |
definition	elements	suggestions
the ability to enlist → ↓	→ leadership:	→ if missing or unclear: make sure that there is one dominant leader.
all actors involved → ↓	→ strategic networks:	→ create, utilise and direct the networks; when implementation comes near, safeguard the commitment of the network by a more formal structure.
and with their help → ↓	→ political & societal support:	→ communicate the problem to society and to the politicians. If societal support is missing, it is to the politicians to do the job.
to generate new ideas and develop and implement a policy → ↓	vision & strategy:	if missing: develop a vision → and strategy and in the meanwhile, safeguard integrality and mutual adjustment of various projects and project elements
designed to respond → to fundamental developments	incentive of spatial-economic problems:	→ communicate the problem to all relevant groups
and create conditions → ↓	coherence of the → elements, momentum:	monitor the change of the → elements and organise for change!
for sustainable development	→ in the metropolitan area:	→ problems nor solutions do not stop at the city's borders.

Note

---

1 See: Van den Berg, Van Klink, Van der Meer (1993), *Governing Metropolitan Regions,* and Van den Berg, Van der Meer, Pol (1995)' *The audit of European policies on metropolitan cities,* Stage II.

Discussion partners

Report on Antwerp

- Mr F. De Beul, Coordinator Strategic Plan Antwerp Region
- Mr E. Cop, Head Department of European Affairs, International Relations
- Mr P. Crombecq, Director CIPAL/ICA
- Mr E. Duysters, PLATO-manager Strategic Plan Antwerp Region
- Mr L. Van der Veken, Manager Antwerp Office, National Bank of Belgium

Report on Bilbao

- Mr I. Areso, Deputy Mayor, Bilbao City Council
- Mr I. Atxutegi, International Relations, Bilbao Metropoli-30
- Mr H. Cirarda Ortiz de Artiñano, Mayor, Getxo City Council
- Mr X. Gallarraga Aldanondo, Department of Economic Analysis, University of the Basque Country
- Mr J.M. Gorordo, Secretary-Director, Chamber of Commerce
- Mr J.L. Iparraguirre, Institute Development Manager, European Software Institute
- Mr A. Martínez Cearra, General Director, Bilbao Metropoli-30
- Mr D. Moyano Padilla, Deputy Mayor, Barakaldo City Council
- Mr P. Otaola, Director, Bilbao Ría-2000
- Mr C. Pera Tambo, Mayor, Barakaldo City Council
- Mr O. Rivero, Head of International Relations Office, University of the Basque Country

Report on Bologna

- Mr W. Brunelli, Association of Small and Medium Industries Bologna
- Mr. D. Cocchianella, Director of the Metropolitan Area Department of the City Council of Bologna
- Mr G. Gotti, Secretary General of the Entrepreneurs' Association of Bologna
- Mrs F. Gualdi, Coordinator of Metropolitan Railway Network
- Mr G. Nicoli, Mayor of San Giovanni in Persiceto
- Mr R. La Monica, Marketing and Innovation Department, City of Bologna
  Mr D. Nigro, Coordinator of Metropolitan Railway Network
- Mr G.F. Poggioli, Assindustria Bologna
- Mr L. Vandelli, Vice President of the Province of Bologna, Institutional coordinator of the Metropolitan Area project

Report on Eindhoven

- Mr H. Bouman, Coordinator STIMULUS, Economic Development Programme Region Eindhoven
- Mr Y. Brouwer, Head Policy and Legal Department, Environment Department Eindhoven Region
- Mr A. van Daal, Director Propery Development, Royal IBC, Best
- Mr C. van Dijk, Head Department of Town and Country Planning, City of Eindhoven
- Mr J. Lucassen, Chairman Executive Board, Academy for Industrial Design Eindhoven
- Mr P.C.J.M. van Run, Secretary Employers Organisation BZW
- Mr. T. Schut, Director of NV Rede
- Mr N.M. van der Spek, Alderman of Town Planning and Urban Control

Report on Lisbon

- Mr M. Edwards, Director of Lusoponte Public Relations, Lusoponte
- Mr A. Laplaine Guimarãis, Director of the Department of International Relations
- Mr C. Lobo Gaspar, Director of Expo'98 Public Relations, Parque EXPO'98

- Mr A. Magalhães, Representative from the Ministry of Environment and Natural Resources
- Mr P. Mattos Chaves, Commerical Director Expo Urbe, Parque EXPO'98
- Mr J. Metello, Advisor to the City Councillor for Environment
- Mrs C. Santos, Director of the Municipal Department of Supplies and Expenditure
- Mr L. Viana Baptista, Architect, Expo'98, Parque EXPO'98
- Mr A. Vaz, Technician Municipal Department of Strategic Planning of Lisbon
- Mr A. Ventura, Technician Municipal Department of Strategic Planning of Lisbon
- Mr J. Zuniga, Road Autonomous Board (Representative Junta Autónoma dos Estrados)

Report on Munich

- Mr Bialucha, Landratsamt München
- Mr Christmann, Landrat Dachau
- Mr O. Goedecke, Regionaler Planungsverband München
- Mr H. Knüttel, Director Münchner Verkehrs- und Tarifverbund GmbH
- Mr R.W. Obermeier, Chamber of Commerce Munich
- Mr H. Rogge, Head Department of Traffic, Chamber of Commerce Munich
- Mr K. Schussmann, Referat für Arbeit und Wirtschaft München
- Mrs. E. Steinberg, Referat für Arbeit und Wirtschaft München
- Mr Weber, Landratsamt München

Report on Rotterdam

- Mr A.J. Doe, Projectoffice ROM-Rijnmond
- Mr G.H.J. Peters, Director Department for Environment, Public Works Rotterdam
- Mr J. Peters, Programme manager ROM-Rijnmond
- Mr J. van der Vlist, former Member of the Provincial Executive Zuid-Holland
- Mr H.W.H. Welters, Director SVZ
- Mrs H.E. Bakker, former director City Development, City of

Rotterdam
- Mr J. Laan, former alderman Town and Country Planning, City of Rotterdam
- Mr P.J. Rodenberg, Projectmanager Kop-van-Zuid, Rotterdam

Report on Turin

- Mr C.A. Barbieri, Polytechnic University of Turin
- Mr C. Beltrame, IRES Piemonte
- Mr L. Bobbio, consultant
- Mr R. Cogno, IRES Piemonte
- Mrs L. Conforti, IRES Piemonte
- Mr M. Demarie, Fondazione Giovanni Agnelli
- Mr L. Ferlaino, IRES Piemonte
- Mr T. Garsci, IRES Piemonte
- Mr P. Gastaldo, alderman for Economic Affairs
- Mr R. Guazetti, Finpiemonte S.P.A.
- Mr R. Lanzetti, IRES Piemonte
- Mr M. Maggi, IRES Piemonte
- Mrs. A. Marucco, Softech
- Mrs L. Mazza, department of Town Planning, City of Turin
- Mr A. Mela, Polytechnic University Turin
- Mr S. Piperno, director IRES Piemonte
- Mr F.B. di Pralormo, director Lingotto SRL
- Mrs S. Saccomanni, Polytechnic University Turin
- Mr J. Vernetti, alderman for Environment and Sustainable Development

Bibliography

General

Berg, Leo van den, H. Arjen van Klink and Jan van der Meer, (1993), *Governing Metropolitan Regions*, Avebury, Aldershot, UK

Berg Leo van den, Erik Braun, Jan van der Meer (1994), *Economic attractiveness and social exclusion: the case of Rotterdam*, EURICUR, Rotterdam.

Braun Erik (1994), *Een sociaal-economische tweedeling in Rotterdam?*, Erasmus Universiteit, Rotterdam.

Bruijn de, J.A., (1992), W.J.M. Kickert, J.F.M. Koppenjan, *Management van complexe beleidsnetwerken*, Erasmus Universiteit Rotterdam

Bruijn de, J.A., (1995), E.F. Ten Heuvelhof, *Netwerkmanagement: strategieën, instrumenten en normen*, Erasmus Universiteit Rotterdam

Dicken P. (1992), *Global Shift: The Internationalization of Economic Activity*, Londen.

Eurocities Social Welfare Committee (1992), *European Social Policy and the City*.

Jarillo J.C. (1993), *Strategic Networks: Creating the borderless organization*, Butterworth-Heinemann, Oxford.

Klijn, E.H (1994), *Policy networks: an overview*, Working paper no 11, Rotterdam.

Kooiman, J. (1993), *Modern governance*, London SAGE publications.

Kouwenhoven, V.P. (1991), 'Publiek-private samenwerking mode of model?', PhD-Series in *General Management* no 2, Faculteit Bedrijfskunde, Rotterdam School of Management, Erasmus Universiteit, Eburon.

Meer J. van der (1992), *De steden en Europa*, een bijdrage voor het colloquium: De uitdaging van de stad, EURICUR, Rotterdam.

Nijkamp, P. (1993), 'Succcess Factors for High Speed Rail Networks in Europe', in: *International Journal of Transport Economics* Vol XX No.3 October 1993.

Parkinson M. (1992), F. Bianchini, J. Dawson, R. Evens, A. Harding, *Urbanisation and the Functions of Cities in the European Community*, European Institute of Urban Affairs, Liverpool John Moores University.

Porter M. (1990), *The Competitive Advantage of Nations*, The MacMillan Press, London.

Report on Antwerp

Antwerp Information Technology Centre (ICA), not dated, *Antwerp, an Intelligent City*

Berg, Leo van den, H. Arjen van Klink and Jan van der Meer (1993), *Governing Metropolitan Regions*, Avebury, Aldershot, UK

City of Antwerp (1993), *Statistical Yearbook 1993*

City of Antwerp, not dated *a*, *Een strategie voor de Antwerpse regio*

City of Antwerp, not dated *b*, *Antwerpen, een Intelligente Stad of informatietechnologie in dienst van de samenleving*

City of Antwerp (1994), *Antwerp Newsletter 2*, September 1994

City of Antwerp, not dated *c*, *Bestuursakkoord 1995-2000*

Gazet van Antwerpen, edition 29 September (1995), Interview with Marc Francken, Chairman, Chamber of Commerce Antwerp

Maatschappij voor de Vernieuwing en Promotie van Antwerpen (1992), December 1992, *Strategic Plan Antwerp Region*

Maatschappij voor de Vernieuwing en Promotie van Antwerpen (1995), April *Stand van zaken in het Strategisch Plan Regio Antwerpen*

Vandekerckhove, Freddy, not dated, *Memo to the Leden van het college (project Stad in Beweging)*

Vranken, Jan en Youssef Ben Abdeljelil (1995), *Sociale kaart van Antwerpen*, Studies over de samenleving nr. 1, Acco, Leuven

Report on Bilbao

Pablo Otaola (1995), *Cities: Space of problems and opportunities*, Madrid, 7 November 1995

Bilbao Ría 2000, Brochure

Berg, Leo van den, H. Arjen van Klink and Jan van der Meer (1993,) *Governing Metropolitan Regions,* Gower, Avebury

Berg, Leo van den, Jan van der Meer and Peter M.J. Pol (1995), *Audit of European Policies on Metropolitan Cities*, Euricur, Rotterdam.

Ayuntamiento de Bilbao (City Council of Bilbao) (1992), *Plan General de ordenacion urbana.*

Bilbao Metropoli-30 (1993), *Informe Anual de Progreso,* Bilbao.

Bilbao Metropoli-30 (1994), *Informe Anual de Progreso*, Bilbao.

Bilbao Metropoli-30, several brochures.

Bilbao Metropoli-30, *Plan Estrategico para la revitalización del Bilbao Metropolitano* (Fase 1-4).

Bilbao Metropoli-30, Internet site

Report on Bologna

Commission of the European Communities, Directorate-General for Regional Policy (1993), *Portrait of the Regions*, Luxemburg: Eurostat

Comune di Bologna (1994), *Governare le Città. L'Accordo per la Città Metropolitana di Bologna*, Bologna: Società Editrice il Mulino

Conferenza Metropolitana Bologna (1995), *Documenti*, Bologna

ERVET (1993), *Emilia Romagna Region. Main Indicators*, Bologna

Ministero dei Transport, Commune di Bologna, Provincia di Bologna, Regione Emilia-Romagna e Ferrovie dello Stato (1994), *Per la definizione di un nouvo assetto dei trasporti pubblici nell'area metropolitana Bolognese. Il trasporto pubblico ed il servizio ferroviario metropolitano*, Bologna

Provincia di Bologna (1995), *Progetto Città metropolitana. Note per il Programma di mandato*, Bologna

Unione regionale camere di commercio dell' Emilia-Romagna (1995), *Statistiche Regionali*, Numero 81/1, 1995

Report on Eindhoven

Commissie van de Europese Gemeenschappen, Europees Fonds voor Regionale Ontwikkeling, Europees Sociaal Fonds (1996) 1994-1996, *Doelstelling 2 Nederland, Zuid-Oost Brabant*, ENIG Programmeringsdocument

Gemeente Eindhoven - Dienst Stadsontwikkeling (1989) *Eindhoven op weg naar 2015*

Gemeente Eindhoven - Dienst Stadsontwikkeling (1991), *Structuurschets Eindhoven binnen de ringweg - samenvatting*
Gemeente Eindhoven - Dienst Stadsontwikkeling (1991) *Profielschets internationaal stedelijk knooppunt Eindhoven*
Gemeente Eindhoven - DSO-RO (1995), *Evaluatie en Herijking Sleutelproject Westcorridor, Evaluatie 1995*
Gemeente Eindhoven - DSO (1995), *Duurzaamheid en het sleutelproject Westcorridor*
Gemeente Eindhoven, Dienst Stadsontwikkeling, *Documentatie sleutelproject Westcorridor*
Kamer van Koophandel en Fabrieken voor Zuid-Oost Brabant, not dated, *Economisch actieplan, een samenvatting*
Lucassen, J. (1994), *De Witte Dame*, Stichting De Witte Dame, Eindhoven
NV Rede Economische Ontwikkelingsmaatschappij Regio Eindhoven (1994), *Jaarraport 1993*, Eindhoven
NV Rede Economische Ontwikkelingsmaatschappij Regio Eindhoven (1995), *Jaarraport 1994*, Eindhoven
NV Rede Ontwikkelingsmaatschappij Regio Eindhoven (1992), *High-tech Guide Eindhoven Region*, Eindhoven
Samenwerkingsverband Regio Eindhoven (SRE) (1995) *Nieuwe rol regio Eindhoven*, Meerjarenbeleid, Ontwerp, Eindhoven
Samenwerkingsverband Regio Eindhoven, VLEHAN, FIAR, *Projectbeschrijving Nationaal proefprojekt inzameling en herverwerking wit- en bruingoedapparaten in de regio Eindhoven*
Stichting Emmasingel (1993), *De Witte Dame*, Eindhoven
Stuurgroep Regiovisie - Stadsregio Eindhoven-Helmond (1993) *Regiovisie, een ruimtelijke ontwikkelingsstrategie Stadregio Eindhoven-Helmond*
Stuurgroep Sleutelproject Westcorridor (1992), *Eindrapportage Aanwijzing Sleutelproject Stedelijk Knooppunt Eindhoven*

Report on Lisbon

Câmara Municipal de Lisboa (1992), *Plano Estratégico de Lisboa*
Câmara Municipal de Lisboa (1994), *Plano Director Municipal - Regulamento*
Câmara Municipal de Lisboa (1993), *Lisboa, the Atlantic Capital of Europe building the future*
Parque Expo '98, EXPO URBE, not dated, *Plan Overview*
Parque Expo '98, EXPO URBE, promotial material

Parque Expo'98, Lisboa EXPO'98 (1995), *Relatório & Contas - Exercício de 1994*

Parque Expo'98, not dated, *EXPO URBE, A Unique Investment Opportunity*

Report on Munich

City of Munich (1994), *Munich - the city and its economy*, Department of Labour and Economic Development

Federal Ministry for Regional Planning, Building and Urban Development (1993), *Guidelines for Regional Planning*

Gillessen, Joachim, not dated, *Zum Stand der Diskussion über die Neuorganisation des Münchner Verkehrs- und Tarifverbundes (MVV)*, Landrat des Landkreises München

Goedecke, O. (1995), *Die Stadt und ihr Umland - Zur Zukunft von Stadtregionen am Beispiel der Region München*, Presentation Symposium Bayerischen Akademie für Naturschutz und Landschaftspflege in Eching, 4 May, 1995

Industrie- und Handelskammer für München und Oberbayern, (1994), *Competition between Metropolitan Areas in Europe - and Munich?*

Industrie- und Handelskammer für München und Oberbayern (1990), *Standort M*, ed. by A. Röhrich

Industrie- und Handelskammer für München und Oberbayern (1995), *Bericht '94*

Industrie- und Handelskammer für München und Oberbayern (1994), *Neuer Verbund für den Nahverkehr, Nachfolgeorganisation für den Münchner Verkehrs- und Tarifverbund*

Landeshauptstadt München, Referat für Stadtplanung und Bauordnung, (1995), *Analysen zur Stadtentwicklung,*

Landeshauptstadt München, Referat für Stadtplanung und Bauordnung, (1995), *Zukünftige Chancen und Risiken der Landeshauptstadt München als Wirtschaftsstandort*

Landeshauptstadt München, Referat für Arbeit und Wirtschaft (1992), *Wege zur wirtschaftspolitischen Kooperation für den Raum München*, Protokol der Tagung 10 April, 1992

Landeshauptstadt München, Referat für Arbeit und Wirtschaft (1994), *Jahreswirtschaftsbericht 1993*

Landeshauptstadt München, Referat für Arbeit und Wirtschaft (1994), *Münchner Jahreswirtschaftsbericht 1994*

283

Landeshauptstadt München, Referat für Arbeit und Wirtschaft (1993), *Der Standort München und die Öffnung Osteuropas: Auswirkungen und mögliche Strategien*

Landeshauptstadt München, Referat für Arbeit und Wirtschaft (1992) *Wirtschaftspolitisches Konzept für die Landeshauptstadt München*

Münchner Verkehrs- und Tarifverbund GmbH (1993), *Report - Geschäftsbericht 1993*

Planungsreferat der Landeshauptstadt München, Hauptabteilung Stadtentwicklungsplanung I/43 (1994), *Zur Räumlichen Entwicklung der Region München, Anforderungen an ein neues Siedlungsleitbild*, Abschlussbereicht des Arbeitskreises "Räumliche Aspekte der Regionalentwicklung"

Planungsverband Äusserer Wirtschaftsraum München (1995), *Dokumentation 5 - 20 Jahre Regionalentwicklung Vergangenes verstehen - Zukünfiiges gestalten*

Wirtschaftsraum Südbayern, München, Augsburg, Ingolstadt (1995), *MAI-Aktivitäten des zurückliegenden Jahres und Ausblick*, contribution to the 3rd May conference on 5 May, 1995, Ingolstadt

Wirtschaftsraum Südbayern, München, Augsburg, Ingolstadt (1994), *MAI - Europe's prosperous center*

Wirtschaftsraum Südbayern, München, Augsburg, Ingolstadt e.V., not dated, *Entwurf der Satzung des Vereins -*

Report on Rotterdam

Aart, Y.F. van, P.P.J. Driessen and P. Glasbergen,(1993), *Evaluatie van het ROM-gebiedenbeleid: deelstudie Rijnmond*, The Hague: Ministry of Housing, Regional Development and Environment

Berg, Leo van den, H. Arjen van Klink and Jan van der Meer (1993), *Governing Metropolitan Regions*, Aldershot: Avebury

College van Burgemeester en Wethouders van Rotterdam (1987), *Vernieuwing van Rotterdam*, Rotterdam

Commissie Sociaal Economische Vernieuwing Rotterdam (1987), *Nieuw Rotterdam, een opdracht voor alle Rotterdammers*, Rotterdam

Mik, G.(ed.)(1989), *Herstructurering in Rotterdam: modernisering en Internationalisering en de kop van zuid*, Rotterdam: Economisch-Geografisch Instituut, Erasmus University Rotterdam

Programmabureau ROM-Rijnmond (1994), *Voortgangsrapportage 1994 ROM-Rijnmond Hoofdrapport*, Rotterdam

Stuurgroep ROM-Rijnmond (1993), *ROM-project Rijnmond: Plan van Aanpak, Beleidsconvenant.* The Hague, SDU.

Report on Turin

Dicken (1986), *Global shift - industrial change in a turbulent world,* London: Harper & Row.

Ferlaino, F., and S. Piperno (1994), *La réforme du government local en Italie: l'nstitution des aires métropolitaines,* Journées d'études Ecole Normale Supérieure de Cachan, 6-7 May, 1994

Gabert, P.(1968), *Turin: ville industrielle,* Paris: Presses Universitaires de France

IRES (1995), *Cento progetti cinque anni dopo - l'attuazione dei principali progretti di transformazione urbana e territoriale in Piemonte,* Turin: Rosenberg & Seller

IRES (1996), *Relazione sulla situazione economica, sociale e territoriale del Piemonte 1995,* (draft version) Turin.

Il Lingotto - 1915-1939, Turin: Umberto Allemandi/Lingotto srl. (1992)

Mény, Y. (1990), *Government and politics in Western Europe - Britain, France, Italy and West Germany,* Oxford: Oxford University Press,

Ohmae, K. (1989), 'The global logic of strategic alliances', *Harvard Business Review,* March-April, pp.143-154

Sustainable urban projects - international workshop on principles of implementation, Turin, December 1994

For Product Safety Concerns and Information please contact our EU
representative GPSR@taylorandfrancis.com Taylor & Francis Verlag GmbH,
Kaufingerstraße 24, 80331 München, Germany

Printed and bound by CPI Group (UK) Ltd, Croydon, CR0 4YY
08/05/2025
01864366-0010